The
Postmodern
Imagination of
Russell Kirk

The
Postmodern
Imagination of
Russell Kirk

GERALD J. RUSSELLO

University of Missouri Press

Columbia and London

Library of Congress Cataloging-in-Publication Data

Russello, Gerald J., 1971–
    The postmodern imagination of Russell Kirk /
Gerald J. Russello.
        p.   cm.
    Summary: "Examines such concepts of Russell Kirk's
thought as imagination, historical consciousness, the
interplay between the individual and tradition, and the
role of narrative in constructing individual and societal
identity. Focuses on Kirk's role in the development of
the new conservatism of the 1950s and 1960s and his
critique of modernity"—Provided by publisher.
    Includes bibliographical references and index.
    ISBN-13: 978-0-8262-1720-2 (alk. paper)
1. Kirk, Russell.   2. Conservatism.   I. Title.
    JC573.R87 2007
    320.52092—dc22

                                            2007006111

Designer: Jennifer Cropp
Typesetter: The Composing Room of Michigan, Inc.
Printer and binder: The Maple-Vail Book Manufacturing
    Group
Typefaces: Palatino, Bailey, and Letter Gothic

Frontispiece photo courtesy of Annette Kirk

carissimae Alexandrae uxori et
Emmae Georgiaeque filiis meis
magna cum amore

Contents

Acknowledgments

This book would not have been possible without the extensive assistance of many people, for which I am deeply grateful. I would like to thank Gleaves Whitney, Jeffrey O. Nelson, William J. Gould, James Person, John Kekes, Bruce Frohnen, Gregory T. Doolan, Sean T. Keely, and Joshua Silverstein for reading earlier drafts of the manuscript and for their comments and suggestions. John Connelly, of Regis High School in Manhattan, has been a mentor for many years, and my interest in Russell Kirk is due in large measure to him. His advice on this project was of immeasurable help. Adam Schwartz tirelessly and generously discussed this volume with me during its long evolution and read large portions of it in manuscript.

Annette Kirk has been a continuous source of materials, references, and advice since she hosted me on a trip to Piety Hill during the summer of 1995, as have the various assistants at the Kirk Center, particularly Charles Brown and Claudia Henrie. Scott D. Moringiello provided critical assistance during the summer of 1999, spending much time rooting about New York libraries tracking down sources for me while working full-time. Thomas Molnar, Robert A. Herrera, Lee Edwards, George Nash, William Fahey, and Mitch Muncy were kind enough to share with me their thoughts on Dr. Kirk, and they helpfully referred me to relevant primary and secondary works. The Heritage Foundation and the Wilbur Foundation provided me with fellowships to do necessary early research and writing.

Finally, thanks are due to Beverly Jarrett, Sara Davis, Susan King, and the rest of the marketing and editorial staff at the University of Missouri Press for helping me shape the manuscript into a publishable book and to Kay Banning for compiling the index. Any errors or omissions, of course, remain solely my own.

I would also like to thank *Modern Age, The American Journal of Jurisprudence, Humanitas, Publius, The New Criterion,* and *The University Bookman* for permitting me to republish work that first appeared in their pages.

Finally, deep gratitude is owed to my wife, Alexandra, for her patience and support.

The
Postmodern
Imagination of
Russell Kirk

Introduction

Russell Kirk Today

I t is an exceedingly strange time to be a conservative. Radio talk shows with a conservative tilt flourish and best-seller lists burst with conservative titles. The FOX television network has made itself into a forum friendly to conservatives and has emerged as a strong competitor of the older television networks. Magazines, daily newspapers, and the Internet are filled with discussions of neoconservatism and extended, sometimes abstruse reflections on political philosophers such as Leo Strauss and Carl Schmitt and their intellectual relationship to conservatism. Staid publishing houses such as Penguin have developed new series to appeal to right-leaning readers. Even the *New York Times* has a reporter whose "beat" is American conservatives and their world. Arguably, the attention devoted to conservative ideas rivals anything in the history of conservatism, including during the Reagan years.

Most oddly of all, perhaps, have been the fortunes of Russell Kirk. Kirk (1918–1994) was a principal architect of the conservative resurgence in America after the Second World War. The 1953 publication of his doctoral dissertation, originally titled *The Conservative Mind: From Burke to Santayana,* was a major intellectual event in America. It has been translated into a number of languages, and the "canons" of conservatism with which it begins are perhaps the most well-known touchstones for conservatism. Excepting perhaps *National Review* founder William F. Buckley Jr., Kirk was the most prolific conservative author of the last century. Throughout the 1960s and 1970s, he was a fixture on the national lecture circuit and routinely considered among the most influential conservative thinkers.

Yet despite his recognized influence, his place in American conservative historiography remains ambiguous. On the one hand, conservatives of almost every stripe recognize his importance and influence. For example, Buckley, who approached Kirk to write a column for his fledgling magazine of conservative opinion, has said that the founding of *National Review,* and American conservatism itself, would not have been possible without Kirk. William Rusher, another major figure from the early days of postwar conservative organizing, identifies Kirk as the man who gave "this great [conservative] movement its name." On the other hand, Kirk too often has been the subject of undue adulation and hagiography. As Wesley McDonald says in his well-received introductory study, Kirk's admirers "sometimes venerate him at the expense of understanding the substance of his thought or quote him selectively to promote agendas that would have been foreign to his thinking and nature."[1] Most surprisingly, perhaps, is that Kirk is now being enlisted into contemporary disputes over the future of conservatism, a debate he generally shied away from.

Kirk's carefully crafted eighteenth-century persona does not help those seeking to find out why his works remain so influential. His antiquated writing style and general reluctance to become involved with specific policy disputes do not fit within any typical conservative posture, and they in fact have served to sideline his influence in contemporary debates. As Clinton Rossiter once jibed, Kirk had the sound of a man "born one hundred and fifty years too late and in the wrong country."[2] Was he a wise Burkean or an anachronism? A storyteller or an intellectual? An American traditionalist or a misplaced Tory? While remaining well respected, Kirk developed few clear followers or doctrines to carry forward his influence. Kirk charted his own course, which did not always coincide with public conservative niceties.

Although there are occasional nods to the figures Kirk reintroduced into the conservative self-definition—W. H. Mallock, John Randolph, Irving Babbitt, Christopher Dawson, and Bernard Id-

1. William F. Buckley Jr., "Russell Kirk," *Right Reason,* 402–9; James E. Person Jr., ed. *The Unbought Grace of Life: Essays in Honor of Russell Kirk,* 50; W. Wesley McDonald, *Russell Kirk and the Age of Ideology,* ix.

2. Clinton Rossiter, *Conservatism in America,* 222.

dings Bell, among others—the tradition of political and literary figures he identified no longer serves as the fulcrum of conservative critique. The type of literary conservatism evident in his major books
is rarely seen in today's conservative magazines. In an early essay on
Kirk's thought, Donald Atwell Zoll locates Kirk's "aesthetic" conservatism in part in his "luxuriant sense of beauty" and hatred of
vulgarity. It is perhaps no surprise that the figure with which Kirk
initially ended *The Conservative Mind* was the cosmopolitan philosopher and essayist George Santayana, whose contribution to conservative thought lay in precisely his defense of the necessity of beauty to societal health. For Santayana, "a good society is beautiful, a
bad one ugly. Upon this ground, [Santayana] builds his conservatism and his condemnation of the direction modern life has taken."
Kirk eventually replaced Santayana with Eliot as the book's closing
figure, perhaps because Eliot's Christian conservatism became more
attractive to Kirk than Santayana's aesthetic agnosticism; nevertheless, the Spanish philosopher's conviction that the coming industrial world would be characterized for its ugliness and uniformity
strikes a chord in Kirk's early writings.

Zoll credits Kirk with

> luring ... assorted conservatives into a more politically self-
> conscious phalanx, into an intellectual movement sharply di-
> vorced from the conventional strictures of the Republican Party or
> the "dollar conservatives" (in Eliseo Vivas's phrase) that would
> follow. Under Kirk's neo-Burkean aegis, a basically philosophical
> consort developed from as presumably disparate currents as reli-
> gious neo-orthodoxy, literary agrarianism, moral realism and anti-
> egalitarianism; they found a center in the "prescriptive" social
> thought of the Burkean tradition.[3]

The "prescriptive center" Zoll identifies seems to have little bearing
in the postmodern political landscape, and the coalition that the center forged is in tatters. On the one hand, both major political parties
have largely accepted the same beliefs in the benefits of the free market, global trade, and exporting democracy, all subjects about which
Kirk had deep suspicions. The sentiment expressed in a recent *National Review* essay that conservatives should consider "the oppor-

3. Kirk, *The Conservative Mind: From Burke to Eliot*, 445 (hereafter cited as *CM*);
Donald Atwell Zoll, "The Social Thought of Russell Kirk," 112, 116–17, 118.

tunity to drive larger cars to be a blessing of our consumer society," for example, bears little relation to Kirk's conservatism, as does the magazine's support for the Iraq War.[4]

Moreover, the contemporary Right has adopted some of the intellectual underpinnings of liberalism, such as a belief in equality, the primacy of individual rights, and the universality of American political and popular culture. As Rossiter noted, even in the 1950s Kirk's alliance with mainstream political or economic conservatism was probably always best left unexamined: "Kirk, it seems to me, maintains contact with the conservatism of Goldwater and General Motors only because most of his friends refuse to pay him the compliment that most of his critics have paid him richly: the chewing, swallowing and digesting of his books."[5] The editorials in *Harper's* or alternative outlets such as the *New York Press* or the *Baffler* now are as likely as any conservative publication to contain Kirk-like assessments of political utopianism or consumer culture. Kirk's thinking on community, loyalty to region, and imagination find fewer contemporary echoes in conservative thought, even as they appear with increasing frequency in mainstream discourse.

On the other hand, calls by some conservative intellectuals for a "Middle American Revolution" or a tendency toward religious eschatology represent a strain of nativism that is likewise foreign to Kirk's cosmopolitan conception of American culture. Kirk and traditionalists of the 1930s, 1940s, and 1950s were born into a particular society that they saw slipping away and that they wished to preserve. Kirk, for example, defended the Depression-era Michigan of his youth against the left-wing revisionists and urban planners. To read someone like Garet Garrett, the lead editorial writer of the *Saturday Evening Post* who defended an America of little regulation and traditional values, is to encounter an America that is no more. The world some contemporary conservatives, often called "paleoconservatives," wish to establish is quite different. Indeed, the late Samuel Francis once implied that while respectable, Kirk and the older traditionalists were the "beautiful losers" of conservatism because they lacked a political program or a sufficiently objective eye for the current cultural situation. Francis also stated that "for all the virtues of Kirk's classical conservatism . . . it was simply not adequate to the

4. Dave Shiflett, "The Yappy Warrior."
5. Rossiter, *Conservatism in America,* 221. See also Nigel Ashford, "Russell Kirk as Conservative Thinker," 37, 39.

mission that serious men of the right in the middle of the 20th century journey should have taken up."[6] Conservatives like Francis propose cultural solutions based in a tradition of thought that began with thinkers like Gaetano Mosca, Max Weber, and James Burnham rather than those to whom Kirk looked for guidance.

Kirk illustrates a strand of conservative thought that parts with contemporary conservatism in important ways and mounts a critique of liberalism that differs from other forms of conservatism. The current study seeks to provide an overview of several crucial areas to determine whether the aesthetic, imaginative conservatism Kirk propounded has anything to say in the contemporary world. The first chapter summarizes Kirk's life and thought and emphasizes not only the celebrated "canons," which have become hallmarks of most forms of conservatism since the 1950s, but also other features such as imagination, the sentiments, and religion. The imagination assumes a central place in this study because Kirk thought that disorder in the imagination was an inevitable feature of the modern world. People search for individual identity through the images that surround them, and modern images are based either on the false science of materialism or a debased sensuality, which Kirk denominated the "diabolic imagination."

> The average sensual man and the average sensual woman, though bored with mechanism and materialism and frightened by the loss of self-image, never will get beyond the tricks of Simon Magus—not unless the prophet and the man of genius open the way for them. The crowd perceives by means of images, false or true. But the discoverers or shapers of images are persons of extraordinary perceptions, not governed by the idols of the tribe or of the marketplace.
>
> Images are representations of mysteries, necessary because mere words are tools that break in the hand, and it has not pleased God that man should be saved by abstract reason alone.[7]

And it fell, Kirk thought, to conservatives to fashion the appropriate images to convey this sense of mystery to each generation. Kirk's conservatism was an attempt at reconstruction; it was a recognition that engagement of the sentiments through an imaginative render-

6. Francis, "Holding the Pass," 35.
7. Kirk, "The Rediscovery of Mystery," 4.

ing of history was just as important as an appeal to reason. His conservatism in other words was not merely a defense of existing institutions, an understanding of conservatism first introduced by Karl Mannheim and elaborated upon by Samuel Huntington. It was also a critique of those institutions.

Chapters 2, 3, and 4 concentrate on key substantive areas of Kirk's conservative vision. A society uses history, law, and politics to construct its identity, and each of these factors has been a consistent focus of conservative thought. History shapes the past, through the stories and events a society deems worthy of repeating. The act of repetition, and the choice of what bears repeating, becomes tradition. Like the historian John Lukacs, Kirk was sensitive to the importance of subjectivity in history, and he largely rejected the Enlightenment vision of the objectivity of fact. The historian participates in the creation of history, and the objects of knowledge cannot be separated fully from those who study them. While a commonplace "postmodern" notion now, Kirk used this understanding of history for conservative purposes, as a way to dislodge a seemingly "objective" modern history that seemed merely to confirm liberal premises. The past changes, and how it changes and why are in the hands of the culture generally and the historian in particular.

The role of history and its transformation into tradition provides a key insight into Kirk's conservatism: that institutions or social practices worth conserving must be transmitted in new forms if they are to survive. While traditions should be preserved,

> Some traditions may grow obsolete; all require respectful scrutiny, now and then, in light of the age, lest they ossify. Traditions take on new meanings with the growing experience of a people. And simply to appeal to the wisdom of the species, to tradition, will not of itself provide solutions to all problems. The endeavor of the intelligent believer in tradition is so to blend ancient usage with necessary amendment that society is never wholly old and never wholly new.

As British philosopher Roger Scruton wrote in his study of conservatism, "The desire to conserve is compatible with all manner of change provided only that change is continuity."[8]

---

8. Kirk, *Enemies of the Permanent Things,* 181 (hereafter cited as *EPT*); Scruton, *The Meaning of Conservatism,* 22.

Some have dismissed conservatism's defense of existing institutions as only a mild form of utilitarianism: whatever works should be preserved, because the danger of novelty outweighs the discomfort of what is familiar. Kirk's defense of tradition was not utilitarian in this way, not least because he thought some current institutions and practices did need to be changed despite the danger he saw in novelty. It was based instead on a perception not of superiority, but of familiarity: one is attached to tradition because it is one's own. As Stanley Fish (an unlikely conservative ally) put it, "Our convictions are preferred; that's what makes them our convictions."[9]

Moreover, one cannot escape one's own tradition. The concept of the autonomous individual at the center of much contemporary liberal political theory is false. Some critics of Kirk thought his preference for existing institutions meant merely that conservatives would defend whatever exists. Since change is inevitable, such cannot be conservatives because they ultimately accept it and go on to defend that new state of affairs. This mischaracterizes Kirk as a reactionary and ignores his strong assertion that conservatism is an attitude or set of attitudes that define one's stance toward reality, not devotion to particular social institutions.

The law controls how society orders itself in the present, through widely recognized legal principles shaped by an adversarial legal process. Kirk was a strong proponent of the Anglo-American common law system and that system's judge-made rules. Following John Randolph, the subject of his first book, Kirk disliked the process of legislation, thinking it in some ways less reflective of the popular sentiment than individual judicial decisions. The political process is too easily manipulable by interest groups or demagogues. He thus endorsed structural mechanisms, such as federalism and the common law system to stem the power of political ideology. More provocatively, perhaps, Kirk adopted from the still-obscure American thinker Orestes Brownson the concept of "territorial democracy," which sets out a political theory based not on Lockean natural rights but on the concept that political power must be centered on a geographic unity within which all people participate in governance.

While it was not perfect, Kirk believed that a fractured common law system working through a federalized structure could avoid the dangers of ideology. His criticisms of the Supreme Court focus on

9. Fish, "Don't Blame Relativism," 31.

the legislative-like attributes its decisions have assumed, which anticipated conservative argument against the Court in the mid-1990s. With its emphasis on precedent and adherence to traditional forms, the law also appealed to Kirk as a repository of social cohesion and imaginative respect for the past.

There is also the somewhat complex relationship between Kirk and the natural law. From very early on, Kirk adhered to some form of natural law, though he was never clear about its sources and never discussed its precepts in any detail. Some have taken from this that he should not be considered a natural law thinker at all. Wesley McDonald, for example, believes that Kirk's interpretation of natural law makes for some "exegetic difficulties" because of Kirk's attempted union between the natural law and the moral imagination. In particular, McDonald maintains Kirk never fully examined the disjunction between the natural law as a series of universally applicable immutable precepts and the moral imagination, by which "the good is seen as dynamic, living, and organic [with] particulars that cannot be conceptually predefined but are grasped by an intuitive vision."[10]

Finally, politics permits a discussion of a society's future and its values. Writing of Burke, Kirk concluded that "the prudent reformer combines an ability to reform with a disposition to preserve," a formulation that captures the combination of practical means and imaginative will that Kirk thought represented conservatism.[11] At the center of his political conception were the principles of party and the statesman. Kirk struggled to develop a model of American statesmanship that would not only preserve what he found admirable in Burke's career but remain particularly American in character. Chapter 4 also examines Kirk's economic thinking. Kirk was never a free-market absolutist, and he had harsh words for global capitalism and the destructive tendencies of the free market. In one of his earliest collections of essays, he wrote that the "American industrialist, by and large, has been a liberal, and so has the labor organizer"; the larger cultural questions have been consumed by an "obsession with economics."[12]

Nor did he believe that a particular economic view had been em-

10. McDonald, *Kirk and the Age of Ideology*, 71, 77.
11. *CM*, 45.
12. Kirk, *Confessions of a Bohemian Tory*, 305 (hereafter cited as *CBT*).

bodied in the American Revolution or the founding of the American republic. Economics, as a means of ordering material wants, must remain embedded within the goals of life, and not itself become the goal. In his economics textbook, Kirk tried to offer his interpretive framework for economic life, and this book concentrates just as much on morals as it does on the laws of supply and demand.

The examination of these areas will place Kirk within the intellectual debate over the failure of modernity and the emergence of postmodernity.[13]

The term *modernity* itself is fluid. The terminology of the word, and its cousin, *postmodernism*, has grown quite complex, but for our purposes a few points should be noted at the outset. First, for Kirk modernity was characterized most significantly by what he believed was an excessive reliance on a straitened form of rationalism to solve fundamental moral problems arising from humanity's fallen nature. Liberalism—with its focus on "rational" solutions to social problems, reliance on trained experts, and a mechanistic view of the human imagination—is the political expression of modernity. Second, Kirk saw the liberal order as failing for want of imagination, and he saw emerging from it a new age that had discarded both liberal rationality and the premodern tradition represented in the writings of Burke. This new age, which Kirk called the Age of Sentiments and identified with postmodernism in an early essay, was still inchoate. In his essay "Imagination against Ideology," Kirk opined that the postmodern age was still too early in its development to be defined:

> We seem to be entering upon the Post-Modern Age . . . and new thoughts and new sentiments and new modes of statecraft—or *renewed* thoughts, sentiments, modes—may take on flesh soon. The Post-Modern Age surely will be an epoch of big battalions and Napoleonic figures; possibly it may be also a time of renewed poetic imagination, and of the reflection of poetry in politics. Thus Americans may learn for instance that the sanguine response to the dreary abstraction called Marxism is not a dreary counter-abstraction called Capitalism (embracing Marx's own jargon), but rather a reaffirmed poetic vision of the splendor and misery of the human condition.[14]

13. For a good summary of this divide, see Stephen M. Feldman, *American Legal Thought from Premodernism to Postmodernism*, 28–45.
14. Kirk, "Imagination against Ideology," 1578.

Kirk wrote this essay in 1980, at the very beginning of the Reagan era and of eight years of conservative dominance of the executive branch. His prediction, however, was not the sanguine hope in the "end of history" that Francis Fukuyama and others would be advocating by the end of the decade. As post-1989 and September 11, 2001, events have shown, religious and cultural passions and sentiments, some long buried, have reemerged as important forces on the world stage and as an important alternative to modernity. This shift has been noted in the United States not only by conservatives. After the 2004 presidential election, for example, essayist Garry Wills wrote derisively of the "Day the Enlightenment Went Out."[15] What will replace it, however—technological nightmare or fundamentalist theocracy, the dislocations and inequalities of global capitalism or the resurgence of ethnic and religious tribalism—remains a matter of intense debate. A full consideration of the implications of postmodernism for conservatism is considered in the final chapter of this volume.

Yet, Kirk's identification of a postliberal era based in imagination and sentiment has resonance in contemporary conservative writing on postmodernism. As it happens, Kirk's consistent refusal to concede to the claims of modernity, and his conviction that modernity had dissolved into a new age that was characterized by imagination and sentiment, echoes 1960s and 1970s postmodern critiques. Conservatives, nonetheless, have had a contentious relationship with postmodernism, which for many has been what Kirk called a "devil term." To the mainstream Right, it stands for everything they oppose: relativism, amorality, lack of respect for tradition, and a slavish devotion to innovation. Postmodernism, however, need not be only a form of hypermodernism, as some liberal opponents of postmodernism, such as Bernard Yack, have claimed.[16] Postmodernism contains a range of expressions, to which some conservatives have responded favorably. Indeed, as we will see, conservatives have long had a cool respect for the idea of the postmodern, if not for its proponents. This history is largely unknown or ignored by current conservatives. Recently, however, that cool respect has blossomed into warm accommodation. For example, Peter Augustine Lawler argues that "postmodernism, rightly understood," is in fact conservative:

15. Wills, "The Day the Enlightenment Went Out," A25.
16. Yack, *The Fetishism of Modernities.*

Postmodernists in the usual sense often do well in exposing liberal hypocrisy, but they can do so in the name of completing the modern project of liberating the individual's subjective or willful and whimsical perspective from all external constraints. Conservative postmodernism, by acknowledging and affirming as good what we can really know about our natural possibilities and limitations, is radically opposed to liberated postmodernism—and to the modern premises it radicalizes.

Kirk was one of the first conservative thinkers to see in postmodernism an opportunity for conservatism to reassert itself amidst the collapse of modernity. Ted McAllister highlights this specific type of "conservative imagination" in his recent book, *The Revolt against Modernity*. By the end of the nineteenth century, he contends, "The conversation had shifted, and knowledge had been reconfigured to exclude those realms of human experience not amenable to the scientific method," including most important the imagination, which allowed individuals to "transcend the moment to capture a glimpse of the timeless."[17] This shift deprived conservatives of their accustomed voice, which was the voice of narrative and tradition rather than of science. Since then, conservatives have scrambled to defend what they saw as enduring values in a language that was increasingly no longer accepted, or even recognized. Those formerly disdained modes of communicating and transmitting cultural knowledge would return to favor.

On several occasions Kirk spoke approvingly of the beginning of a postmodern era to replace an exhausted modernity. This new period would dispense with liberalism's reliance on "defecated rationality" and empty theory. Instead, Kirk envisioned an Age of Sentiments to supplant the modern Age of Discussion; which will be discussed more fully in chapter 5. Sentiment, which Kirk defined as "a moving conviction; by a conviction derived from some other source than pure reason," would replace the cold reason Kirk found characteristic of modernity.[18]

This new age would recognize that humanity is moved by the heart first. Sentiment must be disciplined, however, by tradition and

---

17. Mark C. Henrie, "The Road to the Future," 19; Lawler, "Conservative Postmodernism, Postmodern Conservatism," 16, 17; McAllister, *Revolt against Modernity: Leo Strauss, Eric Voegelin, and the Search for a Postliberal Order*, 265.
18. Kirk, *Redeeming the Time*, 131 (hereafter cited as *RT*).

imagination to serve as a coherent basis for an individual or a society. Kirk's vision intersects with postmodern thought in surprising ways, although the distinctions are equally sharp.

In some respects this affinity for some postmodern themes in Kirk's criticisms of modernity should not be surprising. Kirk was always something of an oddball in the conservative firmament, and he never quite fit in with any of conservatism's varied camps. His ambivalence toward capitalism, for example, while passed over by the business-class supporters of early conservatism in the 1950s for the sake of a united front against communism, as the Rossiter quote suggests, became a liability for him by the 1990s. Moreover, Kirk's inclination to limit America's foreign engagements did not sit well with those who thought it a conservative mission to spread democracy or "global capitalism." Kirk's strong affection for the British example and his disdain for nativism, which he thought was "always a plague of the Right," stood in contrast to those in the conservative movement who wanted to carve out a distinctly American conservatism apart from its European connections.[19]

Kirk was faulted for thinking that this Burkean past was necessarily connected to a living American conservative tradition.[20] In particular, Kirk's tendency to "Burkify" American issues by finding parallels in the thought of Edmund Burke for every conceivable problem rankled other conservative thinkers who thought that American conservatism was a separate phenomenon from its British and Continental cousins.

But Kirk becomes a more complex figure from the vantage point of a decade or more after his death. The typical caricature of Kirk as an ersatz eighteenth-century gentleman was wrong, made by a too-hasty assessment based on appearances. It is belied by Kirk's own expressed distaste for the time of Burke and Johnson, which he described as "an age of gilded selfishness and frivolous intellectuality —an age almost without a heart."[21]

Kirk has been too often simplistically characterized as a reactionary, his subjects "woefully archaic and detached."[22] But Kirk

---

19. Kirk, *Beyond the Dreams of Avarice: Essays of a Social Critic,* 58 (hereafter cited as *BDA*).

20. Although some conservatives, most notably Robert Nisbet, made just such a connection from reading Kirk's books (see George H. Nash, *The Conservative Intellectual Movement in America since 1945,* 361n117).

21. *BDA,* 184.

22. Alan Lawson, "Is There a Usable Conservatism?" 17.

was keenly aware of his time and more sanguine about the present than is usually acknowledged. His invocation of Burke, for example, was not a nostalgic look backward for its own sake. Indeed, Burke was a conservative hero precisely because he was "essentially a modern man, and his concern was with our modern complexities."[23]

Further, the genealogy and "conservative mind" Kirk developed over four decades of writing bear striking resemblances to contemporary thought. The internal weaknesses he found in liberal modernity are now commonplaces, appearing among not only conservative writers but liberals and radicals as well.

Indeed, even as Kirk became only a "half-remembered legacy" on the Right,[24] liberals seemed to discover him anew. His death in 1994 inspired a number of sympathetic eulogies and retrospectives in the mainstream media, which up until that point had tended to overlook him. The *New Republic*, for example, published a favorable analysis of Kirk by critic John Judis and featured a glowing review of Kirk's posthumous memoir, *The Sword of Imagination*, by the southern historian and former Marxist professor-turned-conservative sympathizer, Eugene D. Genovese. Deflecting criticism that Kirk's opinions were antiquated or no longer viable, Genovese wrote, "In so many ways, Russell Kirk seems like a creature of the mothballs. As we survey the wreckage of a century that he did his best to civilize, let's hear it for the mothballs."[25]

Kirk is also beginning to attract the attention of television, a medium he despised. The network C-SPAN devoted a segment of their "American Writers" series (which has profiled major figures such as Benjamin Franklin, William Faulkner, and Walter Lippmann) to Kirk and his legacy. Even the *Chronicle of Higher Education* favorably discussed Kirk, if only to enlist him in the arguments against a "neoconservative" foreign policy. The magazine failed to notice the irony of praising this excoriator of "Behemoth University" and much of modern education who would have found little merit in its pages.

The fractured circumstances of conservatism itself have contributed to Kirk's uncertain place. As it entered the twenty-first cen-

23. Kirk, *Edmund Burke: A Genius Reconsidered*, 8 (hereafter cited as *EB*).

24. Bruce Frohnen, "Has Conservatism Lost Its Mind? The Half-Remembered Legacy of Russell Kirk," 62.

25. Judis, "Three Wise Men," 20–21, 24; Genovese, "Captain Kirk," 35–38. Similarly, Ralph C. Wood finds the source of the strength of Kirk's social criticism in his deliberate old-fashionedness ("Russell Kirk, Knight of Cheerful Countenance," 10).

tury, the conservative movement split into numerous new groups, each going in its own direction. This, too, was an echo of the past: almost as soon as conservatives coalesced into a broad-based political and social "movement" in the 1950s, the movement itself began to dissolve. The conflicts among these different camps have been at times so pronounced that scholars have called the political—and, in some cases, personal—controversies that enveloped the Right during the 1980s "the conservative wars."[26] As recently as 1997, three years after the so-called Republican revolution in the House of Representatives, the publishers of the journal *Commentary* organized a symposium, titled "On the Future of Conservatism," the prospects of which, some thought, were less than sure. (More recently, in the fallout of the Iraq War and the 2006 elections, *Commentary* published an article titled "Is Conservatism Finished?")[27]

The lines of this "conservative crackup" have been variously drawn. Some commentators have determined that the basic conservative division is between those who "mourn the loss of the old world and still urge us to flee an America that has become indistinguishable from Gomorrah" and those who "believe in the continuing possibilities of liberal democracy and the fruits of Enlightenment culture." Sociologist Peter Berger distinguishes between the neoconservatives, who accept modernity, and "Old Right" conservatives, who do not. Hilton Kramer, critic and editor of the *New Criterion*, defends a high (conservative) modernism from the depredations of cultural philistines of both the Left and the Right.[28] Modernity in this context means reason, high art, and universal truth against deconstructionist philosophy, political correctness, and the degradation of art into shallow posturing.

The early debates about the meaning of conservatism were centered in the efforts at self-definition and consolidation against communism abroad and statism at home. This coalescence of conservatism brought socially conservative Catholics, libertarians, and anti-Communists together in a common struggle. The enormity of

---

26. Paul Gottfried, *Conservative Movement*, xxiii. A popular history of political conservatism is Lee Edwards, *The Conservative Revolution: The Movement that Remade America from Robert Taft to Newt Gingrich*.

27. Wilfred M. McClay, "Is Conservatism Finished?" http://www.commentarymagazine.com/cm/main/viewArticle.aip?id=10812.

28. Adam Wolfson, "Apocalypse Now?" 31; Berger, "Our Conservatism and Theirs," 65–66; Kramer, "Modernism and Its Enemies," 3.

the Communist threat enabled them to dampen their differences, at least for a time. The entry of the neoconservatives into the conservative fold in the 1960s and 1970s precipitated the second series of debates, as the older alliance of business leaders and agrarians, populists, and East Coast intellectuals, such as Buckley, began to weaken. The story of the neoconservatives has been told often: mostly ex-liberals who came of age as members of the Left, the neoconservatives joined the conservative ranks in large numbers as a result of their distaste at the anti-Americanism and growing political radicalism of the New Left in the 1960s and 1970s. Irving Kristol, one of the early forebears of the movement, recounts the history of the neoconservative "persuasion" as "the erosion of liberal faith among a relatively small but talented and articulate group of scholars and intellectuals, and the movement of this group . . . towards a more conservative point of view." Louis Filler, in his *Dictionary of American Conservatism*, describes neoconservatism as "arising out of disillusionment with both radical-socialist programs and Democratic Party developments deriving from the New Deal."[29]

Generally speaking, the neoconservatives did not oppose government power to effect social change as did some of the traditionalist and libertarian conservatives. Instead, the neoconservatives' shift to the right began with an examination of the unintended social and cultural consequences of large-scale government planning. Like other conservatives, the neoconservatives believed in the primacy of order and community but rejected what Mark Gerson described as the "conservative emphasis on the authority of tradition and the glorification of the past."[30] Order and community, in the neoconservative vision, rested more on a common allegiance to the principles of the Declaration of Independence, in particular that of equality, rather than to a shared history or religious communion. By the 1980s and 1990s, neoconservative scholars and policy analysts had assumed a large place in the Reagan and Bush administrations, conservative

29. Patrick Allitt, *Catholic Intellectuals and Conservative Politics in America, 1950–1985*, 1–16. For one ex-liberal's odyssey, see Norman Podhoretz, *Ex-Friends*; Kristol, *Neoconservatism: The Autobiography of an Idea*, x; Filler, ed. *The Dictionary of American Conservatism*, 222–23.

30. Gerson, *The Neoconservative Vision: From the Cold War to the Culture Wars*, 8–9. Other studies are Gary J. Dorrien, *The Neoconservative Mind: Politics, Culture, and the War of Ideologies*; John Ehrman, *The Rise of Neoconservatism: Intellectuals and Foreign Affairs, 1945–1994*; and Nina J. Easton, *Gang of Five: Leaders at the Center of the Conservative Crusade*.

journals, and think tanks.[31] Many neoconservatives, such as Jeanne Kirkpatrick and William J. Bennett, took on prominent roles in Republican administrations, and neoconservative journals, such as *Commentary*, gained increasing influence. Their efforts led in part to the electoral success of Ronald Reagan in 1980.

Kirk stayed out of much of this intraconservative strife, but his reluctance to side with any of the factions may have cost him long-term influence. Despite his support for its general mission, for example, in the 1950s Kirk acknowledged he had "little in common with some of the people on *National Review*'s lengthy masthead—on which he declined to have his name appear."[32] Kirk named in particular Willmoore Kendall and Frank Meyer, whose disputes with Kirk in the pages of *National Review* did much to shape the debate over conservatism in the 1950s and 1960s. Many years later, in the midst of the split between the neoconservatives and the traditionalists Kirk asked to have his name removed from the masthead of the paleoconservative *Chronicles*.[33]

Although he praised the neoconservatives for their practical successes in founding journals of opinion and offering practical solutions to issues that had long been dominated by liberals, he thought them "often clever, seldom wise." Kirk rated highly the work of a few neoconservatives, in particular that of Michael Novak, Nathan Glazer, and Diane Ravitch, but ultimately he thought that they would eventually lose their influence because of their importation of liberal categories such as progress and capitalism into their thought.[34]

The third series of conservative infighting during Kirk's life began in the late 1980s and early 1990s. The Cold War had ended, and the half century of efforts by conservatives to fight the Soviet Union was over. Although there were some political triumphs, such as the Republican takeover of Congress in 1994, conservatives once again began to dispute first principles. The watershed year was perhaps 1996, when former Nixon aide and political commentator Patrick J.

---

31. McAllister, *Revolt against Modernity*, 60–64. For a more acerbic view of the neoconservatives, see Andrew Sullivan, "The Scolds," 46.

32. Kirk, *The Sword of Imagination: Memoirs of a Half-Century of Literary Conflict*, 188 (hereafter cited as *SI*).

33. For a summary of Kirk's relationship with *Chronicles*, see Scott P. Richert, "Russell Kirk and the Negation of Ideology," 28–30.

34. Kirk, *The Politics of Prudence*, 178, 172 (hereafter cited as *PP*).

Buchanan announced his run for the Republican nomination for the presidency. Buchanan offered a sharp challenge to the conservative mainstream for losing its bearings in the "culture war." Although he lost the nomination, Buchanan illuminated the strong fault lines between the differing conservative groups. Buchanan later left the Republican Party over conflicting positions on immigration and free trade.[35]

Buchanan did not lack for intellectual supporters among the paleoconservatives who emerged during this period as a recognizable segment of the Right. The paleoconservatives broke with the other conservative groups in a series of public disputes during the 1980s, the most important of which was the rejection of paleoconservative scholar M. E. Bradford for a post with the National Endowment for the Arts, which the paleoconservatives attributed to neoconservative influence in the Reagan administration. By the 1990s, the paleoconservatives had attacked the conservative establishment on a range of issues. For example, the editor of *Chronicles* echoed Buchanan's derision of free trade, calling it the "point at which socialism converges with both individualism and globalism—three roads that lead to world government."[36] Samuel Francis, another *Chronicles* editor, lambasted American pretensions to international activity in the name of democracy or human rights.[37] Joseph Scotchie described such critics as seeing the issues facing the American Right as part of a "grand battle royale waged between a mostly rural and small-town Middle America, and their Washington-Manhattan-Hollywood tormentors," including mainstream conservatives.[38]

The paleoconservatives have since attempted to outline a new American populism, based on a regionalist conservatism, drawing in particular from the South and Midwest, and featuring a renewed economic nationalism, a resistance to immigration, a stronger concern for protecting localities from federal interference, and a suspicion of American international involvement.[39] As Adam Wolfson

35. See Buchanan, *The Death of the West.*

36. Thomas Fleming, "Selling the Golden Cord," 10; George Watson, "Conservatives and the Free Market," 23.

37. See, for example, Francis, "The Price of Empire," 15. For an extended discussion of southern conservatism, see M. E. Bradford, "Where We Were Born: The Southern Conservative Tradition," in *The Reactionary Imperative*, 115.

38. Scotchie, ed. *The Paleoconservatives*, 13.

39. Gottfried, *Conservative Movement*, 81, 91, 147–48; Nash, *Conservative Intellectual Movement*, 338–39. For a detailed account of the other incidents that have

has noted, the paleoconservative program is fundamentally different from that proposed by traditionalists such as Kirk, despite certain similarities. The paleoconservative "spirit," Wolfson contends, quoting paleoconservative scholar Paul Gottfried, "is far more Nietzschean than neo-Thomistic" and is characterized by a belief that the modern world is "irrevocably cut off" from the Western tradition.[40] Traditionalists such as Kirk, on the other hand, do not see the disruptions in the tradition to be as irrevocable.

The events of September 11 brought on another period of conservative self-evaluation. Prominent conservatives were split over the proper response to the terrorist attacks and what the attacks meant for American policy at home and abroad. The attacks forced conservatives to reassess cultural questions that had preoccupied them for the last ten years, such as the debate over civil liberties, the role of religion in public life, and indeed the nature of the society those liberties are intended to preserve. The debates became increasingly vitriolic, as witnessed by former George W. Bush speechwriter David Frum's accusation that the paleoconservatives are "unpatriotic" for failing to support the war in Iraq, and the paleoconservative retort that Frum and others have hijacked the conservative name.[41] Jacob Heilbrunn argued that in fact the conservative coalition *National Review* helped forge has basically dissipated in the aftermath of the Iraq War.[42]

Commentator Andrew Sullivan has contended that the terrorist attacks have undermined all the major elements of the conservative movement: the traditionalist conservatives and religious Right, the neoconservatives and the libertarians. Sullivan maintains that the neoconservative "ideology" was unprepared for the flexible response required in the face of terrorism. "Like most ideologies, neoconservatism has a tendency to ossify, to fail to see new opportunities or realities." Instead, Sullivan implies, the neoconservatives remained mired in a Cold War mindset, preferring unilateral international action and stark ideological positions.

The traditionalist conservatives are, according to Sullivan, even

---

led to the conservative realignment, see John Judis, "The Conservative Crackup," 30–42.

40. Wolfson, "Conservatives and Neoconservatives," 39, 42.

41. Frum, "Unpatriotic Conservatives," 32.

42. Heilbrunn, "The Great Conservative Crackup," http://www.washington monthly.com/features/2006/0605.heilbrunn.html.

more out of touch. Their efforts to reintroduce religion into public life—strengthened with George W. Bush, a professed evangelical Christian, in the White House—is now the least appropriate political philosophy after September 11. "The terrorist attacks emanated from the total fusion of religion and politics," Sullivan wrote, and the message the traditionalist conservatives offer—that American culture is completely secularized and corrupt—merely plays into the hands of terrorists and has no chance of success with the American people.[43] Conservatives such as Dinesh D'Souza have taken a similar line. D'Souza argued in his book, *What's So Great about America,* that America should be defended because of its secular, postreligious social order, and he largely rejected any connection between religious faith and American identity.

While it is of course impossible to say how Kirk would have reacted to the September 11 attacks, it is instructive to look at what Kirk did write that may have some bearing on conservatism's present circumstances. Order is the first need of society, he wrote in 1973, and order is almost always grounded in a religious faith, though faith need not be established in any formal constitutional sense. Social order requires belief, but that belief cannot be manufactured from ideology. While "we must reject political religion, ideology," nevertheless we "must affirm, with all the strength that is in us, the high part of religion in the civil social order."[44] Belief, then, must spring from the people themselves and be reflected in social customs and politics.

During the controversy surrounding Senator Joseph McCarthy's investigations, Kirk cautiously supported the right of the Congress to investigate "un-American activities" by suspected Communists. He criticized McCarthy himself, however, for being in "a long line of destructive critics in the American Congress whose function it is to bedevil the executive arm for good or ill." He wrote that a country has the right to defend itself if attacked from within:

> Any ordered society has a right to protect its own existence, and, if the choice must be made, that right of society transcends the lesser right of individuals to follow their own humor to tamper with existing institutions after some predilection of their own. A people

43. Sullivan, "Right Turn: What Conservatives Should Learn from 9/11," 22.
44. Kirk, "Religion in the Civil Social Order," 306, 309.

have the right, in consequence, to expect that their officers shall obey the established laws of the land. . . . A nation so "liberal" that it cannot bring itself to repress the fanatic and the energumen under any circumstances will be reduced to a condition thoroughly illiberal.

But Kirk parted company with those conservatives who sought to impose conformity to an "American way of life," a term he considered "meaningless or positively baneful unless . . . attached to particulars. I have not the slightest idea of what 'the American way of life' in the abstract, may be." As the above quote indicates, Kirk was no pacifist, and he did not believe that the Constitution was "a suicide pact" that prohibited the nation from defending itself, either from enemies abroad or what he described as "ideologues" at home. But as long ago as 1954, Kirk condemned the doctrine of "preventive war" as "morally ruin to us."[45]

The dispute over the first Gulf War also may shed some light on how Kirk might fit within the current spectrum of conservative opinion. He broke sharply with mainstream conservative opinion about the 1991 Gulf War against Iraq, which he considered ill-advised and not in accordance with conservative principles. In making his argument against an activist foreign policy, Kirk did not rely on the "America First" tradition of Charles Lindbergh and others that has become a resource for contemporary conservatives opposed to "nation building," which rests on a characterization of the "American nation," often in racialist terms that Kirk did not use. Nor did Kirk's opposition rest primarily on the belief that government would increase in both size and intrusiveness as a result of an expansive foreign policy, though Kirk did often voice opposition to a "behemoth state."

Rather, Kirk's distaste for a more avowedly interventionist foreign policy grew out of two conclusions: first, that the elements of the American system would not be welcomed by people in other countries who cherished their own cultural traditions, and that the principles of this system could not be readily transferred to other nations in any event; and second, that the proponents of an expansive foreign policy usually represented what Kirk called the "universal monotony and mediocrity" of the basest forms of American consum-

45. Kirk, "Conformity and Legislative Committees," 347–48, 345; Kirk, *Prospects for Conservatives,* 225.

erist materialism. Therefore, it would not be prudent to engage in exporting the "American way" to other nations. Instead, in "Toward a Prudent Foreign Policy," Kirk concluded, "The differing nations of our time must find their own way to order and justice and freedom. We Americans are not appointed their keepers." This conclusion is in keeping with Kirk's conviction that a temporary respect for diversity is a cornerstone of the conservative temperament, which should influence even foreign policy, whose object should not be "to secure the triumph everywhere of America's name and manners, under the slogan 'democratic capitalism,' but instead the preservation of the true national interest, and acceptance of the diversity of economic and political institutions throughout the world."[46] Thus, Kirk's rejection of an extreme capitalism dovetailed with his rejection of a foreign policy that would place advancement of American "values" across the world.

The contrast between Kirk and other conservatives becomes even sharper in light of Kirk's statements that indicated that liberalism, as such, was no longer conservatism's enemy, but rather was passing away as a coherent intellectual position. As early as 1956, only three years after the publication of *The Conservative Mind*, for example, in an essay on John Stuart Mill, Kirk wrote that the liberal individualism in *On Liberty* "was *dated;* written at the summit of what Bagehot calls the Age of Discussion, it is a voice out of the vanished past of nineteenth-century meliorism."[47] He concluded that liberalism, by its own internal premises, would exhaust itself while at the same time depleting the accumulated wisdom upon which it by necessity relied. Like the British writer Malcolm Muggeridge, with whom he was friendly, Kirk saw in liberalism a "death wish." Liberalism, with its belief in progress, economic leveling, passion for novelty, and disdain for tradition, was only one aspect of an anticonservative position; with its passing Kirk glimpsed a possibly darker future. Whether the coming age would be a conservative one, or reflect something far worse than liberalism, was the deeper question that underlay most of Kirk's work.

Kirk is usually placed in the "traditionalist," or paleoconservative, camp. In retrospect, however, as we have seen, the distance between Kirk and the other major conservative camps becomes more evident,

<hr />

46. *PP,* 215, 221.
47. Kirk, "Mill's 'On Liberty' Reconsidered," 23.

and his traditionalism assumes a rather idiosyncratic cast.[48] Despite his consciously old-fashioned pose, his thought was not as congruent with that of the paleoconservatives as some have thought. Although his early books, particularly his study of John Randolph, endeared him to southern conservatives, as the years passed the South did not assume a central role in his construction of conservatism (as it did, for example, in that of thinkers such as Bradford or Richard Weaver). *The Conservative Mind* is largely a study of New England and British figures. In *The Politics of Prudence,* one of his last books, Kirk names only two southerners—his first subject Randolph and his old friend Weaver—among ten "exemplary conservatives." His open admiration for Abraham Lincoln as a conservative figure further separated him from the paleoconservatives' ranks. Yet his interpretation of Lincoln as a democratic Burke, born of the same Christian Western culture, differed as well from the neoconservatives' understanding of Lincoln as the president who inserted the ideals of the Declaration of Independence into the Constitution.

Likewise, Kirk's reading of the American founding did not find favor with the neoconservatives or the conservative academics influenced by the political theorist Leo Strauss. Both groups placed Locke, Hobbes, and the "new political science" at the center of the creation of the United States. The founding was a break from, rather than a continuation of, Western political history that began with Jerusalem, Athens, and Rome. Instead, Kirk eclipsed Locke and Hobbes with Burke and Hooker and argued that the founders were more influenced by their Protestant Christianity, political experiences, and common law backgrounds than by political philosophy. The political theorist Willmoore Kendall criticized Kirk on precisely this point. Kendall argued that Kirk improperly reached over to Burke to supply an American tradition of slow change while ignoring two facts: first, that slow change was not properly a part of the American tradition; and second, that the manner in which change was regulated was *already* included within the American tradition, through the amendment provisions of the Constitution, as were the criteria by which to judge change (for example, in the preamble to the Constitution).

48. See Robert Heineman, "Conservatism in the U.S.: 1976 to the Present," 1451. Heineman organizes conservatives into traditionalists (including the agrarians), libertarians, neoconservatives, and what he calls "populist" conservatives, emerging largely from evangelical religious groups.

Kirk had described the founding generation as representing an American conservative resistance to change. Kendall in contrast argued that in fact "change . . . was the watchword on these shores from the moment of the Mayflower Compact, which in and of itself was a breathtaking political innovation," as were the Declaration of Independence and the Constitution. Likewise, Kendall hammered at Kirk's evocation of an "eternal contract" binding the generations. While perhaps appropriate in a British context, in which there is no written compact, in America "we know perfectly well what contract we are referring to, namely that of the Declaration of Independence as renewed and specified in the Constitution." Without the principles of the Declaration, there would be no way to distinguish good traditions from bad. The political theorist Walter Berns made a similar point in reviewing Kirk's *A Program for Conservatives:* "To limit ourselves to just one example, consider [Kirk's] definition of loyalty as love of 'the prescriptive values of American society' or of the 'nation's traditions.' The question to which this assertion is exposed cannot be asked too often: which values and which traditions?"[49] Kirk would spend a lifetime elaborating his answer to this challenge.

Charles R. Kesler has updated Kendall's critique. In a lecture entitled "What's Wrong with Conservatism," Kesler singled out "traditionalist conservatism" in general and Kirk in particular as being "alienated . . . from the American political tradition." While nodding approvingly in the direction of some American figures, such as John Adams, Kirk, according to Kesler, found the founding generation wanting. George Washington, James Madison, Alexander Hamilton, and the other founders were of little interest to Kirk, because they did not endorse "the quasi-Burkean love of prescription, inequality, and the Romantic-organic view of society that Kirk himself embraced."[50] The corollary to Kirk's neglect of the major figures of the founding led to his underemphasizing the uniqueness of the American Revolution, in preference to his creation of a "consciously Anglo-American" hybrid, which obscured in the name of prescriptive rights and a hatred of abstraction the real "natural rights" that the American revolution sought to preserve.

Kirk's interpretation of the cultural development of American so-

---

49. Kendall, "The Benevolent Sage of Mecosta," in N. D. Kendall, ed., *Willmoore Kendall Contra Mundum,* 36–37, 46–47; Berns, review of *A Program for Conservatives,* by Russell Kirk, 683, 685.

50. Kesler, "What's Wrong with Conservatism," 7.

ciety could not be more different, and it places in sharp relief the difference between his conservatism and that sketched in the views of thinkers like Kendall and Berns. "It is a sad error," he wrote, "to fancy that the American Revolution and the Constitution broke with the British past and the American past. . . . It is no less intellectual folly to argue that the Constitution was written in conformity with the ideas of John Locke, subjecting the American people to perpetual obedience to what are alleged to be Locke's political principles."[51] In contrast to the Straussians and the neoconservatives, Kirk did not interpret the Constitution as a defense of any abstract "ideas," but rather as a legitimate elaboration of the American colonial tradition arising from its British heritage.

Kirk's argument emphasized continuity and devalued the quasi-ideology of American "exceptionalism" in favor of inserting it into a wider tradition. Writing against Clinton Rossiter, Kirk argued that "National historical experience, though it matters a great deal, is not all."[52] His understanding of the development of culture in general and America in particular placed him at odds with other conservatives on issues such as free trade, immigration, government power, and even the meaning of America. In 1986, for example, Kirk was already separating himself from conservatives who would "urge us to sell the National Parks to private developers" or "Those who fancy that foreign policy can be conducted with religious zeal, on a basis of absolute right and absolute wrong."[53] And he absolutely rejected any equation of American culture with "Democratic Capitalism." Kirk's vision of the American founding accords more with republican scholars such as J. G. A. Pocock than with the now-standard conservative account. Scholars such as Barry Alan Shain and Donald Lutz have supplied a more complex picture of the history of the founding, showing its deep roots in the Protestant covenantal tradition rather than in the natural rights theories of the seventeenth and eighteenth centuries.[54] This interpretation of America, however, and Kirk's criticisms made him a somewhat ambivalent figure among

51. Kirk, *Rights and Duties*, 45 (hereafter cited as *RD*).
52. *BDA*, 59.
53. Kirk, "Enlivening the Conservative Mind," 25, 27.
54. See, for example, Shain, *The Myth of American Individualism: The Protestant Origin of American Political Thought*; Lutz, "Religious Dimensions in the Development of American Constitutionalism," 21. The classic works remain Pocock, *The Machiavellian Moment: Florentine Political Thought and the Atlantic Republican Tradition*, and Bernard Bailyn, *The Ideological Origins of the American Revolution*.

conservatives, who were more accustomed to fighting the liberal vision of American rather than quarreling about their own.

The emphasis Kirk placed on tradition and social custom has also found renewed interest among postmodern thinkers looking for a refuge from and an alternative to liberal culture. Wayne Gabardi, for example, defines culture as "the historical transmission of a learned repertory of embodied human practices expressed in symbolic codes through which individuals and social groups develop and perpetuate a way of life."[55] Postmodern figures help to throw light on Kirk's criticism of modernity, despite their great differences with conservative ideas. Kirk himself emphasized the social construction of much of our lives by tradition and custom that rendered the modern "autonomous self" simply no longer credible. Other postmodern thinkers, such as Hans-Georg Gadamer in his *Truth and Method*,[56] have voiced understandings of tradition similar in some respects to those of Kirk.

Kirk's emphasis on tradition, not surprisingly, differs from postmodern culture in certain critical respects. First, the conservative places an importance on the individual in creating and participating in tradition that postmodern culture does not. Postmodern thought tends to create monolithic cultures of "oppression" even as it criticizes modernity for doing so. The postmodern concern with fluid "structures of power" in which individuals are inescapably caught and from which they cannot break free does not allow for the exercise of the moral sense in the way Kirk understood it. This view therefore leaves little room for free will and the fallen nature of humanity, which forms a central element of the conservative understanding of tradition. Kirk proposed a different understanding. Tradition is created and re-created through the decisions of individuals acting in time. The ambient tradition, while always of course preexisting the individual, nevertheless is constantly being changed and adapted. Yet, that individuals always act within a tradition, even if they change it, is an opinion shared by Kirk and the postmoderns.

Second, tradition implies value judgments, while postmodern "culture" often does not. Such value judgments are made by authority, but there are in fact numerous authorities: institutions,

---

The republican literature is reviewed in Gerald J. Russello, "Liberal Ends and Republican Means."

55. Gabardi, *Negotiating Postmodernism*, 89.

56. Gadamer, *Truth and Method*.

churches, and the individual conscience all act as sources of authority. The postmodern view of culture as an endless play of symbols does not accord any particular set of symbols prominence and does not "privilege" any particular authority over the others. There is thus no reason to prefer one set of cultural practices over another, and the resulting position to adopt is the philosophical shrug of Rorty's "liberal ironist," who cannot explain why he believes as he does or why others should do so. Further, because of the postmodern delight in "overturning prejudices" and seeing a mass of conflicting voices in every social construct or practice, they lose the ability to judge among those practices. For Kirk, on the other hand, we are tradition-making animals and will always seek a stable expression of agreed-upon social custom. Authority comes into play to make decisions as to which traditions will be accepted and extended, and which will not. And given the long time-horizon of tradition, judgments can be made among particular social practices.

All this is not to say that Kirk was a "postmodern," which may lend an air of trendy relativism to his thought that it does not have. Kirk advocated core truths based in human nature, in what he called the "Permanent Things" of human existence. Postmodern thought, because of its opposition to Enlightenment "essentialism" relies heavily on historicist arguments (in the sense that there are no transhistorical truths). This is a criticism to which conservatism, too, has been vulnerable. Kirk's thought is historically conscious but does not reject the possibility of seeing eternal truths within historical events. That is, he sought transhistorical truths from the materials of history itself. Postmodernism, while sensitive to the complexity of human experience, too often gives up the search for truth in a welter of conflicting "symbols" or explains meaning away within an updated version of the Enlightenment "story," this time focused on race or gender rather than economics. And while politically most postmodernists have succumbed either to reaction or revolution, Kirk proposed that prudence, not ideology, should remain at the heart of the political.

There is a growing realization among some conservatives that a conservative postmodernism may avoid the same crises that have befallen liberalism upon the conclusion of the modern age. Mark C. Henrie has written that "Conservatism remains a rebuke to modernity," and "Precisely in refusing to make its peace with the modern age, conservatism will retain its voice even when modernity shall at last have been overcome."[57] Kirk's concerns over modernity—its quest for domination, obsession with technical efficiency, cult of the "emancipated" individual, progress, and drab uniformity—all find resonance in postmodern critiques. This is Kirk as, in Rod Dreher's phrase, a "crunchy con," that is, one of those conservatives who "fly below the radar of the media and Republican politicos" because their views do not fit what is considered the conservative mainstream. In an inventive grafting of Kirk onto a countercultural bourgeois bohemianism—conservatives and others who shop organic, prefer smaller communities, and disdain chain stores—Dreher identifies an emerging trend that has Kirk as a (sometimes unacknowledged) intellectual inspiration. Dreher singles out Kirk as "the most reliable guide to [a crunchy] sensibility" because he understood that conservatism was not "a political agenda" but "a fundamental stance toward reality."[58] The major themes of this stance are not reducible to a mere choice of a "crunchy" lifestyle, which is more easily enveloped within a wider individualistic free market than the orientation toward what Kirk considered the permanent things of existence.

57. Henrie, "Opposing Strains," 24, 29.
58. Dreher, "Crunchy Cons," which he later expanded into a book-length study also entitled *Crunchy Cons.*

1

Life and Thought

> The perennial problem for the conservative is . . .
> whether the present allows any sort of action that
> might preserve a cherished past.
>
> Pierre Schlag, "The Problem of the Subject"

Historian George Nash has written that Kirk supplied American conservatives with the identity and history they had been lacking.[1] *The Conservative Mind*, published in 1953, could not have come at a better time, because conservatism in America seemed to have neither an identity nor a history at midcentury. The political and literary history that Kirk provided for conservatives served as a rallying cry, and his "Permanent Things" supplied ammunition against the charge that conservatives were mere temporizers without any firm beliefs. Just three years before *The Conservative Mind* was published, the critic Lionel Trilling famously stated in his book *The Liberal Imagination* that liberalism was "not only the dominant but even the sole intellectual tradition" left in America. And Louis Hartz concluded in his influential study *The Liberal Tradition in America* that the lack of a true conservatism in America was almost inevitable because America "never had a real conservative tradition" in the first place,

1. Nash, *Conservative Intellectual Movement*, 67.

such as that existing in Europe. Two decades later, literary historian Robert Crunden, looking back on the early part of the twentieth century, found thinkers of a conservative cast to be the "superfluous men," lacking much influence or many prospects in liberal America.[2]

By the mid-1950s, however, despite these dire diagnoses, prospects had begun to improve. *National Review* had already announced its intention to stand athwart history, yelling "stop" to the rush of progress. Kirk used his early books as exercises to retrieve the past for a century he felt was heading for disaster. Others joined him. In those years, conservatives began to articulate a comprehensive intellectual opposition to liberalism and, as the slow emergence of politicians calling themselves "conservatives" was to show, a political one as well. What Kirk called his "prolonged essay in the history of ideas" was one of a small cluster of books—including Friedrich von Hayek's *The Road to Serfdom* (1944), Richard Weaver's *Ideas Have Consequences* (1948), Whittaker Chambers's *Witness* (1952), and Robert Nisbet's *The Quest for Community* (1953)—that enabled American conservatives in the 1940s and 1950s to collect what had been a disorganized and splintered body into a coherent social force.

With the publication of these books, a history of conservative thought that was half-hidden and half-created began to come into focus. Indeed, one of the purposes of *The Conservative Mind* was to compose a narrative that placed conservative principles at the very core of Western and, with Kirk's later *The Roots of American Order*, American culture. Most prominent among these "preconservatives" were the humanists Irving Babbitt and Paul Elmer More of Harvard; the individualist Albert Jay Nock; members of the "Austrian school" of economists (only later, and never fully, embraced by Kirk); the group of critics and poets connected to Vanderbilt University known as the Southern Agrarians; and above all T. S. Eliot. It was Eliot, supplanting the philosopher George Santayana by the third edition, who served, along with Burke, as the bookend thinkers in *The Conservative Mind*.[3] In different ways, each of them opposed what they

2. Trilling, *The Liberal Imagination: Essays on Literature and Politics*, 5; Hartz, *The Liberal Tradition in America*, 57; Crunden, *The Superfluous Men: Conservative Critics of American Culture, 1900–1945*.

3. See Kirk, "The Conservative Movement: Then and Now." Babbitt's best-known work may be *Democracy and Leadership*. Babbitt's thought is analyzed in Claes Ryn, *Will, Imagination, and Reason: Babbitt and Croce and the Problem of Re-*

perceived (variously) as the excessively democratic, industrial, centralizing, secularizing, or intellectually impoverishing drift of American and Western culture. Although seemingly moribund before the New Deal and of no importance if compared to the regnant liberalism of the 1950s and early 1960s, Crunden concluded that conservative writers nevertheless produced a significant body of work that challenged liberalism's central premises.[4]

Missing from Kirk's pantheon, however, were several figures some admired for their conservatism. For example, Kirk omitted Lord Bolingbroke and Alexander Hamilton and southerners such as George Fitzhugh. As will be discussed more fully in chapter 4, Kirk suggested that Bolingbroke was a reactionary rather than a true conservative, seeking to reinstate an aristocratic politics that could no longer exist. Hamilton, too, was something of a reactionary, a "grand old-fangled gentleman," who sought to transport English life to the New World, ignoring that "it is difficult to reproduce social classes from a model three thousand miles over the ocean."[5] While Hamilton has received new attention from conservatives for his emphasis on an "energetic" executive, for Kirk he did not embody the mainstream of conservatism. Nor did Kirk ever warm, in his published writings at least, to the "Old Right" populists such as *Chicago Tribune* publisher Colonel Robert R. McCormick or Charles Lindbergh, who have received increased attention from some paleoconservatives.[6] *The Conservative Mind*, in other words, was a conscious attempt to shape the conservative past and not merely to "retrieve" a set of objective historical facts, as some argued at the time.

The scattering of conservative intellectuals soon became a self-conscious "movement," dedicated as much to political victory as they were to intellectual sophistication. Their efforts resulted in one political near miss—the failed candidacy of Barry Goldwater for the presidency in 1964—before achieving political victory with the election of Ronald Reagan as president in 1980. During these years, Kirk

---

ality. Recent discussion of More's importance can be found in Stephen L. Tanner, "Paul Elmer More and the Critical Temper." A selection of Nock's essays are collected in *State of the Union: Essays in Social Criticism.* The Southern Agrarians' position is stated in their 1930 manifesto, *I'll Take My Stand* (Baton Rouge: Louisiana State University Press, 1977).

4. Crunden, *Superfluous Men*, xii–xiii.

5. *CM*, 80.

6. Justin Raimondo, *Reclaiming the American Right: The Lost Legacy of the Conservative Movement.*

founded the scholarly journals *Modern Age* and *The University Bookman*. He also participated directly in politics, most importantly during the campaign of Barry Goldwater but extending through the Nixon and Reagan eras.[7] Any full analysis of American intellectual and political history in the postwar period must account for Kirk's influence on the formation of conservatism in the wake of the Second World War through the first Gulf War.[8]

Since his death, Kirk has been the subject of several Festschriften and has been graced with titles such as "Apostle of Ordered Liberty," "Knight of Truth," and (borrowing a term once used to describe Taft) "Mr. Conservative." It is unclear whether Kirk would have welcomed this iconic status; indeed, toward the end of his life, he warned younger conservatives not to take "Kirk's Works" as a bible of conservatism.[9] When Kirk arrived on the American intellectual scene in the 1950s, he was more than a mere guru of the "conservative movement": he was seen as a sophisticated exponent and interpreter of the primary alternative system of thought to liberalism, and not just by other conservatives. It was common, for example, during the 1950s through at least the early 1970s for Kirk's reviews and essays to appear in such seemingly unlikely places as the *New York Times Magazine*, the *Annals of the American Academy of Political and Social Science*, and even *Cosmopolitan*.[10] Kirk was often paired with a recognized liberal figure to present a conservative account of public events.[11] Just as important, Kirk's books were reviewed in major journals and newspapers in the United States, Britain, and Europe, from the *New York Times Book Review*, the *Chicago Tribune*, and the *Baltimore Sun* to the *Manchester Guardian* and the *Observer*, from *Time* (which devoted the whole of its book review section to *The Conservative Mind*) to the *Yale Review* and the *Political Science Quarterly*.[12] In reaching beyond an audience already favorably disposed toward

7. Lee Edwards, *Goldwater: The Man Who Made a Revolution*. Kirk's own account can be found in *SI*, 254–304.

8. James E. Person Jr., *Russell Kirk: A Critical Biography of a Conservative Mind*. My thanks to Mr. Person for letting me see his study in manuscript. In addition to the memorial issues noted below, more personal accounts of Kirk can be found in Michael Jordan, "Me and Mecosta: Studying with Russell Kirk," 35; and Christopher O'Brien, "Liberal Studies through International College," 159.

9. *PP*, 47.

10. Kirk, "You Can't Trust Perpetual Adolescents," 62.

11. See, for example, Kirk, "A Republican View of the Democrats," 49; and "Is Social Science Scientific?" 30.

12. For a complete listing through 1980, see Charles Brown, *Russell Kirk: A Bibliography*, 105.

conservatism and the somewhat insulated conservative intellectual community, Kirk was almost as successful as William F. Buckley Jr. in attracting a wider public audience. Indeed, Thomas Fleming, a leading paleoconservative and editor of the journal *Chronicles*, described the Kirk of the 1950s as "on his way . . . to becoming one of America's great literary celebrities."[13]

Yet that celebrity never quite happened. While remaining well respected, others took his place in the conservative limelight. Kirk is usually grouped with those conservatives who find refuge, as Samuel Francis has written, in "species of romanticism or archaism."[14] This image, perhaps more than the substance of his thought, has hindered his continued prime of place as an expositor of conservative thought. The conservative battles during the 1980s, in which he was an indifferent participant, also put him on the sidelines. Yet far from representing a "literary and romantic" nostalgia or an unsophisticated approach to social and political analysis, Kirk's works set out a multilayered interpretation of Western culture and a critique of modernity.

The delight Kirk took in his fiction, which was not often considered of great importance by those more interested in Kirk's critical or historical works, indicates that his role as a "conservative intellectual" or the "godfather of the conservative movement" was for him only part of the story. In 1987, for example, Kirk published his *The Wise Men Know What Wicked Things Are Written on the Sky*, a collection of lectures given at the Heritage Foundation, a conservative think tank in Washington. That same year Kirk's story "There's A Long, Long Trail A-Winding" appeared in *The Color of Evil*, a collection of horror stories that also featured Stephen King, H. P. Lovecraft, and Shirley Jackson. When first published in 1974, this story won the short fiction award at the third World Fantasy Convention. Kirk used stories such as this one to give narrative form to his arguments about human nature and society. As James Person noted, fiction permitted Kirk to indulge his imaginative bent to clothe his concerns about the confrontation between religion and secularism and his distrust of progress. In particular, the fantastic tales Kirk devised enabled him to express his conviction, which will be discussed more fully in chapter 3 of this volume, that the past is never far from the present and

13. Fleming, "Thunder on the Right," 43.
14. Francis, *Beautiful Losers: Essays on the Failure of American Conservatism*, 4.

that beneath the surface of our materialist age, spiritual forces still exist.[15]

The "Two Kirks:" A Brief Biography

Much of Kirk's early work was perhaps unexpected for those looking for "typical" American conservative writings of the 1950s. Kirk wrote of drinking with Scottish lords and adventuring with the poet-translator Roy Campbell, and he spent more time wandering through the haunted castles of old Scotland than commenting directly on the United States and its affairs. His early life is more reminiscent of those American modernists of the preceding generation who sought authenticity and adventure away from the United States than the staid conservatives with whom Kirk is often grouped. His essay collection entitled *Confessions of a Bohemian Tory*, published in 1963, but containing his reflections from the mid and late 1950s, provides a glimpse of how Kirk saw himself. In the opening lines, Kirk described himself as "A connoisseur of slums and strange corners, I have dwelt in more garrets and cellars, forest cabins and island hovels, than I can recall," and he argued that one could easily be both bohemian and Tory.

> A Tory, according to Samuel Johnson, is a man attached to orthodoxy in church and state. A bohemian is a wandering and often impecunious man of letters or arts, indifferent to the demands of bourgeois fad and fable. Such a one has your servant been. Tory and bohemian go not ill together: it is quite possible to abide by the norms of civilized existence, what Mr. T. S. Eliot has called "the permanent things": and yet to set at defiance the sot securities and sham conventionalities of twentieth-century sociability.[16]

Although a Tory, Kirk was not yet attached to religious orthodoxy: his conversion to Catholicism still lay some years in the future. Nor do his condemnations of the "bourgeois fad and fable," "sot securities," and "sham conventionalities" trace usual conservative pieties;

15. Kirk, "There's A Long, Long Trail A-Winding," 87; Person, *Kirk: A Critical Biography,* 111. See Robert Champ, "Russell Kirk's Fiction of Enchantment," 39–42.
    16. *CBT,* 3–4

were not these the very things conservatives ought to be preserving? Kirk was charting a different course: of orthodoxy, yes, but not of the expected kind.

As Kirk recalled in his memoir, "Some readers began to fancy that there were two scribbling Russell Kirks." And indeed, in a sense, there were two: the one who composed long works of biography or intellectual history; and the other who produced stories of the occult for collections such as *Love of Horror* and who was given the "high distinction" of being made a "Knight Commander of the Order of Count Dracula" by the Count Dracula Society, for his books *The Surly Sullen Bell* and *The Old House of Fear.* The historian John Lukacs noted this duality in a tribute to Kirk, whom he described as "both Tory and Puritan." According to Lukacs, Kirk "has propagated the restoration of medieval and bourgeois virtues sometimes within the same book or essay or article."[17] For those already familiar with Kirk, his 1995 posthumous memoir, *The Sword of Imagination,* contained few surprises. Kirk was accustomed to reciting his personal experiences in his columns and essays. *National Review* readers had long ago been treated to the story of the courtship of his wife, whom he invariably called the "beauteous Annette" and whom he married in 1964. Similarly, stories of Kirk's family and ancestors, his boyhood experiences, and his many travels found their way into his writings, and it is these stories that make up the bulk of his autobiography.

The son of a railroad engineer, Russell Amos Kirk was born in the railroad town of Plymouth, Michigan, in October 1918. Although they were not wealthy, Kirk's forebears had long been in America. According to Kirk, one of his ancestors was brought up on charges in the Massachusetts Bay Colony in the seventeenth century for "neglect of public worship and spending the Sabbath slothfully." His family had achieved some prominence in their adopted state of Michigan, and his ancestor Amos Johnson had been a founder of the hamlet of Mecosta. As a boy Kirk spent his summers in this small village and later made his home there. His Mecosta relations had a reputation for being "spiritualists" and for hosting séances and ghostly summonings at their house, which the locals called "Piety Hill." Looking back on his boyhood, Kirk imbued Piety Hill with a faded grandeur: "Over everything at Piety Hill brooded an air, by no

---

17. *SI*, 251, 339; Lukacs, "An Exceptional Mind, an Exceptional Friend," in Person, ed., *Unbought Grace*, 53.

means oppressive, of vanished lands, frustrated ambitions, forgotten expectations. One learned not to lay up treasures on earth, where moth and rust doth corrupt. The vanity of human wishes was writ large at Mecosta."[18] This of a town of which, it should be said, never numbered more than two thousand residents and during Kirk's writing career may have had less than half that many.

From his youth, Kirk identified two major influences on his thinking. The two—somewhat opposed to each other—can serve as counterpoints for understanding his later work and from which one can trace the emergence of the "two Kirks." On the one side was Frank Pierce, his maternal grandfather. Pierce owned a local bank in Plymouth and seems to have been something of a self-made man. While it was Kirk's grandmother who provided young Kirk with his first history books—including one composed by the family genealogist of the Pierce clan—it was his grandfather who would become the stronger influence.

Pierce passed on to Kirk his love of history and serious conversation, as well as his fondness for long walks, for which Kirk was later to become famous. Pierce seems to have been a sober, serious man, and Kirk was often to have recourse to his grandfather when needing an example of the "real shapers of public opinion," for whom he wrote. British constitutional thinker Alfred V. Dicey said that it was these individuals who illustrated the advantages of a localist culture that emphasized small communities and who ultimately shape national affairs. The story, which Kirk recounted many times, of his grandfather matching wits with the gangster "Machine Gun Kelly" outside the safe of his bank concentrates into a narrative all the characteristics of Kirk's ideal citizen: resourceful, pious (in the Roman sense of the word), honorable, and self-assured in the face of danger.[19]

Kirk's other major influences were the Swedenborgians and spiritualists who inhabited Piety Hill. They inspired Kirk's love of ghost stories and his feel for the occult. Indeed, his memoir is filled with stories of his and other people's encounters with ghosts at Piety Hill. Kirk later used some of these stories as bases for his fictional works. Indeed, at times the border between his "eldritch tales" and the odd events at Piety Hill is hard to distinguish. Kirk did not have a par-

---

18. *SI*, 4; Kirk, "The Quickening of Imagination," 284.
19. *CBT*, 11.

ticularly religious upbringing: his parents were apparently fallen-away Protestants, and as he himself confessed, "No member of my family had been baptized since time out of mind, nor did any of them go to church."[20] Yet exposure to these marginalized spiritualists formed a core part of his thinking. From the repeated stories of hauntings, séances, and odd happenings, Kirk developed his critique of rationalism. Sole reliance on reason could not take account of such things and so could not provide an explanation for basic human emotions such as terror, redemption, or forgiveness.

In the fall of 1936, Kirk began his studies at Michigan State College of Agriculture and Applied Science, now Michigan State University. Kirk supported himself at Michigan State largely by entering contests and competing for prizes. He also began to write for academic quarterlies—significantly, his first published piece, "Mementoes," was a reflection on artifacts found in his family's house. Another early essay, written during the Second World War, was drawn from the diary of an ancestor who had fought in the Civil War. After graduating in 1940 with a degree in history, Kirk entered Duke University, where he wrote his master's thesis on John Randolph of Roanoke, which was years later to become his first book.

After graduating from Duke, Kirk faced an uncertain future. As he recalled in his memoir, during that time he sank into a deep sense of apathy.[21] In what turned out to be a fortunate event, Kirk was drafted into the army shortly after Pearl Harbor. He spent the majority of his time in the military at the Dugway Proving Ground in Utah. His duties were light and involved mostly office work. At Dugway, Kirk was able, almost without limit, to indulge his reading habits and to expand his intellectual horizons; it was during this period, for example, that he exchanged a series of letters with the libertarian thinker Nock. It was also at Dugway that Kirk read Marcus Aurelius's *Meditations,* which had a long-lasting effect on his work.

During the war Kirk began to form the ideas that would later characterize his life's work: "In the Great Salt Lake Desert . . . he began to perceive that pure reason has its frontiers and that to deny the existence of realms beyond those borders . . . why, that's puerility." Despite his admiration for the great minds of the modern age, "His was no Enlightenment mind, Kirk now became aware: it was a Gothic

20. Ibid., 14.
21. *SI,* 53.

mind, medieval in its temper and structure. He did not love cold harmony and perfect regularity of organization; what he sought was a complex of variety, mystery, tradition, the venerable, the awful."[22] This conclusion combined an intellectual conviction with temperament, and it defined Kirk's rejection of the Enlightenment mind. He came to advocate modes of thought that departed from the Enlightenment vision in fundamental ways. Tradition and mystery, for example, were to become cornerstones of his own conservatism.

After the war, Kirk returned to Michigan. Eventually, he found a job as an instructor in history at Michigan State and opened a small used-book store in East Lansing, Michigan. Still unsure of what he might do, in the fall of 1948 Kirk decided to begin doctoral studies at St. Andrews University in Scotland. For his dissertation, he chose to write on the thought of Edmund Burke. Kirk's time in Scotland during the 1950s and in Europe during the early 1960s and the friends he acquired there were to have a lasting effect on his character and his writing.

Always shy and laconic, Kirk found the courtly and reserved manners of St. Andrews and rural Scotland more to his liking than the brash attitudes of postwar America. The many ghostly tales and stories of hauntings surrounding the Scottish great houses continued to fuel Kirk's fascination with the occult and the Gothic. And although Kirk bore many of the marks of his low-church Puritan ancestors (indeed, in a certain way, Kirk's family was not that much different from many other WASP families brought low by one too many financial adventures, but still retaining the house in the country and sets of old books), the aristocratic and medieval trappings of Scotland's peers appealed to him, especially in light of his rising appreciation for the Gothic mind. The initial result of this close connection with Scotland, as reflected in his writings of the time, was the creation of Kirk's lasting persona in the United States. So strong was the Scottish stamp that when he returned to the United States some conservatives suspected him of harboring a preference for aristocracy or an established church rather than postwar American democracy. Kirk did little to alter this perception, even after he settled in the United States and began writing for American periodicals. Instead, Kirk appropriated the persona and crafted an image of himself as a

22. Ibid., 68–69.

"figure of antique grandeur,"[23] an image that assisted him in sharpening his critique of modernity. Pictures of him from this time—still a relatively young man—show him severely dressed in old-fashioned costume, complete with walking cane and watch fob. He combined this façade as lower-case Scottish laird with his interpretation of the Roman philosopher-emperor Marcus Aurelius's Stoicism. Yet his writings reveal not a dour fustiness, but a real sense of fun even as he engaged in serious intellectual battle.

The end result of his studies in Scotland was *The Conservative Mind,* which was published in 1953 by the small conservative publishing house of Regnery, after being rejected by Knopf. Later, with the assistance of T. S. Eliot, it was published in Britain by Faber and Faber. The extensive press the book received, both positive and negative, helped launch Kirk as a conservative standard-bearer. Four decades later, Kirk commented on its reception in his memoir: "Few politico-historical books in the twentieth-century have enjoyed such a record—or so much influence, direct or indirect."[24] *The Conservative Mind* was widely reviewed, and after Gordon Keith Chalmers's favorable assessment of the work appeared in the *New York Times, Time* magazine devoted its entire book review section to it.

Not all reviewers, however, thought so highly of the young scholar's tome. Prominent representatives of the liberal order accepted Kirk's challenge. Norman Thomas, for example, focused on Kirk's alleged ignorance of the class struggle. In *United Nations World,* Thomas disparaged Kirk's espousal of a "democracy of elevation" simply because he did not appreciate "socialism, the welfare state and the income tax." The *New Republic* published a negative review titled "The Blur of Mediocrity" by Francis Biddle, who had served as attorney general under President Roosevelt and as a judge at Nuremberg. The critic and poet John Crowe Ransom, Clinton Rossiter, and Peter Gay all criticized portions of Kirk's argument. But as Nash noted, aside from any substantive merits it may have had, the book arrived at the right time: "these were the early days of the apparently conservative administration of President Eisenhower; perhaps Kirk's book could yield clues about the aspirations of the resurgent Right." Kirk himself expressed some surprise that the book had made such "a splash."[25]

23. Ibid., 116.
24. Ibid., 150.
25. Brown, *Kirk: A Bibliography,* 105–7; Nash, *Conservative Intellectual Movement,* 67; *SI,* 149.

Kirk, nominally still on the staff of Michigan State when he came back to the United States in 1952, resigned his position and returned to Scotland the following summer. Kirk had little patience for the politics of a small university, and the university in turn had little time for a now well-known conservative writer. In 1953, after some months in Scotland, he returned to Mecosta to make his way by writing. The town was still home to a number of Kirk's relatives, in whose house he lived and later inherited. From that point, Kirk began to assume his place among major conservative thinkers. Shortly after the publication of *The Conservative Mind*, Kirk received a Guggenheim Fellowship for study abroad. The result of his travels in Britain on the fellowship was the collection *Beyond the Dreams of Avarice: Essays of a Social Critic*.

During this period, at the suggestion of William F. Buckley Jr., Kirk agreed to contribute a regular column—entitled "From the Academy"—to a new conservative journal, the *National Review*. The column ran for more than two decades, and for much of the 1950s and 1960s Kirk wrote on a wide range of educational matters. As noted above, he also founded his own journal, evocative of the old monthlies and quarterlies that he admired. Initially entitled the *Conservative Review*, the first issue was published under the title *Modern Age* in 1957. The new journal was intended to diagnose and correct the ills of the modern age, not to celebrate its successes. Kirk sought to reverse the universalist "notions" of modernity, whose "overweeningly arrogant" proponents had, Kirk thought, brought the world almost to ruin.[26]

Kirk became more prominent in intellectual and political circles as the years passed. Although he was a prolific writer, Kirk also made his living by lecturing, and he was much sought after as a representative of "the conservative position." This was especially so during the 1960s, when Kirk frequently engaged liberals or radicals of the day, such as Tom Hayden or William Kunstler, on issues ranging from educational policy to Vietnam. As a result of his relative isolation and freedom from regular academic duties, Kirk used his time to follow up the success of *The Conservative Mind* with a series of books that further established his reputation. Kirk's studies of Edmund Burke and Robert Taft both appeared in 1967, followed four years later by his study of T. S. Eliot, entitled *Eliot and His Age: T. S. Eliot's Moral Imagination in the Twentieth Century*. The Eliot study was

26. *SI*, 187–88, 191–93.

widely noted and reviewed by writers such as Denis Donoghue and Paul Theroux.[27] After this series of discrete subjects, Kirk once again returned to the grand narrative style with his *Roots of American Order.*

It was also during these years that Kirk became actively involved in Republican politics. As will be discussed in chapter 4, he campaigned vigorously for Goldwater in 1964, supporting him first in the primaries against Rockefeller, and then defending his reputation against Johnson. However, he pointedly noted that he was kept at a distance from the campaign itself and was not consulted in matters of policy.[28] Kirk also was consistently active in Michigan politics. He campaigned, for example, to retain rural schools against centralized education and later served as justice of the peace for the township in which Mecosta is located.

Yet, despite the fact that the conservative political message began to gain more force in the 1970s into the 1980s and that Kirk continued to publish, his fortunes within conservatism began to change. There were several reasons for his relatively decreased visibility, including the improved self-confidence of American conservatives, who were able to proffer alternative standard-bearers, and the lifelong reluctance of Kirk to assume the spotlight. Wesley McDonald, writing on Kirk's reputation, attributes his decline to the larger disputes among conservatives during the 1980s, particularly the entry of neoconservatives such as Norman Podhoretz and the group of political theorists influenced by Leo Strauss.[29] These new arrivals, according to McDonald, replaced an earlier generation of conservatives, particularly traditionalists such as Kirk, at the forefront of antiliberal thinking in America.

But as with other changes in conservative opinion during his career, the controversies did not change Kirk's own program much. Through the 1980s, Kirk published books and essay collections on a regular basis. He presented two important series of lectures at the Heritage Foundation: one on "political errors of the twentieth century"; and another on law and justice. In 1992, he received from President Ronald Reagan the Presidential Citizens Medal in public recognition of his work. He died at home two years later, after pub-

27. Ibid., 405–14. See also Theroux, "The Way to East Coker," 4–5.
28. *SI*, 285–88.
29. McDonald, "Russell Kirk and the Prospects for Conservatism."

lishing *The Politics of Prudence,* an essay collection that surveyed the conservative landscape.

Beyond the Canons: Major Themes

In a well-known passage of *The Conservative Mind,* Kirk set forth what he considered to be the six basic "canons" that had defined conservative thought since the French Revolution. They were, largely, opposites of those features that Kirk believed defined the modern world: (1) a belief in a transcendent order, which Kirk described variously as based in tradition, divine revelation, or natural law; (2) an affection for the "variety and mystery" of human existence; (3) a conviction that society requires orders and classes that emphasize "natural distinctions"; (4) a belief that property and freedom are closely linked; (5) a faith in custom, convention, and prescription; and (6) recognition that change is not reform, which entails a respect for the political value of prudence.[30] These canons were not static, and Kirk's formulation of them changed over the years. In his last enumeration of these principles, for example, the requirement of orders and classes in society was muted. Perhaps in recognition that with the end of the Cold War the allure of large-scale government schemes was waning, Kirk added instead an explicit canon favoring "voluntary communities" rather than opposing social planning.[31]

In retrospect, these canons are perhaps the weakest part of the book. Such a catalog played right into the hands of his critics, who thought these principles exemplified a conservative abstraction at odds with the historical texture of the remainder of Kirk's argument. He had, in other words, fallen into a rationalistic mode more akin to liberal theorizing and had, some thought, failed to connect the two halves of his account. One reviewer, Gordon Lewis, concentrated on this precise point: "any attempt to build philosophic foundations for [the conservative] attitude is invariably evidence that the attitude no longer claims the instinctive allegiance" of the culture; "far too much of genuine conservatism . . . is a matter of feeling and instinct and emotion to be satisfactorily reducible to the forms of logical asser-

---

30. *CM,* 8–9. For an extended introductory gloss on these canons, see Person, *Kirk: A Critical Biography,* 37–47.
    31. *PP,* 17–24.

tion and proof."[32] Although Kirk never renounced the canons, they continued to change, perhaps as a sign of his discomfort with such abstractions. In his later works there were as many as ten, and in more recent editions of *The Conservative Mind*, Kirk admonished that "if one seeks by definition more than this, the sooner [one] turns to individual thinkers, the surer ground [one] is on." Indeed, in one of his last books Kirk acknowledged that his understanding of these conservative principles was fluid: "The diversity of ways in which conservative views may find expression is itself proof that conservatism is no fixed ideology. What particular principles conservatives emphasize during any given time will vary with the circumstances and necessities of that era."[33] Rather, other themes implicit in *The Conservative Mind* such as the imagination (not mentioned in the canons) were instead brought to the fore in his other works.

This fluidity in defining conservative principles offers an obvious conceptual difficulty for conservatives: if different institutions or traditions can be defended, depending on the circumstances, is there any core to conservative thought? Kirk never answers that question with any finality. Conservatism, he seems to say, cannot be known in itself—any reduction of its propositions to a list of "dogmata" destroys what makes conservatism worth advocating, namely, its resistance to rigidity and tolerance of multiplicity. To contend otherwise would, in Kirk's formulation, reduce conservatism to "ideology." "The triumph of ideology would be the triumph of what Edmund Burke called 'the antagonist world'—the world of disorder; while what the conservative seeks to conserve is the world of order we have inherited. . . . The conservative mind and the ideological mind start at opposite poles."[34] Yet that distinction deserves more analysis. The ideological mind is orderly, after a fashion: indeed, in other places Kirk criticizes ideologues for being too rigid and logical according to their premises. Rather, the ideological world is based on false assumptions about man and society; therefore, its order is a false one.

Yet, conservatism and conservatives can be known through their effects and their actions. Over time, adherence to custom and convention builds a pattern that cannot be anticipated and that defies

32. Lewis, "The Metaphysics of Conservatism," 728, 729.
33. *CM*, 10; *PP*, 17.
34. *PP*, 14.

the categorical explanations of ideology. Like Heisenberg's particles, isolating a set of concrete conservative propositions freezes them into a reactionary ideology and negates their influence and vitality, while an attempt to trace that influence though a myriad of historical and social circumstances over time renders the definition of enduring conservative principles problematic. Kirk expressed this understanding when he situated conservatism between determinism, "which equates good and truth with whatever happens to succeed," and relativism, which denies "the very existence of truth and good."[35] The former focuses too much on temporal location—what is here now is good. The latter places too much emphasis on flux— since everything changes, there can be no center. Conservatives have, at one time or another, been prone to embrace either position. Kirk tried to steer a middle path, believing that chance and variety were good and necessary, both in individuals and societies, but also holding that such flux could provide a way to see, even if only partially, a stable center.

While there is no reason to doubt that the six canons set out in *The Conservative Mind* provided the scaffolding for much of Kirk's thinking, they should be distinguished from other important themes that inform his work. For example, as noted, the imagination is barely implied in this list, though it does appear elsewhere in *The Conservative Mind* and assumed a large place in Kirk's thinking beginning in the 1950s and in his later work. The several types of imagination, and the imaginative structuring of reality in which Kirk engaged, were at the center of Kirk's critique of modern life and are therefore crucial to a proper understanding of his work. The importance Kirk placed on individual conscience and the necessity of narrative and story are likewise absent from this list. The canons establish a starting point for a different account of the development of Anglo-American (and, by extension, Western) civilization, from what Kirk saw as the dominant mode of the 1950s.

Religion is another feature that is absent from the canons, except as it is implicated indirectly in the belief in the transcendent. It has rarely been examined by interpreters of Kirk's thought, and some prominent conservatives have maintained that religious belief is not essential to a conservative position. Roger Scruton, for example, has stated that the contemporary conservative return to religion is itself

35. Kirk, "Conservatism Is Not an Ideology," 59.

an Enlightenment phenomenon. It represents not the world-shaking faith of traditional Christianity, but "the image of religion, held in the aspic of a law-governed state."[36] Kirk may have had some sympathy with that opinion earlier in his career—hence his respect for nontheist conservatives such as Nock and Babbitt. Later, however, he held a contrary opinion. Even before his conversion, which occurred in the 1960s after his marriage, he believed "orthodoxy in church and state" to be a part of the very definition of a "Tory," bohemian or no. And subsequent study convinced him that organized forms of religious worship were the mainsprings of culture. What "orthodoxy" Kirk meant, however, has not been too closely examined.

Indeed, the exact contours of his thinking on religious belief have not been fully explored. Christopher Dawson, one of Kirk's favorite historians, contended that, viewed historically, religion has always been bound up with the development of culture, yet religion is never solely a conservative force. Christianity tore apart the fabric of the pagan Roman Empire, and the emergence of Protestant Christianity had a similar effect on the political and theological unity of late medieval Europe. The idea of a "Christian culture" is not, as some of Kirk's opponents have implied, a monolithic theocracy espousing a reactionary politics. Indeed, at least with respect to the United States, Kirk distanced himself from such an idea. In an essay on Eliot, Kirk wrote that religion forms the basis of every society, that "Liberalism and democracy cannot stand unsupported," and that support must come from either the religious beliefs of the people or "else the inverted religion of ideology." For Kirk, the former was preferable, because he saw in ideology no limiting principle to protect society from corruption or barbarism. Nevertheless, Kirk did not endorse for America a national or established church; indeed, in that very same essay, he noted that Eliot condemned the "millenarianists," whom Kirk described as wishing to impose theocracy, and who would sweep away the institutions and traditions of America in the hope of ushering in the kingdom of God.[37]

Kirk rejected the contention that religion has a merely utilitarian purpose and decried efforts at inventing religious faith, such as the Cult of Reason during the French Revolution. He likewise disdained

---

36. See, for example, Dermot Quinn, "Religion and the Conservative Mind"; Scruton, "Godless Conservatism," 8.
37. Kirk, "Eliot and a Christian Culture," 5, 10, 15.

finding a substitute for a lost faith, such as the proponents of "civic virtue" had argued for in the 1980s. These efforts, Kirk thought, were doomed to failure and in any event were subject to being used as manipulative tools. In 1992, he wrote,

> Some well-meaning folk talk of a "civil religion," a kind of cult of patriotism, founded upon a myth of national virtue and upon veneration of certain historical documents, together with a utilitarian morality. But such experiments of a secular character never have functioned satisfactorily. . . . Worship of the state, or of the national commonwealth, is no substitute for communion with transcendent love and wisdom.
>
> Nor can attempts at persuading people that religion is "useful" meet with much genuine success. . . . People will conform their actions to the precepts of religion only when they earnestly believe the doctrines of that religion to be true.[38]

However, the features of religion that provide structure and a story of existence to people of that faith are valuable even in a practical way. Kirk also contended that faith will inevitably supply an organizing feature to that people's culture. As an empirical matter, he believed, religious cult is at the root of any culture: "Once people are joined in the cult, co-operation for many other things becomes impossible," such as agriculture, architecture, and government. The problem with modern culture is that it has lost its connections with its religious roots and has instead substituted ideology.[39] In other words, people will always have belief. The question is whether that belief will be the traditional religion of the culture or another belief system imposed on them or invented for the moment.

Religious faith has assumed a larger place in public discourse in the postmodern age. In part, "New Age" and other religions fill a gap that modern rationality leaves wanting. As Joseph Bottum has stated, "premoderns and postmoderns share the major premise that knowing requires [God's] existence," though most of the latter do not believe that God exists, while the former, by and large, did. Religious belief, therefore, need not be incompatible with postmodernism, just as it need not be incompatible with rationalism. It represents a dif-

---

38. Kirk, "Civilization without Religion?" 4.
39. *BDA*, xiv; Kirk, "Religion in the Civil Social Order," 306.

ferent realm of thought and proposes a different methodology with which to approach reality. Indeed, even central postmodern figures like Derrida have engaged seriously with theology.[40]

As will be discussed in the last chapter, the Episcopal cleric Bernard Iddings Bell, whom Kirk admired greatly, was one of the first to use the term *postmodernism* for the contemporary condition. Bell's postmodernism was explicitly religious, the solution to a crisis of faith in an unbounded reason: "dependence upon the scientific method and the appeal to reason, will, as has been said, not suffice in a world convinced that for religious discovery scientific research can be of no service whatsoever."[41] In its place, Bell proposed a postmodernism comfortable with modern science and miracles, which placed the good of existence—sacralized through the Christian understanding of Incarnation—at the center of its understanding of the world.

Kirk too found what he called "scientism," which was a reduction of human existence to material criteria, to be the enemy of religion and a particular characteristic of the modern age. Further, scientism held that true science was incompatible with, and made irrelevant, traditional religious belief. The proponents of scientism, often infused with their own blinkered rationality, "informed mankind how men and women are naked apes merely; have pointed out that the ends of existence are production and consumption merely; that happiness is the gratification of sensual impulses merely; that notions of the resurrections of the flesh and life everlasting are superstitions of the childhood of the human race merely." As Jeremy Beer noted, Kirk's critique of scientism's presumptions, especially its undermining of religious belief, were part of a larger attack on the supposed "value-neutrality" of the hard and social sciences.[42]

A corruption of true science, scientism was used to achieve particular ideological ends, and in general it simply parroted the materialistic assumptions of a previous generation. Materialism, however, is the scientific theory of yesteryear. Significantly, Kirk did not think that scientism had any real connection to contemporary sci-

40. Bottum, "Christians and Postmoderns," 28. See also John D. Caputo and Michael J. Scanlon, eds., *God, the Gift, and Postmodernism.*

41. Bell, *Postmodernism and Other Essays,* 53.

42. *BDA,* xvi. Beer, "Science Genuine and Corrupt: Russell Kirk's Christian Humanism."

ence. Contemporary science, he argued, now "ent[ers] upon the realm of mystery" and imposes no difficulty for religious belief.[43] "As it was at its dawning," Kirk wrote in an essay sharply criticizing "the old-fangled rationalist" C. P. Snow, "science is once more philosophical."[44] Religion, philosophy, and science, split at the time of the Enlightenment, may yet see a reconciliation through the intermediaries of particle physics or "string theory." Indeed, a rejection of scientism would lead to an openness toward theism:

> physicists instruct us that we of this seemingly too-solid flesh actually are collections of electrical particles, held in an ephemeral suspension and arrangements by some "laws" that we do not understand in the least. We are energy—and energy, which we can neither create nor destroy, is incessantly being transmuted into new forms. . . . For the science of quantum mechanics has undone nineteenth-century concepts of matter, and it becomes conceivable that whatever power has assembled the negative and positive charges composing us may reassemble those electrical particles, if it chooses.

In no less a forum than *Wired* magazine, Gregg Easterbrook announced a "new convergence" between science and faith. The discoveries of the last three decades, he wrote, "have left the science-has-all-the-answers script in tatters"; indeed, in fields such as particle physics that confront the basic questions of physical reality "metaphysics is making a comeback." Kirk thought that imagination was as applicable to science as it was to literature or history, and he was fond of recalling the passage in Andre Maurois' *Illusions* in which Einstein and the poet St. John Perse discover from each other that the physicist and the poet work through similar methods.[45] The scientific imagination and method held no fears for Kirk.

Two other ideas featured in the development of Kirk's thought deserve mention: the concept of *place* and the importance of *sentiment*. Uday Singh Mehta, in his detailed study of Burke and liberal political theory in the context of the British empire, discusses how these

43. Kirk, "Civilization without Religion?" 5.
44. Kirk, *The Intemperate Professor and Other Cultural Splenetics*, 68.
45. *SI*, 13–14; Easterbrook, "The New Convergence," www.wired.com/wired/archive/10/12/convergence.html; Kirk, "The Christian Imagination of T. S. Eliot," 123–24.

features of Burke's thought conditioned his reactions to the British colonial experience in India, as well as the French and American revolutions. Mehta contrasts Burke's view of place and the associated concept of territoriality with the liberal view, influenced by Locke and Mill. The liberal "myopia" regarding place "eviscerates that thought's political and emotive significance and thus renders it inert." Specifically, Mehta criticizes Locke for depriving place of any emotive significance. "By divesting a nature given and held in common of any emotive force, Locke blocks an important moment of commonness . . . and, hence, the constituent of a potential political identity." In contrast, Burke has a much fuller political and emotional account. For Burke,

> the link between place and identity is a psychological one in which feelings (such as love) and cognitive associations and not merely preferences, such as those that get mobilized in the expression of consent, are galvanized. . . . Burke takes territoriality to be constitutive of individual and collective identity and associates its denial with the cavalier horror of imperial and Jacobin excesses.[46]

Kirk criticized what he saw as the rootlessness of much of modern life and the associated loss of place as a defining characteristic of existence. As we observed earlier in his ruminations on Mecosta, a standard feature of Kirk's style was to invest even the smallest places with human drama. The emotional and imaginative resources people invest in places are important components of individual and social self-identity and, therefore, a source of loyalty and affection. These places are usually, but need not be, physical places. They can also be social or political spaces. Political boundaries, family homes, old castles, ruins, anything that can be invested with value: each can contribute to the creation and formation of personal identity in the larger culture.

Because of their power, a society should be mindful of the construction of its places; not surprisingly, architecture was an abiding concern for Kirk. In an essay entitled "The Architecture of Servility and Boredom," Kirk sets out the importance of the way buildings look. The art of architecture and city planning "must be concerned primarily with the person, and how he thrives under a large plan;

46. Mehta, *Liberalism and Empire: A Study in Nineteenth-Century British Liberal Thought,* 116, 127, 133. Kirk discusses Burke and India at *EB,* 96–123.

with the republic (or public interest) and what sort of society arises from grand designs. . . . Assuming, however, that urban planning has no limits, the breed of urban planners have given us the architecture of servility and boredom." Over the past quarter of a century and more, "anarchy and desolation have been the consequences of grandiose pseudo-planning." The critique of modern architecture contains a capsule of Kirk's broader complaints about modernity. A small class ("urban planners") controls society by manipulating its architecture and other symbols. The ideas of this class are false, seemingly focused on the public good, but more often devoted to ego or profit. Rather than public architecture, "it has been an architecture of sham: the outward symbol of a society which, despite all its protestations of being 'free' and 'democratic' rapidly sinks into servility."[47] Most important, the planners ignore the sense of scale, preferring large and bureaucratic structures, which reduce the importance of the individual, to a human-scaled community.

The mathematician and architectural critic Nikos Salingaros calls the current practice of modern architecture a "cult," and he accuses this cult of betraying traditional architecture for a false scientism and obsession with ideology. In an essay entitled "The Danger of Deconstructivism," he argues,

> In fact, we find ourselves confronted with a mystical cult that uses scientific terminology just like magical words—whose effect is due only to their sound. The cult intentionally ignores scientific meaning. This works because most people have no scientific background, and because scientists (who should be the ones to expose this fraud) are closed in their own narrow world of research. It is an irony of our times that such a cult, founded on ignorance, survives and blossoms, and has taken control of the media and the Architecture Schools.[48]

Such an orientation deprives architecture of the social role both Salingaros and Kirk believe it needs to fulfill. In a recent theological defense of place, Philip Sheldrake sees the postmodern critique of modern architecture along the same lines. He contends that it seeks "to discover place, to affirm human difference, to facilitate the re-

47. *RT,* 88–90.
48. Salingaros, "The Dangers of Deconstructivism," February 16, 2003, http:// www.2blowhards.com / archives / 000670.html.

covery of territorial identity, to build community, to reshape public space and to plan built environments in accordance with human proportion."[49]

Politically, a strong notion of place assists in reducing the power of a centralized government. At bottom, a love of country—the large nation—is dependent upon a love for one's own. Quoting Randolph, Kirk maintained that "in clinging to [the states] . . . I cling to my country; because I love my country as I do my immediate connexions; for the love of country is nothing more than the love of every man for his wife, child, or friend." As an exponent of "territorial democracy," a term he derived from Orestes Brownson, Kirk believed that, as far as possible, governmental power should be in the hands of those it governs. Thus, the people most directly affected should have a say in the decisions that are made, and if that government were to err in some fashion, any damage would be limited. Kirk opposed large governments, for their inefficiency and for the "moral absolutism" they tend to impose. In a 1989 lecture given at the Heritage Foundation, Kirk advocated "Family farms, farmers' cooperatives for marketing, encouragement of artisans and small traders, the technical and administrative possibilities of industrial decentralization, the diminution of the average size of factories," and other measures to reduce the reliance on a rationalized centralization, which "terribly damages communal existence."[50] In this criticism, Kirk continued in a long line of Anglo-American agrarian or "distributist" thinkers such as G. K. Chesterton, who opposed both economic and political collectivism. With some few exceptions, however, Kirk failed to elaborate on how such a conservative communal vision might be accomplished.

In his own life, Piety Hill encompassed one such vision. Except for the lack of an active farm, Kirk lived on a small scale the sort of life he advocated in his writings. Kirk played host to foreign visitors and displaced persons, often at some cost to himself. Technology or other accoutrements of modern life were conspicuously absent from the grounds. Holidays—especially Halloween—were celebrated with (perhaps slightly exaggerated) old-fashioned pomp, and Mecosta was perhaps as far from the center of intellectual or social ferment as one could get.

49. Sheldrake, *Spaces for the Sacred: Place, Memory, and Identity,* 164.
50. *CM,* 164; *EB,* 173–75; Kirk, "A Conservative Program for a Kinder, Gentler America," 4.

Place embodies a rich vein of experience that cannot be rendered or explained in scientific or rationalist calculus. Personal feelings for particular places, or a society's reverence for places, represent a form of understanding that modernity cannot comprehend using its usual tools. As the prominent American geographer Yi-Fu Tuan wrote in his *Space and Place: The Perspective of Experience,* "A large body of experiential data is consigned to oblivion because we cannot fit the data to concepts taken over uncritically from the physical sciences."[51] Place carries emotional weight that transcends its measurement as mere "space." Like Burke and his defense of the myriad Indian folkways against the leveling influence of the British empire, Kirk thought that historic boundaries and the customs and practices they engender are worth preserving for their own sake, out of respect for the persons who created them and also for those who have grown with and through them. This is not to say that Kirk proposed a standpattism; he believed that individuals have a responsibility to create their communities and to constantly engage the past in that act of reconstruction. For Kirk, however, the settled certainties of place are where one must begin.

Paradoxically, perhaps, although he himself was rooted in Michigan, Kirk spent much of his early adulthood abroad, first at St. Andrews and then on a number of extended trips. Like some other conservatives of a localist bent, Kirk was a wanderer, and he apparently enjoyed seeing the universal idea of place played out in different contexts. And he believed that each place is imbued with emotional and intellectual content that are part of its physicality. Thus Kirk praised Alexander Smith's quixotic and forgotten book *Dreamthorp,* for seeing with "a poet's eye" the pleasures of a real town in Scotland.[52] People are tied to place—as T. S. Eliot to London or John Randolph to Roanoke Plantation and his home state of Virginia. The efforts to enliven those places through imagination are what creates the bonds of affection in the first instance. Kirk's own estate in Mecosta embodied this conviction. The Italianate old house was decorated with cast-off and found items from hotels, churches, and other institutions, rescued from the wrecking ball. On the lands that had belonged to generations of his family, Kirk planted trees as silent reminders of the duty to plant seeds for future generations.

51. Tuan, *Space and Place: The Perspective of Experience.*
52. Kirk, "Dreamthorp and Linlithgow," 102.

A concern with sentiment also loomed large in Kirk's thought, and it was to become more important as he developed his critique of modernity. Kirk defined *sentiment* as "a moving conviction; by a conviction derived from some other source than pure reason."[53] It is sentiment, not reason, that moves us first. Architecture, politics, literature, and history all inspire feelings in us before they make us think. Although Kirk proclaimed himself to be a man more of thought than of sentiment (and hinted at least once that liberalism's reliance on sentiment was a sign of "decay"), his conception of rationality was bound to sentiments. One does not, in Kirk's view, think about something about which one has no feelings, for good or ill. Indeed, he recognized that sentiment may have more power than reason. Sentiment is not, or not only, mere feeling; in Vigen Guroian's words, sentiment is "a human response to the world that lies somewhere between thought and feeling." Without a thorough understand of ourselves and our motivations, Kirk thought rational discourse would be impossible: the passions would rule.[54]

Sentiment assumes a larger importance in Kirk's work because of his assertion that the coming (post)modern age will be an Age of Sentiments, superseding the old, modern, liberal Age of Discussion. The Age of Sentiments will be more concerned with the power of image on the heart, rather than that of logical discourse on the mind. Kirk thought that rhetoric—the creation of image through language—was a critical art for conservatism to perfect. And according to Kirk, rhetoric is only effective at creating those images if it pays careful heed to the sentiments, of both the speaker and the audience.

Kirk's construction of the role of the sentiments, therefore, is tied together with his qualified respect for reason. The first comes before the second, and he deplored those he considered reductive rationalists—John Dewey, for example—who abstracted all thought from feeling and denigrated both. Likewise, he was suspicious of men like Rousseau, whom he considered to have reduced sentiment to mere feeling and to have emancipated it from thought. Thus, when writing of education, Kirk stressed the importance of arousing students' feelings for or against certain things through the use of stories, only later providing a rational explanation for those feelings.[55]

53. *RT,* 131.
54. Guroian, *Rallying the Really Permanent Things,* 77; Kirk, "Reinvigorating Culture," 27.
55. See, for example, *EPT,* 109–15.

Imagination against Ideology

Just as much as place and sentiment, imagination lay at the heart of Kirk's thinking. In a 1976 essay, "Perishing for Want of Imagery," Kirk concluded that "when our minds are deprived of high poetic images, the vacancy will be filled by images of another origin and character," a result that will have damaging consequences. Indeed, if a culture "will not have the moral imagination . . . it will fall first to the idyllic imagination; and presently into the diabolic imagination." He described *The Conservative Mind* as an "exercise in imagination" and entitled his memoir *The Sword of Imagination.* And he wrote a number of essays elucidating the imagination in its various forms. Kirk often quoted Napoleon as saying "Imagination rules the world." He no doubt found it ironic that a man of action, or "master of the big battalions," as Kirk called him, would praise what is often perceived as a passive exercise in daydreaming.[56] (Indeed, Kirk thought himself, as the title of his memoir suggests, fighting battles as well, so perhaps the evocation of Napoleon was more than whimsical.) Imagination appears with great frequency in Kirk's essays, and knowing how he used the term is key to understanding his thought.

Gleaves Whitney has identified no fewer than five types of imagination that contributed to Kirk's program of cultural critique: historical, political, moral, poetic, and prophetic.[57] For Kirk the imagination was clearly more than a passive experience; it was a central feature of the human outlook, critical to understanding the past, selecting among political compromises, or bringing about any social change: "Not pure reason, but imagination—high dream or low dream—is the moving force in private life and in public."[58] The imagination is always to be reckoned with, a notion Kirk thought the modern world had largely forgotten in its quest for perfection and scientific knowledge. And this forgetfulness had consequences, in that the quest for perfection became tainted with doctrines alien to human happiness.

Stephen Spender characterized the modern age as one of "frag-

---

56. See *SI*, 166, 199.

57. Whitney, "The Swords of Imagination: Russell Kirk's Battle with Modernity," 4.

58. Kirk, *The Wise Men Know What Wicked Things Are Written on the Sky*, 129 (hereafter cited as *Wise Men*).

mented values," in which "the imagination cannot illustrate antiquated doctrines, cannot refer to symbolic meanings already recognized. . . . Everything has to be reinvented, as it were, from the beginning."[59] The moral imagination Kirk espoused was different: it
referred precisely to those "already recognized" meanings. Any rein-
vention was to be at the service of eternal values. The imagination
was a force of both creation and destruction, of composition as well
as decomposition; it need not be used, as some postmodernists
would have it, as solely a "deconstructive" force. Like some postmodernists, Kirk recognized that the late modern or postmodern
world was one in which the promises of the Enlightenment and
modernity had become victims of their own total reliance on the
forces of human reason. They were divorced from consideration of
the lessons of human experience and the nonrational elements of society and individuality. Imagination, expressed, for example, in narrative or collagelike collections of past experiences, was a necessary
measure to counteract the modern *libido dominandi.*

Yet, unlike the postmodernists, who often view the imagination as
a mere plaything that ultimately is unable to escape its own ephemeral projections, for Kirk the imagination was a serious and sub-
stantial component that was able to bridge the otherwise impassable
gap between individual minds. The imagination could overcome
the modern dualism, initiated with Descartes, between body and
spirit, nature and history, or reason and belief. As Elizabeth Sewall stated in her essay "The Death of the Imagination," the imagination "can work only by putting together; it has no other mode of
operation."[60] Kirk, though he also contended the imagination
played a role in stripping away the follies of ideology, would have
concurred with Sewall's basic point. The imagination has great potential to unify sentiments, loyalties, and ideas that are usually considered opposed.

Kirk borrowed the term *moral imagination* from Edmund Burke
and Irving Babbitt. In a famous passage in the *Reflections on the Revolution in France,* Burke contrasted the "superadded ideas, furnished
from the wardrobe of a moral imagination, which the heart owns,
and the understanding ratifies, as necessary to cover the defects of
our shivering nature, and to raise it to dignity in our own estima-

59. Spender, *The Struggle of the Modern,* 50.
60. Sewall, "The Death of the Imagination," 153, 183.

tion" with the "barbarous philosophy, which is the offspring of cold hearts and muddy understandings, and which is as void of solid wisdom as it is destitute of all taste and elegance, laws are to be supported only by their own terrors, and by the concern which each individual may find . . . his own speculations, or can spare them from his own private interests."[61]

Burke's tightly wrapped description gives us several elements of Kirk's understanding of the imagination. The imagination is not primarily rational, but embraces the feelings and affections of those subject to it; it is something outside the individual, but which the individual "owns" and "ratifies"; it is not based upon calculation; and it is something in addition to the physical realities of our "shivering nature." Kirk himself explained Burke's meaning as "that power of ethical perception which strides beyond the barriers of private experience and momentary events. . . . The moral imagination aspires to the apprehending of right order in the soul and right order in the commonwealth."[62] While its core remains the same, the imagination must be "expressed afresh from age to age," primarily through literature and art, but also through statesmanship. Further, the moral imagination

> informs us concerning the dignity of human nature; which instructs us that we are more than naked apes. As Burke suggested in 1790, letters and learning are hollow, if deprived of the moral imagination. And as Burke said, the spirit of religion long sustained this moral imagination, along with a whole system of manners. Such imagination lacking, to quote another passage from Burke, we are cast forth "from this world of reason, and order, and peace, and virtue, and fruitful penitence, into the antagonist worlds of madness, discord, vice, confusion and unavailing sorrow."[63]

The imagination, moreover, "as high dream or low dream," is always present, especially in literature. The only question for Kirk is whether the imagination will be respected and employed, or enslaved or ignored. Like Babbitt, Kirk thought the imagination could

61. Burke, *Reflections on the Revolution in France,* vol. 2 of *Select Works of Edmund Burke* (Indianapolis: Liberty Fund, 1999), 171.
62. Kirk, "The Moral Imagination," 37, 38.
63. *RT,* 71.

serve (in Claes Ryn's phrase) both "as a source of wisdom and as a source of more or less dangerous illusion." Babbitt conceptualized the moral imagination as a kind of "inner check" on what McDonald called the "arbitrary will of man." For Babbitt, as well as for Kirk, the moral imagination "draws man back to the 'ethical centre,' or what Kirk would later call the permanent things."[64]

On either side of the moral imagination, Kirk described the idyllic and diabolical imaginations. The idyllic imagination is in one sense the model for modernity. It assumes human perfection, both individually and socially, and wishes away the faults and sins of people as caused by the artificial bindings of society and religion. The idyllic is "the sort of imagination that, ignoring the hard necessities of human existence, would have us surrender to the appetites in primitive simplicity."[65] The idyllic imagination leaves us in lotusland, oblivious to the joys and pains of a full human existence; it "rejects old dogmas and old manners and rejoices in the notion of emancipation from duty and convention."[66]

Kirk found the idyllic impulse most prominent in Rousseau, who is Burke's adversary throughout *The Conservative Mind*, and whom Kirk called "first among the theorists of radical democracy, the most eminent contemner of civilization." The Genevan's great fault, Kirk wrote, was that he "gave the wrong answers to the right questions. He denied the duality of human experience, and relied upon the regime of the senses as the means to general happiness." For Rousseau, the idyllic imagination was a release of the sentiments untethered by reason or tradition; "the surrender of Rousseau to desire . . . end[s] in the dehumanization of the human race."[67] Like Burke, Rousseau understood that emotion is a powerful political force. The coming age would see the struggle between the old symbols of the moral imagination and the new imagination released by Rousseau.

Babbitt described the idyllic imagination in his *Democracy and Leadership*, which according to Kirk was "the most important book" for those studying "social conservatism" and "perhaps the most penetrating work on politics ever written by an American." Rous-

---

64. Ryn, *Will, Imagination, and Reason*, 147; McDonald, *Kirk and the Age of Ideology*, 65.
65. Ryn, *Will, Imagination, and Reason*, 128.
66. Kirk, "Moral Imagination," 38.
67. *CM*, 423.

seau's idyllic imagination casts our glance backward, to the supposed origins of humanity. He created a "golden age" of untrammeled desire, defined by the absence of prescription or tradition. In a chapter devoted to Rousseau and the idyllic imagination, Babbitt connects Rousseau's longing for his golden age with political idealism. Such an idealism begins from the premise that existing society is corrupt and must be destroyed to usher in a new golden age. This imaginative reconstruction has had political effects: the "idyllic fantasy of a free, happy, lawless, propertyless state of nature" results, almost inevitably, in tyranny. Rousseau's General Will brooks no dissent from the individual or minorities.[68] When the "real refuses to vanish in favor of the ideal," unfortunately, it is easy for those in thrall to the idyllic imagination to believe that "the failure is due not to the ideal itself, but to some conspiracy." The idyll, however, cannot last. Once there has been complete emancipation from every restraint, something must fill the vacuum. Kirk called that something the diabolic imagination.

Borrowed from Eliot's early work, *After Strange Gods*, the diabolic imagination is concerned solely with the darker appetites of human nature. Kirk described it as a "narcosis."[69] It is purely materialistic and rejects the transcendent. Kirk was not squeamish, nor did he seek to prudishly hide these passions. Kirk wrote that "fulsome praise of goodness can alienate" and may even cause a rejection of principles. His own fiction, occupied as it usually was with the occult or supernatural, often turned violent. Yet those features existed for a purpose, the same purpose Kirk discovered in the writings of Flannery O'Connor: to lay bare human nature and, despite the ugliness and evil, to find the "grotesque face of God."[70] Imagination was a means of reenchanting the world against the sterility of modernity, which had stripped away all the nonrational and nonscientific aids to human existence.[71] Between the idyllic imagination, which creates a false utopia by ignoring the material realities of existence, and the diabolic, which treats the material as the only existence, Kirk set the moral imagination. This type of imagination sought to use experience—even experience of terror and pain—as a means to deeper understanding.

68. Babbitt, *Democracy and Leadership*, 104; *CM*, 422, 424.
69. *RT*, 71–73.
70. Kirk, "Flannery O'Connor and the Grotesque Face of God," 429–33.
71. Whitney, "Swords of Imagination," 18–19.

While figures as diverse as politicians and historians could promote the moral imagination, Kirk found its presence most evident in literature. Literature releases us from Eliot's provincialism of time; it "is the breath of society, transmitting to successive rising generations, century upon century, a body of ethical principles and critical standards and imaginative creations that constitutes a kind of collective intellect of humanity."[72] Kirk's conception of literature therefore is not of the autonomous reader discovering, *sua sponte*, eternal truths severed from the larger tradition. It is a social project that allows us not only to interact with one another in the present, but also to understand and be connected with the past. Literature therefore has an ethical, as well as an intellectual, purpose: to order the soul, first, and then the larger community. And because the lessons contained in a culture's literature are cumulative and not created for the moment, a grasp of that tradition enables an escape from ideology, which aims at destroying any basis for thought beyond the ideology's premises and what Daniel Boorstin described as "pseudo-events."

But literature does not present a *rational* argument against rationalism. Its strength lies in awakening the sensibility to an awareness of beauty and to the false promises of the diabolic and idyllic imaginations. Again we see the union of sentiment (or emotion) and reason in Kirk's understanding of the person and of society. Kirk wrote that Eliot, or any poet, could not be expected to solve the problems of the age:

> To demand that Dante be didactic after the system of Aquinas would be to efface *The Divine Comedy;* to demand that Eliot, in little more than a thousand lines of verse, should refute modern rationalism—that would be to deny the function of poetry. So it is through a diversity of questing insights, through abstractions illustrated by concrete representations, that Eliot renews the moral imagination. The rest must be left to theological studies, and to one's own experiences of reality.

> All that such a poem as *Four Quartets* may accomplish is to relate one remarkable man's vision of time, self, reality, and eternity: to describe one person's experience of transcendence.

72. *EPT,* 68.

The poet, through these "questing insights," connects reason to tradition and avoids a "defecated rationality," that "arrogantly severed from larger sources of wisdom" that Kirk saw as the condition of modernity. Modern writers, with whom Kirk juxtaposed Eliot—D. H. Lawrence, for example—value their own experiences more than any other source of wisdom. This leads first to ideology and then to the diabolic imagination; in contrast, "Resort to the moral imagination as a path to wisdom liberates the thinker from the narrow limits of personal experience and individual rational faculties."[73]

There is also what Bruce Frohnen has called "the insights of the seer,"[74] which provides another approach to the imaginative. The echoes of the Swedenborgian séances of Kirk's youth are hard to overlook when Kirk describes how some of his favorite figures, such as Burke, descried the coming age. Seers do not engage in mere nostalgia; rather, they hold up society to a mirror and point to ways of life starkly different from the present. They pierce the veil of the temporal to glimpse the permanent things, then convey their insights to the larger society (though of course these insights may go unheeded). These individuals, and the historical institutions and practices they have inspired, collectively make up the tradition conservatives defend. Kirk argues that the lessons of history transcend their contingent usefulness and utility.

The heritage Kirk adopted from Burke, Eliot, and Babbitt provides the language with which to discuss the relationship between conservatism and postmodernism. The imagination is the intersection between the two schools of thought. Babbitt, who so fiercely attacked the romantic imagination he discerned in Rousseau, was himself a proponent of the imagination's power, so much so that a recent commentator stated that it is precisely Babbitt's move from reason to imagination that "allows him . . . to meet postmodernism on its own ground."[75] There are differences, of course, and Babbitt and Kirk would have deplored much postmodern excess. Indeed, Babbitt, by concluding "not only that man may be governed by his imagination but that in all that belongs to his own special domain, the

73. Kirk, *Eliot and His Age: T. S. Eliot's Moral Imagination in the Twentieth Century*, 287, 45, 46–47 (hereafter cited as *Eliot*).

74. Frohnen, *Virtue and the Promise of Conservatism: The Legacy of Burke and Tocqueville*, 172.

75. Michael A. Weinstein, "Irving Babbitt and Postmodernity: Amplitude and Intensity."

imagination itself is governed by words," anticipated some of the postmodern preoccupation with self-creation. Babbitt turned the postmodern emphasis on the fluidity of imagination on its head by using that arena created by imagination as a call to subvert some of the more exotic forms of postmodernism.[76] Nevertheless, a concern for the imagination remains a hallmark of postmodernism and of Kirk's understanding of conservatism.

In *The Wake of Imagination*, Richard Kearney argues that the postmodern imagination must retain a connection between the poetic and the ethical, between the creative impulse and the need to serve larger truths. At the end of the seemingly endless play of self-parody that has characterized the postmodern rejection of the modern project, the imagination must return to its purposes. In striking language, an early postmodern theorist, Ihab Hassan, contends, in the *Dismemberment of Orpheus*, that "imagination cannot abandon its teleological sense: change is also dream come true. . . . I can only hope that after self-parody, self-subversion, and self-transcendence, after the pride and revulsion of anti-art will have gone their way, art may move toward a *redeemed imagination*."[77] A redeemed imagination is startlingly close to Kirk's theologically infused vision of the moral imagination. The moral imagination redeems humanity from its weaknesses and from the provinciality of being trapped in its own time.

Against the moral imagination Kirk arrays ideology, and his opposition to it is a sustained theme in his work. Indeed, Vigen Guroian notes that Kirk's critique of ideology grew stronger with successive editions of *The Conservative Mind*, "to make even more clear how conservatism is different" from ideology.[78] Unlike the imagination, which Kirk believes to be a permanent feature of human existence, ideology is a product of modernity. Crediting introduction of the term to the philosophical writings of Condillac, Kirk contends that ideology "originally was a kind of climax of rationalism of the Enlightenment, an attempt to systematize and apply knowledge from sensory perception."[79] It represents a faulty misguided intellectuality bereft of the nonrational supports of imagination. In Marx's

76. Quoted in ibid., 42–48.

77. Kearney, *The Wake of Imagination*; Ihab Hassan, *The Dismemberment of Orpheus: Toward a Postmodern Literature*, 257–58 (emphasis mine).

78. Guroian, "*The Conservative Mind* Forty Years Later," 23.

79. *EPT*, 154.

works, the term evolved to mean any set of beliefs that served as a cover for power, an understanding taken up by the Frankfurt School and the postmodernists.[80]

Ideology is not, Kirk stressed, equivalent to political philosophy, which inductively draws out particular truths from historical circumstance, and which contains a germ of the imagination in order to be fully effective. Nor is ideology equivalent to a political program, a position that opposed Kirk to other conservatives, particularly during the Cold War. Irving Kristol and others argued that conservatives needed an ideology to contend against communism, and that this conservative ideology needed to be as complete and coherent as its adversary. Kirk opposed conservative efforts at creating an ideology, thinking that it enshrined an objectionable and false abstractness to historically contingent beliefs. He wrote that while "some Americans, conservatively-inclined ones among them, might embrace an ideology of Democratic Capitalism or New World Order," such an embrace was fraught with difficulty. Kirk thought it was a contemporary attempt to impose a civil religion. Even if done with innocent motives, the imposition of such a construct, Kirk maintained, would have disastrous results.[81]

Rather, according to Kirk, ideology is religious dogmatism in a political context—a context that is completely inconsistent with a conservative outlook. Ideology eliminates the nuances and shades of gray that exist in actual political or social life. "For the ideologue, humankind may be defined into two classes: the comrades of Progress, and the foes attached to reactionary interests," who must be destroyed.[82] The proponent of ideology "resorts to the anaesthetic of social utopianism, escaping the tragedy and grandeur of true human existence by giving his adherence to a perfect dream-world of the future. Reality [the ideologue] stretches or chops away to conform to [a] dream-pattern of human nature and society." Ideology, like imagination, is likely to arise anywhere—in education, in literature—especially in politics. Because ideology is a replacement religion, when injected into the public sphere it makes politics, at least as Kirk defines it, impossible. "Ideology makes political compromise impossible"; and this rigidity could lead, at its most extreme, to civil war.

80. *PP*, 3–4.
81. Ibid., 7–8.
82. *EPT*, 157.

American politics has been so successful in part because it has been largely nonideological. Because Americans share some fundamental concepts—most important, about the limits of politics—they are able to accommodate differing belief systems without vying "with one another in fancied fidelity to their Absolute Truth."[83]

Ideology is a quintessential modern product because it divides the real from the theoretical and inflates the latter at the expense of the former. As Gerhart Niemeyer stated in an article on Kirk and ideology, conservatives prefer the real experiences of life to intellectual systems, rejecting "capitalist individualism, libertarian individualism or a Lockean contract."[84] Because an ideological system, by its nature, considers actual historical experience to be important only insofar as favorable abstractions can be generated from it, application of the principles of a particular ideology becomes easily manipulable. Employment of ideology, Kirk argued, had become the primary tool for those who would use it as a means of controlling others. This opinion holds that ideology is usually "closely allied with the interests of a particular social class or political sect," and it resembles in some respects the position taken by Marx in his early writings, as Kirk himself seems to have understood, though Kirk concluded that Marxism had itself become an ideology.[85]

Kearney finds that the concept of the imagination has been weakened in the postmodern era. The premodern age, he argues, invoked the concept of imagination as representational, or mimetic, copying the work of a divine Creator. The modern age departed from mimesis and turned to imagination as invention, creating new worlds from the individual mind. This creative imagination was very closely connected to the similar attitudes toward history and art, which were working toward some ultimate age of emancipation or liberation. Yet, this modern imagination was in the end unable to fulfill its promise. "Given the extravagant claims for man's creative power, it was inevitable that disillusionment would set in sooner or later. The romantic imagination could not possibly deliver on its promises. Confronted with the increasing disabling realities of modern existence . . . [the modern imagination] soon found itself beating a reluctant retreat."[86]

83. Ibid., 157; *PP*, 5–6.
84. Niemeyer, "Russell Kirk and Ideology," 35, 37.
85. *EPT*, 154–55.
86. Kearney, *Wake of Imagination*, 185.

The Age of Sentiments has likewise (and perhaps paradoxically) not been friendly to the imagination. The postmodern critique of modernity included an attack on the idea of the "original." Without an origin, some postmodern thinkers (Kearney notes in particular Lacan and Derrida) have concluded that "the concept of imagination itself collapses. For imagination always presupposed the idea of origination: the derivation of our images from some original presence."[87] Yet, whether this origin comes from an external source (such as a Platonic idea) or an internal source (such as Kantian moralism), neither can withstand the emergence of the postmodern "parodic" imagination, which turns the image back onto itself into an endlessly replicating series of images, in which the notion of origin disappears.

As Kirk uses the term, the imagination is not tied to an "origin" in the sense that Kearney uses with respect to the modern imagination. Rather, the purpose of the imagination is discernment. That is, it supplies the ability to see through the travails of the moment into certain truths; it is that "power to perceive ethical truth, abiding law, in the seeming chaos of many events . . . It is the strange faculty—inexplicable as men are assumed to have an animal nature only—of discerning greatness, justice, and order, beyond the bars of appetite and self-interest." The imagination can supply this ability of discernment through an appreciation of the complexity and mystery of existence. As Kearney contends, for the postmodern imagination "turning back *on* history does not necessarily mean turning our back *to* it."[88] Joseph Baldacchino, in an essay on Babbitt and the concept of ideology, concludes that for Kirk, appreciation of the transcendent occurred through experience of particular actions. A "direct, imaginative, and experiential intuition of the transcendent in concrete history," Kirk argues, can overcome "the difficult problem of mediation between the universal and the particular" that is the central weakness in conservative thought.[89] Ideology, for Kirk, is inadequate not because there are no absolutes, but because an ideological mode of inquiry is insufficient to describe them.

With the demise of progressivism inherent in the deficient modern notion of imagination, Kirk contended that it was time to rein-

---

87. Ibid., 253.
88. *EPT,* 119; Kearney, *Wake of Imagination,* 26 (original emphasis).
89. Baldacchino, "Babbitt and the Question of Ideology," in George A. Panichas and Claes G. Ryn, eds., *Irving Babbitt in Our Time,* 110.

vigorate the moral imagination, to render it both ethical and practical. This "redeemed imagination" would be able to join in the joys and sufferings of others by means of an imaginative reconstruction of the materials that compose the self and community.[90] For Kirk, the highest ends of the imagination were ethical. His conception of the need for imaginative reconstruction for the modern age, of dissolving certainties and the fractured self, represents a form of postmodern imagination that Kearney and others have seen emerging.

Conclusion: Finding "Other Instruments"

Although often treated as a summary of conservatism, the "canons" and other principles are better understood as a beginning for Kirk. What is important is how the principles were translated into actual forms of life, and Kirk was always quick to leave such lists and provide real examples. It is no surprise, for example, that his essay in *The Politics of Prudence* entitled "Ten Conservative Principles" is swiftly followed by "The Conservative Cause: Ten Events" and "Ten Exemplary Conservatives."

Kirk's critics generally fault him for his alleged archaism or presumed dislike of America and its traditions. However, Kirk's "unrealistic" approach is better understood as a deliberate stance against trends he saw as dangerous to the tradition he sought to defend. Even the carefully constructed image of Kirk as a typical eighteenth-century gentlemen, living a life of letters in a rural "Victorian villa, furnished with furniture salvaged from old hotels and churches," evokes the postmodern propensity for self-creation. E. Christian Kopff describes perceptively (albeit perhaps unintentionally, because of his own antipathy toward postmodernism) Kirk's postmodern affinities: "Kirk presented America with an attitude, a style, a persona." Kopff quotes Kirk as asking, "What are you and I? . . . In large part we are what we imagine ourselves to be. William Butler Yeats advises us to clap masks to our faces and play our appropriate part: the image becomes reality." Kopff contends that Kirk's mask became conservatism and his role that of guide, storyteller, and teacher. For Kopff, the abiding trait of Kirk's style is Kirk's mastery of the art of apt quotation from his grab bag of conservative heroes, especially Burke.

90. Kearney, *Wake of Imagination*, 361–71.

Creation, imagination, playfulness, self-reference, and a hint of pastiche: Kopff's description of Kirk could be a list of postmodern commonplaces. Kirk's persona, and his sometimes out-of-the-way subjects—"Will the Habsburg Return?" for example—jar his readers out of their modernist complacency and confront them with a conservative "romance of the marginal."[91] A standard postmodern strategy is to celebrate the "marginal" as oppressed radicals, an idyllic imagination unrestrained by convention or custom. Rather, Kirk uses the marginality of his own conservatism to highlight what he considered a bent world and to lead readers back to the mysteries of the permanent things.

In its devotion to particular types of rationality, the "Enlightenment mind" of modernity Kirk rejected in the Utah desert leaves no room for mystery. Beginning with *The Conservative Mind*, Kirk made a respect for mystery a cornerstone of the conservative temperament. There is the mystery of free will, of individual choice, of divine Providence, and of the creation and sustaining of tradition. These mysteries have been addressed throughout human history, not through science or discussion, but through myth and story. Although eternal questions, "yet modernity has not discovered convincing answers to the questions that these myths raise; rather, modernity has endeavored to shrug away the profound lessons that lie implicit in these myths." Modernity denigrated mystery in the name of a scientific or politically revolutionary metanarrative, which from the conservative view has had disastrous results. The postmodernists, on the other hand, while recognizing mystery, saw it only as an opportunity to engage in an endless play of word games ultimately to no purpose and to no lasting effect.

In contrast to both of these approaches, Kirk believed the central mysteries of life to be an opportunity for creation, through a constructive use of the imagination. All of history and tradition is brought into each moment and projected forward. Into this temporal stream, the individual's action, tempered, Kirk hoped, by the moral imagination, would be added. In an essay on Kirk and the "postmodern" Eliot, Vigen Guroian explained that Kirk's emphasis on the power of the imagination is intended to recover coherence in these "radically disjunctive times." Like Eliot, Kirk rejected the false

---

91. Kopff, *The Devil Knows Latin: Why America Needs the Classical Tradition*, 183; Steven Connor, *Postmodernist Culture: Introduction to Theories of the Contemporary*, 236.

choices advocated by others confronted with this world that the dissolution of the Age of Discussion has fragmented: "Some of our contemporaries stumble over a single shard and take it for the whole. Others sift nervously through the fragments hoping that this or that one might bring peace or pleasure. Still others endeavor to persuade us that what is broken can be put back together, like Humpty Dumpty, just as it was before." Kirk rejected the ideologues described by Guroian in the first category. But he also rejected the devotees of the idyllic or diabolic imaginations in the second and the reactionaries exemplified by Guroian's third.[92]

The "two Kirks" both served the same end: regenerating the tools of the moral imagination for an age that had dispensed with church, nobility, and tradition. His critics largely misread this stance as an ultimately hopeless nostalgia or a mere pose. His admirers, too, misread Kirk, but in the opposite direction. They see him as embracing a static version of some ideal past and rejecting the present in toto. Rather, Kirk himself provided a suggestion of his path in *The Conservative Mind*. There, he stated that the "appeal to the traditional conservative symbols of the imagination" had been disrupted by the romantic allure of Rousseau and the persuasiveness of the utilitarianism Bentham.[93] "Other instruments and methods" were needed if conservatism was to be reinvigorated, which is hardly the call of a reactionary. With his emphasis on place, sentiment, and the imagination, Kirk outlined what he saw as the enduring components of a conservative temperament. How he adapted those new instruments and methods to particular subjects will be discussed in the next three chapters.

92. Guroian, "Moral Imagination, Humane Letters, and the Renewal of Society," 4, 6–7.
93. *CM*, 425.

2

Participant Knowledge and History

Our religion, our culture, and our political rights all
are maintained by continuity: by the respect for the
accomplishments of our forefathers, and by our concern
for our posterity's well-being.

Russell Kirk, *The Roots of American Order*

The Historical Imagination

A common characteristic of conservative thinkers has been a de-
clared fidelity to "tradition" or "history." Robert Nisbet, a prominent conservative sociologist of the twentieth century, has called
the importance of history an "ingrained feature of conservative
thought." Philosopher John Kekes has described what he calls the
"historical method" as a characteristic form of conservative analysis.
For Kekes "the historical dimension of reflection is central, for it is
by its means" that we can discern how to resolve political conflicts
and to live productive lives.[1] However, it is not at all clear exactly
how conservatives think of history. Sometimes conservatives understand the past as a normative order to which we owe deference
to varying degrees. History, accordingly, has some sort of claim upon

1. Nisbet, *Conservatism: Dream and Reality*, 35; Kekes, *A Case for Conservatism*,
18. For an introductory study of Nisbet, see Brad Lowell Stone, *Robert Nisbet*.

us, and to which we conform our actions, or at least a standard by which we check them.

Sometimes, however, conservatives make a more modest empirical claim: that the past is "useful" in some way and should not be disregarded until it can be shown that a deviation from the past is more useful. Jerry Muller has called this conservative outlook "historical utilitarianism." Historical utilitarianism holds that the existence of some practice of life or institution creates a presumption in favor of its usefulness and should not therefore be discarded without sufficient reason. But he also notes that this historical utilitarian approach has created a welter of competing things conservatives have sought to conserve: at different times, conservatives have defended monarchies and republics, capitalism and regulated economies, and have been both revolutionaries and reactionaries. This variety has hampered clarity, as "too many persons have been trying to 'conserve' too many things for too many reasons."[2]

Kirk was no exception to this adherence to history, and indeed a sensitivity to history is a marked characteristic of his work. He employed what Gleaves Whitney described as a "historical imagination." The historical imagination attempts to trace the change and continuity that humankind has experienced over time. In particular, Whitney identified Kirk's ability to enter into other times, and to uncover the sources of the present in the past, as central to his historical imagination.[3] Using that imagination, the historian is able to examine historical circumstances to separate ephemera from lasting conditions, to find answers to present problems in the past, and to provide a counterweight to two dangers: a narrow provincialism and a preoccupation with novelty, which Kirk thought a dangerous modern temptation.[4]

Kirk's historical style was deliberately narrative rather than analytical. In general he preferred anecdote and example to extended argument. As Paul Hamilton observes in a survey of historical thinking, style and metaphor play a crucial role in historical writing. Historians use these to illuminate a past age for the present. These rhetorical techniques necessitate that both past events and their re-

2. Muller, ed., *Conservatism: An Anthology of Social and Political Thought from David Hume to the Present,* 7. The quote is at page 23.
3. Whitney, "Swords of Imagination," 4–5.
4. Frohnen, *Virtue and the Promise of Conservatism,* 172–73.

lationship to the present are of equal importance.[5] This insight is particularly relevant to Kirk's own work, as he sought to connect the past with the present.

Postmodernism in some respects is quite at home with the conservative historical imagination. Drawing on these connections, Claes Ryn states that even Edmund Burke foreshadowed some aspects of the postmodern critique. Postmodernism and conservatism share, for example, an antipathy toward concepts distilled from "objective" facts and a linear notion of progress with no necessary relation to historical circumstances. Both believe that observation is invariably colored by the observer's participation. In Kirk's case, an understanding of historical fact as partially subjective and a focus on narrativity at times sit awkwardly with his professed belief in a natural law. The former seems to imply a relativism: given the vagaries of historical events and the varied interpretations of them, how can we discern which traditions or customs of the past are worth keeping and which should be discarded? Wesley McDonald alludes to this difficulty in separating out a kind of "conservative positivism" from the "ethical role of tradition." Kirk's historical thought constitutes an extended example of Kekes's historical method, focused on what Mark Henrie has called "the normative value of tradition."[6]

Because the postmodern critique finds the Enlightenment account inadequate to explain the variety and contingency of historical events, it tends to deny any intelligible purpose to history. The postmodern rejection of the Enlightenment view of history, which rested on certain universals (such as the definition of progress and civilization), leads the postmodernists to reject even the possibility of the existence of any universals at all. Similarly, because Enlightenment "progress" is considered to be based on a faulty or oppressive worldview (by, for example, positing European political or cultural forms as the highest point of cultural achievement), some postmodernists have concluded that every interpretation of history is similarly arbitrary. Postmodern history, therefore, is reduced to an infinite number of personal histories that cannot be communicated from one person to another; each is stranded in his own universe, and any attempt to reach out is rebuked as intellectual colonization or the construc-

5. Hamilton, *Historicism*, 28–29.
6. Ryn, "Defining Historicism," 87–88; McDonald, *Kirk and the Age of Ideology*, 93–95; Henrie, "Russell Kirk's Unfounded America," 51.

tion of another false metanarrative. Further, some postmodernist historians have been heavily influenced by the Continental literary theory of the 1960s and 1970s and argue that because histories, inevitably, are composed primarily of texts, and because those texts are supposedly always self-referential, history therefore does not in fact refer to any actual set of events outside the texts themselves.[7] Jean Baudrillard's writings on the first Gulf War and the September 11 attacks offer extreme examples of this principle. He argues that these events were, respectively, invented by the media and by the George H. W. Bush administration.[8]

Kirk did believe in a reality outside of any given text; history is one way to determine the norms of that reality. Nevertheless, he shared certain postmodern historical sensibilities. At the most general level, he was in accord with the postmodern reluctance to propose grand statements about the "meaning of history." Like the postmodernists, Kirk incorporated the idea that history, because it is related to the individual historian and the individual reader, can have multiple meanings. Also like the postmodernists, Kirk displayed a certain "presentism" when speaking of the past, an attitude that has not been generally noticed by his admirers, who take at face value that Kirk was looking backward. Rather, for Kirk, every past moment in a very real sense was also a present moment. Taken to the extreme, this view could "flatten" history and render any notion of historical study irrelevant. The postmodern approach to history, because it rejects the modernist view of progress and periodization, must always reinterpret the past. A postmodern historical imagination "reminds us that humanity has a duty, if it is to survive . . . to remember the past and to protect a future."[9] The postmodern sensibility, however, has a tendency to treat the past as a tool for the present; because historical narratives are essentially malleable, they have no specific meanings other than what we choose to give them.

Kirk avoided the postmodern despair at finding any purpose in historical study and endeavored to discover through historical circumstance the lessons of the past. These lessons are not the same as the meaning of history. A "meaning" implies what the postmoderns

7. For a good summary of one type of postmodern approach to history, see David Carr, *Time, Narrative, and History.*

8. Baudrillard, *The Gulf War Did Not Take Place.*

9. Kearney, *Wake of Imagination,* 392.

call an Enlightenment metanarrative, to which all individual acts are subordinated. Rather, while there is an overarching story, the specific lessons of history can be charted only through individual actions, which ramify, but do not completely dissipate, that metanarrative. The multiplicity of human action and motivation, Kirk thought, forces us to recognize mystery as a central element of the historical past and our understanding of it. In that respect, in acknowledging a core of unknowable "fact," Kirk posited that an observer would never know the full metanarrative.

The historian therefore is faced with the limits of knowledge, because of the inability to chart all the possible actions and influences on historical events. The recognition of these limitations imbue the historian with a sense of humility at understanding the past. The historian creates a story, but he does not thereby judge the failures of the past: "The historian's task is to chronicle, and, if he can, to criticize intelligently; he ought not be expected to set the world in order." That order is, in part, a simple chronological chronicle; it is not a "plan." In one sense, history is "the record of a nation's or a civilization's past."[10] In a second, fuller sense, history can reveal "great truths," hidden within the framework of human experience. The bridge that links these two senses of history is the historical imagination. While history has an overarching meaning, in other words, Kirk parts company with the modern contention that that meaning can be completely known.

Since the 1980s, historians have become more chastened in their appreciation of a deterministic approach to history, which projects a fixed, objective vision of the past according to empirical or materialistic criteria.[11] Instead, scholarly opinion has moved in favor of a view that cultures and individuals can be causal historical agents and that the "past" is in part constructed out of the present. This approach has led to a more receptive attitude for narrative histories.[12] Grand narratives have returned in popular histories as well, from studies such as Huntington's *The Clash of Civilizations* to Tom Brokaw's *The Greatest Generation* to Jacques Barzun's recent study of the West over the past five centuries, *From Dawn to Decadence*. Kirk spent a lifetime construing another such story that took into account what

10. *PC*, 4; *RT*, 101.
11. See James M. McPherson, "History: It's Still about Stories," 35.
12. See George G. Iggers, *Historiography in the Twentieth Century: From Scientific Objectivity to the Postmodern Challenge*, 97–99.

he considered important in understanding the human condition. The major facets of this story involve the continuing adjustments between the place of the individual and the community and the roles of tradition and authority in creating historical continuity.

In his private library at Piety Hill, Russell Kirk devoted a large bookcase to the works of "philosophical historians." His shelves held the books of Arnold Toynbee, Christopher Dawson, Herbert Butterfield, John Lukacs, and others whose work fused historical fact with a philosophical approach to the past. The philosophical approach of these scholars, however, does not mean that they composed "philosophies of history": neither the abstract patterns of Comte nor the ahistoricism of Hegel would have found a place of such favor with Kirk. Rather the historians who occupied this privileged place believed that history is the memory of humanity and its interpretation is an attempt to plumb the mysteries of the human condition. Indeed, Kirk contended that the writing and interpretation of history required the historian to participate, as it were, in the explanation of the past; a historian who seeks to explain the past cannot "stand outside it." This may be "metahistory," but only of a truncated kind. When pressed, Kirk largely refrained from offering any but the most tentative conclusions about the "nature of history," and he almost always took refuge in particular instances and individuals that gave flesh to larger principles.

Nowhere is Kirk's method more evident than in his own (re)construction of a conservative tradition. Through his work, Kirk evoked a past from which conservatives could draw their guiding principles and individual models. As Willmoore Kendall observed, Kirk was as much a participant in conservatism and conservative history as he was a historian of it. The stream of books and essays elucidating the conservative body of thought that he produced both contributed to a conservative future and "wrote" a conservative past. With the publication of *The Conservative Mind*, Kirk had established an "intellectually formidable and respectable ancestry" for conservative principles. In a telling phrase, historian George Nash concluded that Kirk had given American conservatism a "genealogy of good men and valuable thoughts."[13] Recovering this patrimony of conservative figures and principles was itself a significant act of imaginative historical scholarship, and it was done with deliberate intent to drama-

13. Nash, *Conservative Intellectual Movement*, 67, 74.

tize the past. Thus readers were given a striking portrait of John Randolph of Roanoke at the Virginia Constitutional Convention of 1829:

> At the Convention, his tall, cadaverous figure; his flaming eyes like a devil's or an angel's; his bony accusing finger that had punctuated the prosecution of Justice Chase nearly three decades gone; his tormented face, half a boy's, half a corpse's framed by his straight black hair that was a memento of his ancestress Pocahontas; his flood of extemporaneous eloquence like a prophet's inspired—for a generation, Congress and America had beheld this Ishmael of politics, this aristocratic spokesman of the Tertium Quids, this slaveholding *ami des noirs,* this old-school planter, this fantastic duellist, this fanatic enemy of corruption, this implacable St. Michael who had denounced Adams and Jefferson and Madison and Monroe and Clay and Webster and Calhoun with impartial detestation.[14]

In an incisive monograph, "The Mystic Chords of Memory: Reclaiming American History," Professor Wilfred McClay points out that Kirk did not often explicitly discuss the nature of history in his writings, or what McClay has called Kirk's "historical consciousness." Rather, Kirk's "Historical consciousness seemed to have been infused into the air he breathed and mixed into the soil of the ancestral land in which he chose to live." History and tradition lay at the very center of Kirk's understanding of human society. As Frederick Wilhelmsen has written, "Nothing he saw was simply itself. With Kirk everything was charged with history."[15] The historical asides and digressions that occur throughout his work are an indication of the multiplicity of meanings that Kirk found within historical events and places.

The tension in Western civilization between the individual and the community confronts most conservative thinkers. The rights-bearing individual is largely an invention of the modern age, and most conservatives are uncomfortable with the conclusion that individuals can assert such rights against the community. Yet conservatives

---

14. *CM,* 151.

15. McClay, "The Mystic Chords of Memory: Reclaiming American History." See also Gregory Wolfe, "Russell Kirk—The Catholic as Conservative," 31–32; Wilhelmsen, "The Wandering Seer of Mecosta," 83.

also believe in freedom and free will and generally disdain a resort to abstractions to explain historical events. Therefore, there must be room for recognition of individual action against the community. Kirk did not solve this conundrum. Conservatives, in his opinion, were supposed to prevent individual action from degenerating into neoterism or revolution and to retain a connection with tradition. Only by understanding individual action within the broader canvas of history (and tradition as a particular type of historical understanding) disciplined by authority and tradition, Kirk thought, could degeneration be prevented.

From the postmodern vantage point, "contingency" renders personal choice meaningless because it is irreducibly unique, and therefore any personal experience cannot be communicated to another person. Because of his Christian understanding of free will, Kirk believed that choices could have been made differently. While it would perhaps be too much to conclude from this observation that Kirk explicitly rejected a "modern" interpretation of historical fact, Kirk's understanding of history does highlight the (very postmodern) place of contingency in historical analysis. Every historical institution or value carries with it connections and antecedents, which, by their very nature, may have happened differently had circumstances been otherwise.[16]

Kirk believed that order could be created from the welter of competing and conflicting possibilities. That is to say, personal choice and action do not obliterate evidence of commonality. In one respect, this is a truism, one known long before postmodernism tried to demonstrate that each person "reads" texts and circumstances differently. Yet this insight should not diminish the work of the individual or deny the possibility that other readers may find meaning— even the same meaning—in the same text or circumstance.

Russell Kirk as Historian

Although not a formal academic for long, Kirk was trained as a historian. His historical approach remained evident in all his work, though he wrote very few standard academic "histories," in the sense of a chronological catalog based upon original research. Per-

16. Cf. José Ortega y Gasset, *History as a System*, 201.

haps his clearest effort in that regard was the history of his alma mater, St. Andrews University in Scotland, which he published in 1954, and which has received only scant attention.[17] Kirk's other books are almost uniformly of one of two sorts. The first sort is composed of biographies of figures whose lives exemplify the conservative principles Kirk held dear, as in his studies of Burke, John Randolph, Eliot, and Taft. The other books are the converse: histories of conservative principles as illuminated through sketches of individuals. The best example of this latter sort is *The Conservative Mind*. In terms of its scholarship, however, Kirk's books compare favorably with its peers, and "remains a valuable corrective to misleading tendencies in even the best current scholarship."[18]

This simplistic dichotomy, of course, does not tell the whole story; the foregoing excludes his essay collections and books such as *The American Cause* that were written in response to particular circumstances and that do not fit into any category.[19] Kirk was perhaps at his best with the essay form, and his several collections—*Confessions of a Bohemian Tory, The Intemperate Professor, Beyond the Dreams of Avarice,* and *Enemies of the Permanent Things,* as well as the more recent, posthumous collections *Politics of Prudence* and *Redeeming the Time,* often show Kirk at his most insightful. Of his remaining book-length studies, *The Roots of American Order* is his most ambitious work. It is a sweeping narrative of the evolving understanding of the sources of American society, and their connection to the larger Judeo-Christian civilization, which itself has drawn much of its own self-understanding from the Greek and Roman civilizations. Clearly echoing Burke, *Roots* closes with the peroration,

> Th[e] patrimony, as traced in this book, is not a dead thing. The roots of moral order twist back to the Hebrew perceptions of a purposeful moral existence under God. They extend to the philosophical and political self-awareness of the old Greeks. They are nurtured by the Roman experience of law and social organization. They are entwined with the Christian understanding of human duties and human hopes, of man redeemed. They are quickened by medieval custom, learning, and valor. They grip the religious

17. Kirk, *St. Andrews.*
18. Mark C. Henrie, "Russell Kirk and the Conservative Heart," 16.
19. For a discussion of the provenance of *The American Cause,* see Person, *Kirk: A Critical Biography,* 76–79.

ferment of the sixteenth century. They come from the ground of English liberty under law, so painfully conceived. They are secured by a century and a half of community in colonial America. They benefit from the debates of the eighteenth century. They approach the surface through the Declaration and Constitution. They emerge full of life from the ordeal of the Civil War.[20]

Many years later, Kirk drew the lessons of *Roots* in miniature with *America's British Culture*, which concentrated exclusively on the British contributions to American society.

However his books may be characterized, Kirk brought a conviction that context was an inescapable element of historical work and reflection. An indefatigable traveler, Kirk sought to see most of the places about which he wrote and to meet the people, if possible. In a short memoir about his own boyhood during the Depression, Kirk approved the "pragmatic" method of the ancient historian Polybius, and he emphasized that it was important, when writing history, to "know the towns, the country houses, the landscape, the whole physical setting, of the country of one's studies; one must talk with old men and women, besides reading other people's books; one must peer imaginatively behind the veil of yesteryear." This attitude places Kirk in good company: historical writers from Cicero to Montaigne all found the sense of the past that comes from actual physical places to be essential to understanding history.[21] The value that Kirk placed on retaining the places where history was "made" in part explains his interest, which became more evident especially in the 1960s and 1970s, in opposing unthinking "renewal" plans that would destroy old buildings or neighborhoods.

Kirk often makes explicit the connection he sees between past events and historical locations to show his readers how the past continues to affect the present day. Physicality aids in the construction of historical memory. Thus, the opening of his study of Burke begins,

> In College Green, at the gate of Trinity College, near the heart of Dublin, stand the handsome statues of Edmund Burke and Oliver Goldsmith. . . . In a house—thoughtfully demolished a few years

---

20. Kirk, *The Roots of American Order*, 472 (hereafter cited as *RAO*).
21. Kirk, "I Must See the Things, I Must See the Men: One Historian's Recollections of the 1930s and 1940s," 1; C. V. Wedgwood, *Truth and Opinion: Historical Essays*, 21.

ago—on Aran Quay, only a few minutes' walk from Trinity College, Edmund Burke was born on January 12, 1729. He may have been baptized in the medieval church of St. Michan, nearby. . . . Charming Georgian Dublin, built mostly in Burke's time, stood virtually intact until recent years, but now is decayed.

In a postmodern touch, he occasionally includes accounts of his own visits to the places and persons about which he is writing, or even the places where he composed the text. Kirk becomes a part of the history he is writing; thus, his study of Eliot opens with a recounting of meetings that he himself had with Eliot. Similarly, Kirk's description of writing *The Conservative Mind*, "chiefly at haunted St. Andrews and in the old country houses of Fife," places us right at the scene, as it were, alongside Kirk as participants in the composition and, indeed, in the story he is telling. These examples are numerous. His essay on "The Question of Tradition," for example, begins with Kirk as a young boy lying "under an oak on the hillside above the mill pond, in the town where I was born, and look[ing] beyond the great willows in the river valley to a curious and handsome house that stood on the opposite slope," whose existence prompted Kirk's earliest reflections on tradition.[22] Needless to say, perhaps we learn before the essay's end that the house was torn down.

Two characteristics of Kirk's historical writings become apparent from these excerpts. First, Kirk disdained theoretical construction, favoring instead an examination of abstract ideas within the framework of individual persons and institutions. "It is through a diversity of questing insights, through abstraction illuminated by concrete representations," that larger truths become known.[23] Kirk saw this technique in Eliot and adapted it for his own use. For Kirk, after he became a Christian, even God was represented in part by a historical person who lived and preached in a particular place and time. Second, Kirk had a penchant for inserting himself (and, by implication, us) into whatever he was discussing. The lines between "history" and commentary are blurred, and the effect is more like history conceived as a joint enterprise rather than a scientific examination of something beyond or outside us.

22. *EB*, 13–14; *Eliot*, 4; *CM*, i; *PC*, 227. Person discusses the not-insignificant family history in forming Kirk's attitudes on tradition and continuity (*Kirk: A Critical Biography*, 9–11).
    23. *Eliot*, 287.

Although he was widely read in the classical and certain modern historians, it was Burke who most strongly influenced Kirk's understanding of history. Burke taught Kirk that history was more than mere chance or a meaningless string of events; rather, it was the "gradual realization of a supreme design," with individuals as the agents of Providence.[24] "The truths of history, the real meanings, are to be discovered in what history can teach us about the framework of the Logos, if you will: about the significance of human existence: about the splendor and misery of our condition."[25] Note the plural "truths": there is no Hegelian World-Spirit, determining the path of history. The significance, splendor, or misery of our existence are largely of our own making and are never fully revealed.

Kirk rejected historical determinism, agreeing instead with Burke that the Christian doctrine of free will provided a better insight into human experience and history. Providence works in natural ways, and individuals can and do resist the divine will. Although this design is never more than partially comprehensible to us, Burke thought it revealed itself through the historical development of cultural institutions, customs, and traditions. History is a "proving ground, testing institutions through circumstances." It combines and transcends contingent facts and provides a standard for personal action. Just as important, this view of history finds a place for both theory and practice, imagination and activity.[26] This view placed Kirk at odds with the progressive historians of his day, who thought humanity was on a sure course forward and who "taught that men, through their own efforts, could fashion a heaven on earth."[27]

Burke was not the only historical writer to influence Kirk. In "The Perversity of Recent Fiction: Reflections on the Moral Imagination," Kirk identifies the authors who gave him an historical sense while he was still a youth, before he had read Burke. The list includes Charles Dickens and even H. G. Wells, with whose atheism and enthusiasm for progress Kirk later came to disagree.[28] These authors

---

24. *CM*, 40.
25. *RT*, 102.
26. Frohnen, *Virtue and the Promise of Conservatism*, 51. See Harold J. Berman, "The Origins of Historical Jurisprudence: Coke, Selden, Hale," 1735; Will Herberg, "Natural Law and History in Burke's Thought," 325.
27. Mark C. Malvasi, "Kirk among the Historians," 147.
28. *RT*, 84.

prepared him for his subsequent study of history. As Whitney notes, for Kirk the historical imagination begins with exposure to great literature, which transports readers to other times and places and imbues them with a sympathetic understanding for those other times.[29] Kirk praises historians such as Francis Parkman, Washington Irving, and Nathaniel Hawthorne, for "creating, out of rude and fragmentary materials, a vision of the American heritage" to which all—even those who did not share that heritage—could join.[30] Two other historians, Christopher Dawson and John Lukacs, helped Kirk build upon these insights and provided him with a fresh approach to history and understanding tradition.

History, therefore, is not an ideology, nor can it be used as a tool. At best, history provides only glimpses of an underlying order. History is not what Gabriel Marcel called the "armed ghost," but rather an intelligible pattern arising out of the free actions of individuals, a pattern that Kirk understood in his later years as reflecting a divine plan.[31] History has no Hegelian "meaning," to be deduced from a collection of facts, not least because we can never know enough about the past to understand it fully. It is instead a series of clues to enduring norms of behavior or a "conceptual order" that, however imperfectly understood at any one moment, nevertheless reveals a latent integrity.[32] The resources of history are embedded within concrete places and customs and supplement the individual's own private stock of reason to provide a framework for decision. The common law, for example, embraces numerous assumptions and presumptions about human behavior and norms that have become entrenched through time and expressed in legal decisions.

We shall address more precisely Kirk's understanding of the relation between the individual and history later in this chapter; suffice it now to say that Kirk allowed for individuals to alter dramatically the path of history and thereby to reveal or to obscure the supreme design, which in any event can never be completely uncovered. Burke himself was just such an individual, Disraeli another; others adorn the section headings of *The Conservative Mind*. In his first books, Kirk profiled two figures—Burke and John Randolph of Roanoke—who represented this historically rooted individualism on ei-

29. Whitney, "Swords of Imagination," 8.
30. *CM*, 251–52.
31. *EB*, 210.
32. Gerald W. Chapman, "The Organic Premise," 240.

ther side of the Atlantic. Their examples, Kirk thought, could move us still: his *John Randolph of Roanoke*, for example, was a deliberate attempt to "rescue from obscurity" the legacy of the great Virginian in order to guide succeeding generations. His study of Burke also was meant to retrieve a Tiresias for our time, who could confront modern mass ideology with the alternative of the "great continuity."[33]

Kirk emphasized the specifically British roots of the American system, even while he placed the United States within the wider tradition of the West. As M. E. Bradford pointed out with respect to *The Roots of American Order*, this approach is a "Burkean preface" to the study of history. It is a narrative of the long development of characteristic Western institutions and habits of thought. As Person explained, *Roots* places America not as the outcome of an "idea" or "experiment" restricted to currents of thought in the eighteenth century, but rather as a still-evolving component of a larger civilization, which has inherited "long established conventions and traditions." That Kirk remained convinced that the British experience was the proper prism through which to judge American history is evidenced by *America's British Culture*, one of his last books, in which he compared the "literary" legacies of Greece and Rome with the "institutional" influence of Britain.[34] Therefore, Kirk rejected the dominate mode of historical reflection on America—that is, that America is an "exceptional nation," torn free of its Western heritage and free to create a truly *novus ordo*, a conviction shared by conservatives and liberals.[35]

The argument Kirk made for emphasizing the customs of the United States before independence places him at odds with secular progressives as well as some of his fellow conservatives. Kirk contended that America, and American conservatives, ought to be oriented toward Europe, especially Britain, if they wished to protect their common culture. Kirk's emphasis on the British experience was not accepted silently by his fellow conservatives during the renascence of conservative thought in the years following World War II. His crit-

---

33. *JRR*, 26; the first edition was published in 1951. *EB*, 19–20.

34. Bradford, "A Proper Patrimony: Russell Kirk and America's Moral Genealogy," in Person, *Unbought Grace*, 74; Person, *Kirk: A Critical Biography*, 69; Kirk, *America's British Culture*, 102 (hereafter cited as *ABC*). Kirk drew on David Hackett Fischer's *Albion's Seed: Four British Folkways in America* (Oxford: Oxford University Press, 1989) to support his thesis.

35. Malvasi, "Kirk among the Historians," 134–39.

ics, such as Clinton Rossiter and Frank Meyer, suggested Kirk had done little more than create a "usable past," and not a very good one at that. America was a new nation, based in the "new political science" of Locke, which had little need for inherited customs because the first principles of political society could be (and, according to some, had been) established rationally.

America's British Culture instead concentrates on the concrete connections between British and American ways of life. It was Kirk's response to the "multiculturalism" debate then raging in America's culture wars, as a sort of conservative complement to the book by Arthur Schlesinger, *The Disuniting of America*. After discussing language and literature, the rule of law and the system of representative government, Kirk turns to "Mores and Minds," perhaps the most important chapter of the volume. It is a powerful argument for the persistence of habits of behavior over long stretches of time, even when the sources of those habits have been forgotten. The "traditional customs, [the] way of regarding the human condition, [and] principles of morality" that compose American culture Kirk traces to America's original British settlers. "All spoke and read English, all lived under English law, all abided by many old English prescriptions and usages. Theirs was Christianity in British forms." The common culture these settlers created still existed and had flourished; indeed, it had attracted immigrants from other parts of the world, and to ignore it was both imprudent and destructive: "Should that cultural heritage be long and widely neglected, the American nation would drift toward brutishness in private life, anarchy or the mailed fist in public life."[36] In *America's British Culture*, Kirk argued that these habits remained in a form recognizable to Tocqueville a half-century later, despite the immigration of other ethnic groups into the United States. These habits must be the basis for the maintenance of political and cultural life. To substitute an ideology based on "multiculturalism" would be disastrous, because multiculturalism has no substance to it and, in particular, no set of customs, mores, or traditions to which people could develop sentiments of affection or loyalty.

Kirk's reply to his critics remained consistent. As he wrote in the early 1960s, the United States belonged to the "grander tradition and continuity" of the Western world.[37] And American history, rich as it

---

36. *ABC,* 11, 70–71.
37. Quoted in Nash, *Conservative Intellectual Movement,* 180.

may be in some respects, simply cannot provide sufficient reserves when it is severed from its European (and specifically British) roots. "The Present . . . is only a thin film upon the deep well of the Past," and that past—even the distant past—continues to live and influence us into the present.[38] In his later works, Kirk continued this approach, contending that Edward Coke and Samuel Johnson were as relevant to American civilization as John Marshall and the founders. Kirk acknowledged the diversity of the Western tradition and affirmed that the roots of American habits were in Athens, Rome, and Jerusalem as much as in London or Edinburgh. This broad vision avoided the trap of treating a certain aspect of tradition as an "idol," to use the term of Jaroslav Pelikan, which points to nothing outside of itself.[39]

Kirk added, however, the implicit qualification that the United States, while heir to the entire history of the West, is shaped primarily by particular portions of that history—that is, history as seen through the prism of the Anglo-American experience. Thus, a conservative in the United States wishing to remain faithful to that tradition does not have open to him the same set of choices that, say, a Georges Bernanos in France or a Hilaire Belloc in Britain (or even a John Adams or John C. Calhoun in America) had open to them in their circumstances, even though each in some way would rely upon a common Western history.

The Emergence of Participant History

In an important early review of the first volume of Eric Voegelin's *Order and History,* Kirk defined the four major schools of historical thought as he saw them. The first school treats history as meaningless, as if it has no purpose: "everything has been 'evolutionary development' or mere flux."[40] The second school, in which Kirk includes Condorcet, Comte, and Marx, are the positivists, whose teachings are repeated, in the main, by the modern tradition of historical study. Positivists see history as the record of advancement toward a terrestrial paradise defined by some economic or political cri-

38. *Eliot,* 82.
39. Pelikan, *The Vindication of Tradition,* 55.
40. Kirk, "Behind the Veil of History," 466 (reprinted in *EPT,* 259).

terion.[41] The ancients, especially the Greeks, originally composed the third school, and some moderns such as Toynbee have revived it. This school thinks of history as a cycle, with predictable and repetitive stages of growth, maturity, and decay. These three schools have dominated historical thinking for the last two centuries.

Kirk's attention was captured, however, by a fourth school, which advocated the "belief that history is the record of human existence under God, meaningful only so far as it reflects and explains and illustrates the order in character and society which emanates from divine purpose." Besides Voegelin himself, the main contemporary exponents of this "transcendent" school in the West were Herbert Butterfield, Christopher Dawson, and Reinhold Niebuhr, but the ultimate inspiration was St. Augustine. This school concluded that history is the slow revelation of general principles of order, both of the individual and of society. History does not, however, predict "the wave of the future."[42] It has not one meaning that can be applied to the regulation of private and public conduct; and the ends to which history leads are not in history but beyond it. Indeed, to the extent that there is one common meaning to history for Kirk (the unfolding of a providential design), that meaning is articulated and fulfilled by each age—and by each person in that age—in distinctive ways.

Two historians deserve special note because of their influence upon Kirk. Christopher Dawson, though mentioned only sparingly in *The Conservative Mind* and *The Roots of American Order,* was to become one of Kirk's favorite historians.[43] Indeed, later in his life, Kirk embarked on a project to publish Dawson's collected works (which was never completed), and one of his last trips abroad was to visit places associated with the British historian.

There are two relevant points in Dawson's work when considering Kirk's historical thought. The first is Dawson's integration of anthropological research into the habits and practices of peoples with more formal historical reflection, an integration that reached the larger historical profession in a significant way only after World War II.[44] The second and more important point that Kirk adopted is Daw-

41. Francis Fukuyama continues this tradition. See his *The End of History and the Last Man,* and his more recent *The Age of Disruption.*

42. Kirk, "Behind the Veil," 467, 468.

43. Kirk, "The High Achievement of Christopher Dawson," 436.

44. See Iggers, *Historiography in the Twentieth Century,* 102.

son's contention that culture springs from cult, from the structure of organized worship, and that without a religious foundation a civilization will collapse of its own weight, despite material or economic success. This does not mean that any sort of "official" recognition of a particular religion is required. Dawson, as a Catholic convert in officially Anglican Britain, saw dangers in such recognition for both the official and minority faiths.

Rather, Kirk, following Dawson, was making an empirical point. Great cultures have grown up with great religions, and that growth need not be accompanied by a concomitant loss of faith. Dawson anticipated by decades the weaknesses of the "modernization" thesis of secular historians. According to this theory, religious faith is inversely proportional to technological or material progress and merely a primitive relic used to understand phenomena now explainable by science. Because it posited progress in this way, the thesis is linear in that the secular West is the "modern," leading edge of history, while other more religious cultures are "behind" it.

Kirk, drawing from Dawson, concluded instead that history does not constitute a linear progression up to a terrestrial paradise. Rather history is "a path fraught with blind alleys and wrong turns." It is therefore a record both of the spiritual progress of the City of God and of the material progress of the City of Man, each of which "works and finds concrete social expression in history." Kirk employed the distinction between secular and sacred history to explain the evolution, for example, of time and order in the thought of the ancient Hebrews. This distinction lay at the heart of the West's understanding of itself and its history. From this standpoint, the great movements of history occur neither on the plane of pure reason nor that of nature. Rather, they are found on the middle ground of history, on which men, according to Dawson, war against "great unknown powers—not merely against flesh and blood, which are themselves irrational enough, but against . . . powers which are more than rational."[45] This view gives place both to the larger forces that act upon human events, most important for Kirk the will of God, and to human action that is able to influence the course of those forces.

The Hungarian-born John Lukacs is the other historian whose influence on Kirk we shall consider. Lukacs's *Historical Consciousness*

---

45. Dawson, *The Dynamics of World History*, 259, 261; *RAO*, 38–45.

is a wide-ranging study of the nature of historical knowledge. He proposes a new understanding of history, which includes not only the study of documents and other traditional instruments of reconstructing the past but also an exploration of the "deepening consciousness of the functions of human memory." This new history will discard the false distinction between objectivity and subjectivity that is a by-product of a scientific worldview and will reconceive historical knowledge as personal or participant knowledge.[46] Lukacs applies to historical inquiry Werner Heisenberg's uncertainty principle of physics, which struck a terminal blow to the idea of scientific objectivity. Heisenberg concluded that there are no "objective" processes or mechanisms working upon us. As Lukacs reframes Heisenberg's conclusions, "we cannot avoid the condition of our participation" in examining reality. In a 1968 essay, entitled "The Myth of Objectivity," Kirk argues that too often "objectivity" meant merely the unexamined and fashionable opinions of the scholar, a position that completely ignores the ethical ends of literature and the other humane disciplines. In his introduction to a new edition of *Historical Consciousness*, later included in the collection *Redeeming the Time*, Kirk incorporates Lukacs's insights into his own view.[47]

There are some hints of this concept in Kirk's early work. In *The Conservative Mind*, Kirk argues that the great fault of the liberal historians is their lack of imagination and a "passionate attachment to fact," which has had "a depressing effect upon the British and American mind." Among other things, liberalism's unimaginativeness has opened liberalism to defeat from Marxism, which was animated by a form of historical imagination that transcended economic calculations. Yet in other parts of the same work, Kirk seems reluctant to follow his thought in the direction of participant history that he later adopted. In his discussion of Sir Henry Maine, for example, one of Kirk's major figures in his chapter on "Legal and Historical Conservatism: A Time of Foreboding," Kirk speaks with approval of Maine's insistence that "Historical truth must be like the truths of the

46. Lukacs, *Historical Consciousness: The Remembered Past*, 33, 227–36. For a striking discussion of historical consciousness, see José Ortega y Gasset, *Historical Reason*. Linda Hutcheon displays some similarities to Lukacs's view from a postmodern perspective in her *The Politics of Postmodernism*, 47–61.

47. Lukacs, *Historical Consciousness*, 278–86; Kirk, "The Myth of Objectivity," 36. For commentary on Lukacs's historical thought, see Allitt, *Catholic Intellectuals and Conservative Politics*, 211–22.

astronomer and the physiologist." Maine had attacked one of Kirk's bugbears—Bentham's utilitarianism, which ignored custom, tradition, and accumulated empirical knowledge in favor of a simple pleasure-pain calculus. Nevertheless, Maine's "conservative history on a scientific plan"[48] is more rigid than the view that would eventually become Kirk's own.

On this point, Kirk decisively splits with historians of the liberal school. The liberal interpretation of history lacks a way to transform empirical facts into what Charles McCoy called "social facts."[49] A social fact allows a value judgment. Whether bound by the laws of evolution or progress or, as some latter-day liberals would have it, the "procedural republic," liberal schools of historical thought generally preclude the possibility of making value judgments or intellectual distinctions between competing goods.[50] In other words, the approach to history suggested by modernity lacks a sense of context. Trapped within their theoretical models, liberal historians are unable to encompass the human story that Kirk sees being played out *sub specie aeternitatis.*

Kirk elaborates on Lukacs's discussion by saying that "Historical consciousness necessarily is entwined with the mystery of personal consciousness," and involves not only history, but also "certain insights of philosophy and psychology."[51] In his study of Eliot, for example, he says that "our present private condition and knowledge depend upon what we were yesterday, a year ago, a decade gone; if we reject the lessons of our personal past, we cannot subsist for another hour."[52] Thus Eliot, in the "Burnt Norton" section of "Four Quartets," could speak of past, present, and future time, each contained within the other. And one can see even from a brief reading of Kirk's works that his personal vision is fused into the facts that he relates, as in his account of Burke's struggle with Fox, or of Eliot's early public reading before the critic Sir Edmund Gosse. Wilfred McClay has described the process of acquiring historical consciousness as that of entering a "community of memory," one that intertwines person-

48. *CM,* 263 and 19–320.
49. McCoy, "The Dilemma of Liberalism," in James V. Schall, S.J., and John J. Schrems, eds., *On the Intelligibility of Political Philosophy: Essays of Charles N. R. McCoy, S.J.,* 74.
50. Cf. Alasdair MacIntyre, *After Virtue: A Study in Moral Theory,* 204–26.
51. Kirk, "Introduction," in Lukacs, *Historical Consciousness,* xiii.
52. *Eliot,* 82.

al memory and experience with "the memories of discerning others, memories of things one never experienced firsthand."[53]

Historical knowledge, therefore, because it is bound up with the personality and outlook of the historian interpreting the events that make up such knowledge, is also necessarily knowledge about the present. This understanding of history as "recapitulated" (to borrow a term from the theologian Paul Quay) in the present is evident in Kirk's work. As we have seen, Kirk was often criticized by his fellow conservatives for not identifying with sufficient particularity the "tradition" that they ought to be defending. Yet, it is his very books that provide the identification. What Kirk discusses as past he is at the same time bringing into the present as a living tradition. As David Frum has noted, "Russell Kirk inspired the conservative movement by pulling together a series of only partially related ideas and events into a coherent narrative.... Kirk did not record the past; he created it." To point to something outside his work and say "that is our tradition" would be to commit the very rationalistic error Kirk condemns. It would reify rather than inhabit that tradition. Oakeshott decries a similar approach as "only in a society already deeply infected with rationalism will the conversion of the traditional resources of resistance to the tyranny of rationalism into a self-conscious ideology be considered a strengthening of those resources."[54]

Seen in this way, the complaints of Kirk's fellow conservatives reflect a modern approach that seeks "definitive answers" when historical knowledge, as encapsulated in history and recapitulated into the present, eludes such easy schemata. The complaints further reveal a latent modern attitude in positing a break between past and present that conservatives are trying to "heal" or "recover." Kirk rejects such an approach, preferring instead to see traces of the past in the present and to imagine the past through the present.

Narrative and Tradition

The idea of history as a narrative, a story of events grand and malign, is central to Kirk's sense of history. As he records in his essay

---

53. *EB*, 187–91; *Eliot*, 14–16; McClay, "History and Memory," 19, 20.
54. Frum, "The Legacy of Russell Kirk," 15; Oakeshott, *Rationalism in Politics*, 26.

about the Scottish island of Eigg and its idiosyncratic and threatened society of crofters, general truths are bound up in the particular.[55] David Frum has written that Kirk could summon nostalgia with a mere list of place names, as he did at the opening of *The Conservative Mind*. Similarly, in *Roots of American Order*, Kirk traces the roots of Western culture to five particular cities—Jerusalem, Athens, Rome, London, and finally Philadelphia.[56] This nostalgia, of course, is intentional. Kirk's sense of tradition is self-conscious, and he expresses in his writings a palpable sense of loss, a sadness, when recalling an almost-forgotten past.

In the course of his discussion of Lukacs, Kirk derides the cult of fact that was a nineteenth-century obsession. A fact, by itself, means nothing. Only by association with other facts can it assume meaning and bring the underlying event to light. This process of association must by necessity partake in the nature of a story. "In the commendable sense," Kirk argues, "the genuine historian must be at home with fiction." The combination of fact and narrative reveals the manner in which Kirk understood history as including both subjective and objective elements. The best historians share with the best novelists some characteristics, and Lukacs contends that modern ideas about history have obscured the narrow but sharp difference between history and fiction. Of course, history and fiction are not identical. As Lukacs notes, the primary difference between historians and novelists is the former's restriction to actual events and to potentialities based on those events. The novelist, on the other hand, can create characters and possible events and ascribe motives to characters without any necessary basis in the historical record.[57] This does not provide an excuse for wholesale fabrication, as historians are bound by certain real events to which novelists are not. Kirk is thus able to accept the benefits of "narrativity" without committing the error of those who, since they believe history has no connection to events outside of the text, feel free to write clear falsehoods as expressions of "their" history.

Because fact is at home with fiction, and because the nature of historical knowledge necessarily involves choice and selection, histori-

55. *BDA*, 280. Kirk's essays on architecture display the same. See his "The Uninteresting Future," in *The Intemperate Professor*, 143.

56. Frum, "The Legacy of Russell Kirk," 13; *RAO*, 6.

57. Lukacs, *Historical Consciousness*, 104–8, xiv, 115, 126–27.

cal inquiry is a moral enterprise and not just a scientific discipline. Every choice, Irving Howe has written of the novel, involves perspective and every perspective involves criticism; the enterprise of history involves a similar pattern.[58] We must, therefore, understand Kirk's historical writing in terms of its ethical ends: as demonstrations of individual vice or virtue. So important was history for this purpose that Kirk places it among the types of literature children should be exposed to as they grow older and outgrow reading only "fantastic tales."[59] James Fenimore Cooper, Washington Irving, and Nathaniel Hawthorne, whose historically informed fiction Kirk discusses in *The Conservative Mind*, create a vision of the past not too different in purpose and effect than the storytellers of Eigg that Kirk describes. These visions shape our understanding of history more than a recondite discussion of facts: "we are moved far more by images than by logic-chopping," Kirk asserts, and his historical works are filled more with the former than with the latter.[60]

Without imagination, what Jerzy Topolski has called the "aesthetic sense of order,"[61] history at best is worthless. At worst, it becomes a servant of ideology. When the historical imagination is replaced by a scientific historical method, imagination is destroyed. The truths of history are removed from human life and are true only within the parameters set by the method itself, "in some other world than that inhabited by the historian and his fellow men."[62] Instead, good history, like good literature, will evoke the realities of (dis)continuity and the responsibilities the present generation has to those preceding and succeeding it. As Alasdair MacIntyre has noted, it is one of the strengths of a true tradition to be able to enter imaginatively into its own past, as well as into the past of other traditions.[63]

Even scholars in full possession of the "facts," therefore, may not necessarily be "standing in the tradition, and will ultimately make little positive contribution—though possibly great harm."[64] Imagi-

58. Irving Howe, "History and the Novel: Variations on a Theme," in *A Critic's Notebook: Essays*, 184, 192.

59. *BDA*, 290; *CM*, 251.

60. Kirk, "The Armed Doctrine in Fiction," in Stephen Tonsor, ed., *Reflections on the French Revolution: A Hillsdale Symposium*, 98.

61. Topolski, "The Role of Logic and Aesthetics in Constructing Narrative Wholes in Historiography," 198.

62. Allen Tate, "What is a Traditional Society?" in *Essays of Four Decades*, 552.

63. Alasdair MacIntyre, *Whose Justice? Which Rationality?* 394–95.

64. Josef Pieper, "Tradition: The Concept and Its Claim upon Us," 220.

native history, on the other hand, at some point becomes tradition. The transformation is slow; Kirk liked to quote Hawthorne's aphorism that it takes a century to make a tradition. The tradition-making process is also a creative and dynamic process. Tradition constantly is being revised, rewritten, and reinterpreted. Each generation has the task of confronting the truths anew and making them present to the next generation through fresh interpretations. Just as not every historical fact can be known with certainty, so the full "story" of tradition cannot be grasped or told at once. Tradition is, as Eliot intimated, a responsibility one must assume, and fully appreciating that tradition and handing it on to the next generation takes effort.

In some ways, history is the opposite of tradition: history presupposes a separate past that can be analyzed and examined, while tradition assumes within itself the continuity of what has been passed on. The past is immediate for tradition in a way that it is not for history.[65] Likewise, history is understood, in its modern sense as least, as a series of actual events occurring sequentially in the past. Tradition, because not all of the past can be fully known, by necessity is more concerned with the past as it is perceived in the present.[66] Indeed, in some ways, a proper understanding of tradition will incorporate events that do not happen according to linear time.[67] For instance, Stanley Parry distinguishes between pragmatic history, which is concerned with chronology, the "series of prior causal acts and decisions," and paradigmatic history, which is the instantiation of the experience of truth through time. Tradition, Parry concludes, is a type of paradigmatic history.[68] Tradition itself comprises two parts: the process of handing down a tradition, and the actual *traditum* that is tradition's substance. Stories and narrative history constitute the former and are necessary to convey accepted patterns of actions and thoughts from one generation to the next. Edward Shils has described the latter as "beliefs, standards, and rules, of varying

65. Kenneth L. Schmitz, "What Happens to Tradition When History Overtakes It," 59, 65.

66. Edward Shils, *Tradition,* 195.

67. Schmitz, "What Happens to Tradition," 63.

68. Parry, "The Restoration of Tradition," in George A. Panichas, ed., *Modern Age: The First Twenty-Five Years,* 18. See also J. G. A. Pocock, *Politics, Language, and Time: Essays on Political Thought and History,* 239–40, in which Pocock distinguishes between the "traditional" and "historical" forms of self-understanding.

but never exhaustive explication, which have been received from the preceding generations." Ideas and practices are therefore combined in the process of handing down traditional knowledge. What changes occur do so within the context of the tradition itself. Jaroslav Pelikan has remarked on the ability of the Western intellectual tradition to develop while maintaining continuity, even in the face of sharp internal criticism.[69]

Muller, in his introduction to an anthology of conservative writing, distinguishes conservatism from what he calls orthodoxy and traditionalism; the key differences are in their approaches to the past. The orthodox differs from the conservative in that the former defends existing institutions and practices because they are in some sense true and accord with a principle of reason or revelation. "Traditionalism," in contrast, is the undue allegiance to the traditions of an earlier time. Muller derives this separation ultimately from the work of German sociologist Karl Mannheim, who distinguished conservatism from "traditionalism." The latter is a general psychological trait or characteristic that signifies "a tendency to cling to ways of life which we may well consider as fairly ubiquitous and universal." Conservatism, on the other hand, is "always dependent on a concrete set of circumstances." It is in that sense historically contingent, where traditionalism, Mannheim thought, was not.[70]

Kirk too distinguishes conservatism from reaction. The "conservative hopes to reconcile what is most important in old customs with the change that any society must endure if it is to endure . . . the reactionary desires a return to conditions of an earlier period." While for Kirk, earlier in his career, "the conservative always has been reactionary," in later years that view becomes less pronounced. The effect of conservative action, he argues, must ultimately be creative. Static tradition cannot be a response to changed circumstances; as Burke states, "change must be a means of our preservation." When faced with a crisis, the conservative—instead of rejection or retreat— must "improvise some reform of society." Both the reactionary and orthodox positions, with their reliance upon abstractions about history and society that are then imposed upon the past, are only conservative-tinged variants to the absolutism of modernity. To balance its occasional oppressive effects, tradition "must be balanced by

---

69. Shils, "Tradition and Liberty," 104–5; Pelikan, *Vindication of Tradition*, 58.
70. Karl Mannheim, *From Karl Mannheim*, 153; Muller, ed., *Conservatism*, 5–7.

some strong element of curiosity and individual dissent." Indeed, Kirk goes on to say that "Some people who today are conservatives because they protest against the tyranny of neoterism, in another age or nation would be radicals, because they could not endure the tyranny of tradition. It is a question of degree and balance."[71] A balance among authority, tradition, and dissent is necessary for a stable society. According to Kirk, contemporary society is troubled by a surfeit of dissent rather than conformity, and he believes that the other two elements have been disregarded.

Kirk, however, is not as precise when addressing the substance of the Western tradition. In his short essay, "What Are American Traditions?" Kirk attempts to describe traditional ways of thinking in the United States that derived from its Western heritage. Kirk lists as American traditions "belief in a spiritual order which in some fashion governs our mundane order; belief in political self-government; belief in the importance to human persons of certain natural private rights; belief in the value of marriage and the family."[72] This approach helps Kirk accomplish his goal of connecting American institutions with those of the Old World. These traditions, however, are more abstract than we would expect from Kirk. The particular habits Kirk mentions in *America's British Culture*—a pioneering spirit, marital fidelity, courage in adversity, and the like—are somewhat more concrete, but still not developed fully enough to amount to a complete account of American traditions. One expects, rather, something like the list of customs that Eliot employs, which encompass concrete events and symbols that every British schoolboy would know.[73] To give one example, Kirk wrote almost nothing about sports, a subject that, among certain conservatives at least, has been a source of reflection on both the necessity of play to a healthy society and the concrete manifestations of national traditions and character.[74]

In "What Are American Traditions," Kirk laments that such things as the migratory habits of Americans and the influx of immigrants

71. *EPT,* 52; *PC,* 247.
72. *BDA,* 61, 63.
73. T. S. Eliot, "Notes toward the Definition of Culture," in *Christianity and Culture,* 104.
74. See, for example, George Will's paean to baseball, *Men at Work: The Craft of Baseball.* For an acidic commentary from a fellow conservative, see Donald Kagan, "George Wills' Baseball—A Conservative Critique," in David Brooks, ed., *The New Conservative Writing,* 208–27.

are detrimental to tradition in the United States. Yet, Kirk does not explain why these patterns of behavior might not at some future time assume the status of traditions. As George Carey has noted, even antitradition has a tradition, and Kirk does not really address how to distinguish between a true tradition and an antitradition in a manner that is fully consistent.[75]

Indeed, one might object even to the traditions Kirk does name. A New Age spiritualism represents, in some way, a belief in a spiritual order, "which in some way governs our mundane order," yet is clearly not what Kirk means by an American tradition. Likewise, we are given no guidance as to when a "pioneering spirit" might devolve into a selfish individualism that eschews connection to or responsibility for the larger community. His descriptions of traditions in "What Are American Traditions" and in his books are only partial answers to the question of defining tradition, and they may too often ignore other intervening changes that make the items he does identify no longer worth preserving. Indeed, this sort of approach has caused at least one commentator to question whether Kirk ever examined how much the traditions of the American nation he defended had changed in the years between *The Conservative Mind* and the 1990s. Paul Gottfried, for example, criticized Kirk on this point: "Instead of imagining that the old America was 'enduring' in the present one, Kirk and his fellow-archaic conservatives should have been calling attention to a successor regime," which was based on principles that were often quite hostile to the placid cultural continuities Kirk implied were just beneath the surface.[76]

In *Prospects for Conservatives,* Kirk acknowledges that "there can be error in tradition, and even a tradition made up of errors. Man always is compelled to choose among conflicting traditions, and to sort out from the mass of inherited precepts the maxims and customs which truly apply to his present situation in the world." To separate true elaborations of tradition from false ones Kirk turns to an interplay between authority and freedom. What remains of history after being tested by authority is tradition. Authority conditions the development of tradition, even as it itself is limited by historical circumstance, long existence, and the reflection of new conditions. The

75. George Carey, "Traditions at War," 237.
76. Gottfried, "How Russell Kirk (and the Right) Went Wrong,"
http://www. vdare.com/gottfried/041104_htm (November 4, 2004).

Illative Sense is the "combined product of intuition, instinct, imagination, and long and intricate experience." Knowledge does not and cannot "rest upon mere facts," Kirk states, quoting Newman, "because we have not got them." Thus, "in such circumstances the opinions of others, the traditions of ages, the prescriptions of authority," and similar sources will provide guidance.[77] Kirk employed John Henry Newman's "Illative Sense" as a source of guidance for individuals. Kirk describes it as combining "intuition, instinct, imagination, and long and intricate experience."[78] The Illative Sense provides a basis for knowledge rather than reason. However, the Illative Sense of one person, no matter how well-formed, may still go astray. Thus, to correct individual error, there exists authority, which exemplifies a particular, collective Illative Sense.

Authority is not a monolith; several potentially legitimate authorities can compete for personal allegiance. In such circumstances, "the conscientious man endeavors, according to what light is given him, to determine which representatives of authority have claimed too much." It is again worth noting the central role Kirk finds for the individual. For Kirk, "Tradition cannot suffice to guide a society, nevertheless, if it is not understood and expounded and, if need be, modified by the better intelligences and consciousnesses in every generation."[79] Yet the role of authoritative institutions—churches, nations, old families, and universities that still respect traditional learning—is to judge whether emerging social forms deserve incorporation into the tradition. It is the accumulated wisdom of authority that provides a standard for assessment.

Because of their own historical existence, the sources of authority are removed from everyday controversies and thus are able to make judgments from an impartial position. Such institutions can, through a "collective Illative Sense," purge individual error from the tradition.[80] Kirk would not dispute that such institutional authority can go astray and do positive damage to the tradition; yet, a properly developed tradition will contain within itself the means of regeneration. The recognized authorities of the Western tradition have at

77. *PC*, 232; *CM*, 284, 286.
78. *CM*, 285.
79. *EPT*, 283; *PC*, 235.
80. *CM*, 286.

times accepted criticism from within and absorbed those critiques into the "mainstream" of that tradition. Two heroes of the Western tradition are, after all, Jesus Christ and Socrates, both put to death by the political power yet whose doctrines went on to become world-changing.

Describing tradition in detail, however, is self-defeating, because tradition is neither static nor entirely comprehensible. This may be one reason that Kirk did not set forth anywhere the full lineaments of the Western tradition or a more specific list of American traditions, being mindful of Pieper's counsel that "Whoever truly wants to hand something on must not speak of tradition."[81] Instead, Kirk preferred to live and "write" it and to convey its lessons in other ways. Another reason for Kirk's reluctance may have been his habitual reluctance to take on the "prophetic afflatus" and to believe that one person could condense into words the habits and mores of an entire culture. Conservatives who attempt to hold "tradition" to a particular place or time inevitably conjure romantic periods of time that cannot be duplicated because they never really existed. Tradition is a "form of life" rather than—or more correctly more than—a set of precepts or maxims. Such precepts and maxims play a role, but tradition must remain never fully reducible to logical explication. To do so would corrupt what Lee Harris called the "visceral code" of a community, which "tells us what behavior must be passed on," through sentiments such as shame, honor, and respect. Such partial articulation of the underpinnings of a community's "code" is an important feature of historical narratives that are transformed into traditions.[82]

The force of tradition is instead present most fully in those moments Kirk describes as intersections of time and the timeless. For example, Kirk recounts in his memoirs playing with his children early one morning and the visit of the British writer Malcolm Muggeridge and his wife to his home as two such moments. The timeless nature of the acts—hospitality, the reverence of children for their parents, and the love of parents for their children—is revealed through their particularity. These acts took place at Piety Hill in the

81. Pieper, "Tradition," 219.
82. Cf. Francis, *Beautiful Losers*, 4; Harris, "The Future of Tradition"; David Carr, "Modernity, Post-Modernity and the Philosophy of History," 45.

state of Michigan at a specific point in the twentieth century, yet reflect the larger tradition for those participating in them.

The Individual in History

Kirk was severely criticized for having allegedly neglected to consider the primary place of individual freedom in the Western intellectual and political tradition. Kirk was accused, for example by Frank Meyer, of elevating tradition to the point of sacrificing that freedom to a common good. Some of Kirk's statements give credence to this charge. He famously said in *The Conservative Mind*, and in other works, that "the individual is foolish but the species is wise," a remark that prompted Walter Berns to quip that its truth was proven by some of Kirk's own work.[83] Yet Kirk clearly moved away from such a position, if he ever held it at all in a strict form, as time passed. As he well knew, entire societies can indeed be foolish collectively and need to be led back to wisdom by a few who possess historical imagination. He came to understand the individual as a crucial component in the maintenance of history, precisely in the role individual freedom had to play in the continual renewal and reconstruction of that tradition.

The fusion of imagination and fact for Kirk occurs not in abstract historical processes but in individuals whose actions can change the course of history. Kirk frequently made use of the following passage from Burke's *Letters on the Regicide Peace:* "The death of a man at a critical juncture, his disgust, his retreat, his disgrace, have brought innumerable calamities on a whole nation. A common soldier, a child, a girl at the door of an inn, have changed the face of fortune, and almost of nature." Burke's insight in this passage rebukes the historical determinists; the actions by, for example, Joan of Arc (the girl) or Hannibal (the child) could not have been foreseen, yet were charged with historical import. The passage reveals instead Burke's Christian understanding of history, an understanding shared by Kirk. God works through individuals, not processes. And human decisions take place not against the backdrop of an idealized world, but in the face of concrete and difficult historical circumstances. Because

83. *CM*, 37; Berns, review of *A Program for Conservatives*, 686.

of the disjunction between a particular historical framework and transcendent norms, history assumes the possibility of freedom and decision and of evil.[84] Humans can confound the divine plan, at least temporarily, in a way that the materialist or Hegelian plans do not permit.

Thus, Kirk intended his work for those individual "shapers of public opinion" who influence their communities. Kirk was an individualist, but his individualism was chastened by his sense that each person should pay homage to the past. Like Burke, Kirk would have everyone "respect the general sense, the accumulated experience of the past that has become embodied in the habits and usages that the superficial rationalist would dismiss as prejudice." Tradition guides individuals, but there must be "vigorous application and prudent reform" by individuals for tradition to remain appealing and persuasive. Tradition cannot be passively accepted or else it becomes the desiccated "traditionalism," which Pelikan decried as the dead faith of the living. Rather, tradition can be made one's own only by great effort, as Eliot noted in his influential essay, "Tradition and the Individual Talent." The most important aid in this effort is the cultivation of what Eliot called the historical sense, and what this study has called the historical imagination. This sense "involves a perception, not only of the pastness of the past, but of its presence."[85] Kirk, too, as we have seen, thought the development of this sense critical in understanding both history and tradition, and he believed that it was as necessary to those who would act against the tradition as for those acting "in the tradition." Seen in this way, the conservative emphasis on tradition does not impede individual action; in some sense, it is necessary for that action to make sense. As Kekes wrote,

> Traditionalism does not lead conservatives to deny that individuals must make good lives for themselves and that making them requires making choices and understanding and evaluating their significance. Conservatives think, however, that individuals do all this by participating in traditions because traditions provide the

84. Dawson also makes use of this passage in *Dynamics of World History*, 259. Josef Pieper, *Hope and History*, 40.

85. *CM*, i; Babbitt, *Democracy and Leadership*, 125; *EPT*, 286; Pelikan, *Vindication of Tradition*, 65; Eliot, "Tradition and the Individual Talent," in *Selected Prose of T. S. Eliot*, 38.

alternatives among which they choose, the standards of understanding and evaluation they employ, and the elements out of which they form their conception of what a good life would be.[86]

Tradition, therefore, does not simply exist; there is a constant interplay between the teachings of tradition and the choices of the individual.

Further, the development of the sense of the presence of the past affects and changes the past even as the past affects and changes the present. Each addition to the tradition affects all the previous elements of that tradition, which are now subtly shifted into an arrangement slightly different from their arrangement before the addition. Thus, the past does not stand still as modernity assumes. It is here where the individual has such a vital role to play. For the constantly shifting alterations of the elements making up the tradition of a culture are replicated, in miniature, in the slow adaptation of the individual whose knowledge of the past is subtly changed as the individual enters the tradition more fully. As Kirk recognized in his discussion of Eliot's essay, the alteration of the past occurs when individuals take the initiative, and even when that initiative is required to break up parts of the tradition in order to accommodate the tradition to changed circumstances.[87]

Conclusion: History as a Moral Enterprise

The study of history is at a crossroads. One path leads to the historical determinists, descendants of Kirk's positivists, who see larger forces, either material or historical, at work that dwarf individual human actions. They maintain the dream of "progress" and the creation of a universal objective history. The other path is an extreme postmodernism, which doubts that there is any purpose to history at all; every act is random and irreducibly individual and has no meaning.[88] Both schools have little use for tradition or the historical imagination and say little to the individual presented with a welter

86. Kekes, *A Case of Conservatism*, 209.
87. *Eliot*, 60–62.
88. For a commentary on the state of the historical profession, see Keith Windschuttle, "The Real Stuff of History," 4.

of conflicting traditions and masses of historical material. The former approach flattens the individual and the individual's role in history into insignificance. The latter path, while providing in some sense beneficial correctives to the modern view, is ultimately a counsel of despair and deprives its positive contributions of any lasting importance.

Kirk proposed a different approach, contending that "notions about history and its lessons will be powerful in the post-modern age." Although he did not develop a complete historical vision, an outline of such a vision is readily apparent in his writings. Kirk's view of history recognizes that facts are important for human society only when they are embedded in narrative. Narrative gives a sense of identity that the "science" of history cannot provide. Such a history is useless to daily existence or to penetrate history's larger meaning as an illustration of the divine plan. History must be a part of the lived experience of both the individual and the culture as a whole in order for it to assume any coherence. As Ryn suggested, this approach provides a way to understand history as an exercise in self-knowledge against the backdrop of the passage of time.[89]

Indeed, Kirk's practical criticisms of the contemporary teaching of history revolved around history's nonnarrative character. That is to say, Kirk thought history at its weakest when presented as a jumble of distorted and unconnected facts. Recounting the elementary school education given to his daughters, Kirk noted that they were presented with "a pastiche of snippets about Cro-Magnons, Babylonians, Greeks, Romans, medieval folk, and modern revolutionaries, and so forth, and so forth."[90] There was no coherent story in this melange; what was substituted for an appreciation of one's civilization and the role of individuals within it were "sociological generalizations" and the temptation to impart "approved attitudes," using selected bits of history as proof-texts. This, for Kirk, was the very opposite of forming historical imagination. He believed that it is especially critical in the postmodern world, with its explosion of images and information, to construct a coherent story through education, even if not all parts of that story can be defined or controlled.

Richard Delgado has written that stories and "counterstories" can

89. Kirk, "Foreword," iv; Ryn, *Will, Imagination, and Reason*, 110.
90. Kirk, "Historical Consciousness and the Preservation of Culture," 491, 494.

"open new windows onto reality [and] enrich imagination."[91] The postmoderns emphasize, perhaps more than is warranted and certainly more than Kirk does, the destructive power of stories. They reduce the historian's role merely to exposing structures of oppression or exploitation. Kirk prefers the approach of a "constructive imagination" that seeks to renew as much as to condemn.[92] As a Christian, Kirk believed that sin is always present, and thus stories or traditions will be used as often for evil as for good. Yet he also contended that one cannot discard the structures by which societies understand themselves on that basis alone; within the tradition itself, redemption can be found. Indeed, *The Conservative Mind* may be considered one of the more successful conservative "counterstories" of the last century. Kirk's shifting assemblage of persons, who, some argue, did not constitute much of a conservative tradition at all, were examples for Kirk of the stability and flexibility of that tradition. Indeed, Kirk's volume provided a critical "vision of alterity" that offered an alternative to the then-reigning liberal and progressive understandings of American history mentioned by Trilling and Hartz.[93]

While Kirk may have disagreed with some of the postmodernists' conclusions, his area of concern is similar. J. M. Balkin, a prominent postmodern theorist, has described postmodernism as being concerned with the relationship between thought and action and the conviction that "knowledge is always inscribed in a form of life." Postmodern writers have concentrated on the way late twentieth-century America assimilated and passed on knowledge and values. Balkin, for example, contends that an "emphasis on cultural practices and ways of living" is a characteristic feature of postmodern thought.[94] Kirk shared a concern for how the stories that constitute our ways of life are told and transmitted and by whom. Thus, while both Kirk and the postmodernists realize that tradition is "invented" to some degree, the latter are quick to dispose of tradition entirely and to dismiss its value, while Kirk's view would instead engage tradition as necessary for personal and cultural identity.

Because of his belief in a community of souls, Kirk believed that

91. Delgado, "Storytelling for Oppositionists and Others: A Plea for Narrative," 2411, 2414–15. See also Roberto M. Unger, *Knowledge and Politics,* 42–43.
92. *CM,* 68.
93. The phrase is borrowed from David Gross, "Rethinking Traditions," 6.
94. Balkin, "What Is a Postmodern Constitutionalism?" 1966, 1975–76.

history, though composed of a collection of individual narratives, nevertheless was intelligible enough to be communicated to others because these narratives are all attempts at expressing similar things. Speaking of Eliot, he wrote, "it is possible for some other human beings to apprehend the poet's symbols of transcendence; and to draw analogies between those symbolic images and their own fleeting glimpses . . . of [the] permanent things."[95]

Although speaking of poetry and the poet's role, Kirk's words clearly apply to his own conception of history as well. For these stories point to truths beyond themselves, indeed beyond history. Kirk therefore would have disagreed with José Ortega y Gasset's famous formulation that "Man, in a word, has no nature; what he does have is . . . history."[96] While Kirk accepted the idea of an identifiable human nature, he never attempted to reduce it to particulars. Instead, he argued that human nature could be understood only through individual action and reflection upon the larger patterns of conduct in which the historian plays a central role. The historical imagination therefore avoids the "false alternatives" of a hazy universality and a solipsistic individuality.

Yet there is a tension between his obvious enjoyment of out-of-the-way minorities such as the Eigg crofters and his reluctance to absolutize even American culture, and his strong defense of overarching cultural wholes such as "the West" or "Anglo-American culture" in books such as *The Roots of American Order* and *America's British Culture*. Yet he clearly understood the limits of his own culture. Thus, for example, in 1963 Kirk rejected a liberal "planned Americanization of the world," because "diversity, not uniformity, is the blessing of mankind, in public affairs as in private life."[97] Moreover, imposing Americanization might destroy legitimate elements of other cultures, in the name of a consumerism Kirk criticized as representative of American interests abroad. Balancing a just regard for one's own culture while respecting others was not just a problem for Kirk. As Angela Dillard noted in a recent book, American conservatism has historically had difficulty encompassing other traditions that may themselves have conservative roots. Because conservatives by and large reject the liberal understanding of tolerance, conservatives do

95. *Eliot*, 288.
96. Ortega y Gasset, *History as a System*, 217.
97. *CBT*, 302.

not have a history that permits them to be easily inclusive of others, even others who may share some conservative views.[98]

Because of his extensive travels, Kirk had formed favorable impressions of local cultures around the world, which he thought should be defended against the depredations of modern Western ideology. His studies of Eliot, Burke, and others, however, had also convinced him of the need for a common culture that would exist on the basis of "the man of genius and the culture of the educated classes," which again exemplifies Kirk's understanding of the close relationship between the individual and the larger society. Yet the culture of the genius and the educated may betray its principles or may be deceived by a false adoration of the "mass" culture. "The high culture and the common culture, by necessity, are interdependent; so are the national culture and the regional culture. What American culture urgently requires just now is solidarity: that is, a common front against the operations of Chaos and Old Night." Kirk wrote *America's British Culture* because he believed that the "multicultural" position was not representative of a true defense of culture; for him, it was an ideological argument based upon a politicized understanding of culture. Because of its ideological basis, it could not serve as a positive reworking of culture for the new era.

Kirk believed history to be a moral enterprise, which fully engages the historian who seeks to reconstruct the past for the present. Historians are morally and individually engaged at every moment, both in their choice of sources from which to draw their stories and in their choice of words and phrases with which they describe their story.[99] This lends a seriousness of purpose to Kirk's understanding of history that is lacking in some postmodern alternatives. For some postmoderns, writing history with a moral purpose is a fruitless task, not only because of their general moral relativism, but also because they do not think that moral lessons for one individual can affect another. Kirk's approach is folly as well for the positivist or modern approach, in which individual action cannot really interfere with the march of progress or regress that follow immutable laws that the historian only "discovers."

However, Kirk's conception of history is not complete. For exam-

---

98. Dillard, *Guess Who's Coming to Dinner Now? Multicultural Conservatism in America.*
99. Lukacs, *Historical Consciousness*, 111.

ple, although Kirk sees a difference between history and tradition, the boundaries between the two are sometimes murky. Sometimes a tradition is a concrete social custom or habit, sometimes a more fluid pattern of thought or belief. Kirk also varies his definition of history, sometimes meaning past events, past events as we understand them, or the stories or narratives we construct of these past events. At a basic level, however, Kirk sees history in its original sense of inquiry or search: it is a means through which we can find answers, but is not itself an answer.[100] In discussing tradition as both the experience of humanity, expressed in story and custom, as well as the role individuals play in preserving and moving forward tradition, Kirk acknowledged the parts "charisma" as well as "routine" play in human society.[101] He wrestled with the problem of tradition in several ways and tried to balance its static and dynamic aspects, avoiding traditionalism while celebrating the living tradition. While his analysis of historical or traditional elites, and their role in maintaining tradition, is incomplete, he identified particular individuals who embodied the best of Western tradition or who by their actions moved this tradition into new directions without severing it from its roots. Kirk also defined tradition through stories and essays of particular places and events. In this regard, his memoir, *The Sword of Imagination,* is another example of Kirk's exercises in creating tradition through the life of one man—himself. Authority, which is given legitimacy by its long existence and embodiment of tradition, has an important role to play in governing the development of tradition. Individuals must create tradition anew for each generation, yet they must also be chastened in their choices by the teachings of authority and the accumulated wisdom of prior generations.

100. For Kirk's concern over proper definition, see Henry Regnery, "Russell Kirk: An Appraisal," in Brown, *Kirk: A Bibliography,* 132.
101. Pocock, *Politics, Language, and Time,* 244.

3

Kirk's Politics and the Role of the Statesman

Not abstractions, but prudence, prescription, custom, tradition, and constitution have governed the American people.

Russell Kirk, *Enemies of the Permanent Things*

The Art of the Possible

Perhaps to emphasize what he considered the ephemeral nature of most political controversies, Kirk liked to quote the aphorism that nothing was deader than dead politics. And although he consistently disdained exercises such as drawing up platforms or party programs, Kirk expressed great interest in the subject of political leadership and the creation of an enduring political principle embodied in the idea of party. Even his writings purportedly directed at conservative political action approached the subject obliquely. His early *Program for Conservatives,* for example, explicitly "ignore[s] many of the political controversies of the hour" to focus on broader themes of a "conservative program." The book is organized around a series of "Questions," in which Kirk considers the conservative approach to the issues of "Power," "Wants," and "Tradition," among others, but does not offer any detailed political solutions. Kirk's political writing is not without some concrete political commentary, such as the series of essay-debates between himself and liberal figures such as Arthur Schlesinger Jr., and he also published sketches in *National Review* of conservative politicians, including what is perhaps his most famous political essay, "The Mind of Barry Goldwater."[1] Occasionally, Kirk wrote on specific public policies such as the budget or the federal bureaucracy, but these commentaries rarely rise to the level of his more trenchant pieces that include discussions of political ideas.[2] When he did address public policy proposals it was usually to deride them, either as overly centralizing or too abstract to succeed. Yet Kirk was not completely above offering practical advice for success. A clear indication of Kirk's position may be taken from the advice he gave young admirers to study rather than engage in political "activism," which he believed was incompatible with the conservative outlook. In one of his last public lectures, given to an audience of young "conservative activists," Kirk outlined a tongue-in-cheek strategy for a political career. After exhorting his young audience to "volunteer" in political campaigns, he opined that "you will find, indeed, that a number of your fellow volunteers are rather peculiar people, almost Outcasts of Poker Flat, but welcome in a local political organization (if not welcome in many other circles) because, whatever their peculiarities, they are willing to work for a common cause." Kirk further advised his charges that when attending a convention, "endeavor to sit at the chairman's right hand; then others may take you for his right-hand man."[3] Given in 1991, the lecture was in part a counterpoint to the proponents of "movement conservatism," deep into their victories of the Reagan-Bush years, which threatened to conflate Republican Party governance with conservative principle.

Nevertheless, Kirk thought he himself had a political function: "to work upon the body politic by endeavoring to rouse the political and moral imagination among the shapers of public opinion."[4] Kirk used examples to do the rousing. Thus, in invoking the example of Burke for contemporary America, Kirk asked his readers to determine not

1. *SI*, 254; *PC*, ix. This essay was written as part of a new foreword in 1988 (Kirk, "The Mind of Barry Goldwater").
2. See, for example, the following essays by Kirk: "The Federal Budget," 2; "HEW May Get You Too," 34; "Salvation by Bus," 1065; "Killing with Regulatory Kindness," 406.
3. Kirk, "May the Rising Generation Redeem the Time?" 6.
4. *SI*, 307.

"If Burke were elected President of the United States . . . would he" but rather "to put on the mind of Burke [and] to look at the future of American politics as he looked at the future of European politics."[5] This imaginative replacement of Burke was intended to help those involved in politics transcend contemporary political concerns, while retaining the core elements of Burke's outlook.

In the 1950s, Burke, the center of this political conservatism, was receiving new attention as a political thinker. Kirk was among a group of conservatives, including Ross Hoffman and Peter J. Stanlis, who sought to "rehabilitate" Burke from the utilitarian interpretation they thought had misconstrued him. This school, which was identified primarily with Henry Buckley and John Morley, thought Burke's preference for "expedience" was a poor foundation for lasting conservative principles.[6] Some conservatives such as Richard Weaver and Frank Meyer agreed with this negative assessment. Weaver wrote a chapter in his book *The Ethics of Rhetoric* on Burke, whom he compared unfavorably with Lincoln.

Stanlis and the others thought Burke should instead be considered part of a British political tradition, reaching back to Hooker and, ultimately, to the Roman jurisprudents. Stanlis, for example, in his book *Edmund Burke and the Natural Law,* first published in 1958, argued that far from being a utilitarian, Burke was completely familiar with and a promoter of natural law thinking. Kirk, commenting on Stanlis's interpretation, contended that Stanlis clearly established that the "grand Natural Law tradition of Cicero and the Schoolmen, though battered by Hobbes and confused by Locke, re-emerges in all its strength in Burke's reply to the French revolutionaries."[7] The natural law tradition, properly understood, was a rejection of both utilitarianism and the "Rights of Man" of Paine.

Other scholars rejected the interpretation of Burke as a natural law thinker. They criticized Kirk and these other conservatives for using Burke as part of an anti-Communist project during the Cold War. Isaac Kramnick, for example, included Kirk among Burke's "Cold War disciples," in whose work, Kramnick argued, one "senses this aristocratic nostalgia for an era when Christian and humanist men of letters, men of learning and breeding, dominated public life."[8] The

5. Kirk, "Edmund Burke and the Future of American Politics," 107, 109.
6. Nash, *Conservative Intellectual Movement,* 150–53.
7. Stanlis, *Edmund Burke and the Natural Law,* vi.
8. Kramnick, *The Rage of Edmund Burke: Portrait of an Ambivalent Conservative,* 45–47.

Irish intellectual Conor Cruise O'Brien also took this position in his introduction to his 1986 edition of Burke's *Reflections*. O'Brien accused Kirk of selectively misreading Burke and argued that the rediscovery of Burke by conservative scholars in the 1950s was only a cover for their anticommunism. O'Brien wrote that Kirk erred "when he invoked the authority of Burke, and of Burke's England, in support of America's 'imperial duty' today."[9] More recently, David Frum, though appreciative of Kirk, nonetheless argued that books such as *The Conservative Mind* conveyed primarily a political rather than a cultural message. According to this view, Kirk is one of many intellectuals who have distorted history and logic in the hopes of advancing a particular political program.

Although this charge has some weight to it, Kirk does not fit easily into this caricature. Kirk did write one book for an explicitly political purpose. Shocked by stories of American soldiers captured during the Korean War who had displayed little knowledge of the American political system or reasons to defend it, Kirk wrote *The American Cause* as a primer to educate soldiers and others about the basic principles of American political life. But while believing Americans had an international role to play in resisting the expansion of communism, Kirk, to the chagrin of some conservative allies, was no cold warrior. Although he opposed the extension of communism throughout the world, Kirk was consistently harsh on those who thought "American-style democracy" could be packaged for other nations. O'Brien's claim of "imperial duty," therefore, falls short, especially considering the Gulf War, which Kirk strongly opposed. In any event, Kirk discovered Burke well before his participation in the "natural law" reading of Burke. Neither *The Conservative Mind* nor the individual study examined Burke's natural law thinking in any depth. The only clear reference connecting the two stated merely that Burke adopted natural law precepts "in the historical and expedient sense." Kramnick's "nostalgic" reading of Kirk's Burke is a common one, but Kirk himself described Burke as "essentially a modern man, and his concern was with our modern complexities."[10]

Exactly *how* Burke was modern for Kirk is not always clear. In a general outline, Kirk thought Burke was proposing a modern politics that was better suited than the aristocratic reaction of Boling-

9. O'Brien, "Introduction," in Edmund Burke, *Reflections on the Revolution in France*, 65–66.

10. Kirk, *American Cause; CM*, 118; *EB*, 8.

broke. Burke foresaw the coming age of ideology—political ideals based on abstractions and held with religious fervor—that were to shape the coming century. Kirk, writing in a century that saw two ideologies battle one another across the globe, contended that Burke's insight into ideology was of crucial importance. In his battle with ideology, Burke invoked nonpolitical institutions and social traditions as bulwarks against revolution. This strategy led to two centuries' worth of reflection and argument on the role of social institutions in political life by conservatives. This rhetorical approach also, Kirk believed, required employment and development of the moral imagination to conjure the sentiments of loyalty and affection for the ways threatened by ideology. In this too Kirk thought Burke modern in the way that Rousseau and Paine were modern.

As with politics, the nostalgic picture of Kirk and economics is not as simple as his critics' quick dismissal might suggest, although almost no one until recently has considered Kirk's writings on the subject of any serious note.[11] Martin Morse Wooster, for example, faulted Kirk's conservatism because it purportedly did not contain an "appreciation of capitalism and economics." Kirk did boast of assiduously avoiding the business pages, and economics did hold a relatively small place in his work. Yet Kirk composed a lengthy introductory economics textbook, and he was consistently interested in "alternative" economics movements, such as those described in the writings of the Southern Agrarians or the British Distributists. The German economist Wilhelm Roepke, who tried in *A Humane Economy* and other works to develop an alternative program to the standard economics of midcentury, was a favorite of Kirk's. Kirk described the Roepke program as "suited to human nature and to a human scale in society. . . . [Roepke] was a formidable opponent of socialist and other 'command' economies; also a fearless, perceptive critic of an unthinking 'capitalism.'"[12]

With respect to economics, Kirk saw in the devotion to a free market system the same weaknesses he saw in socialism. Favorably discussing the thought of Brooks Adams, Kirk wrote that the cycle of capitalism resulted in destruction: "the capitalist lacks capacity suf-

11. John Attarian has done the most work in this area. See his "Russell Kirk's Political Economy," 87–97; see also Person, *Kirk: A Critical Biography,* 201–12.

12. Wooster, "Captain Kirk," 74. See also James Neuchterlein, "The Paleo's Paleo," 46; *SI,* 29. For a recent study of Roepke, see Patrick M. Boarman, "Apostle of a Humane Economy: Remembering Wilhelm Roepke," 31; *PP,* 114–15.

ficient for the administration of the society he has made his own." A staunch capitalist is opposed to the conservative, according to Kirk, because the former has as reductive a view of the human person as any doctrinaire disciple of Rousseau or Paine, as Kirk argued in a sharp essay on the libertarians.[13]

Kirk's economic thinking is characterized by favoring small rather than large-scale businesses, both as a cultural preference and as a political one. Kirk rejected, almost from the beginning of his career, the notion that economics could constitute a full way of life. While he appreciated the importance of economics as a field of study, he did not consider it the most important field, and he did not think that it should be the prism through which political or social issues should be examined.

For much of his career, Kirk was able to support himself as a writer; therefore, he knew the advantages of a free and relatively unregulated economy, which had allowed him to pursue the life he desired. Yet, he also argued that a myopic concern for the bottom line created not only social stagnation, but ultimately economic loss and political degradation. So, for example, in discussing the economic concerns of the founders, Kirk recognized that finances and economics were of deep interest to them—both personally and with respect to the fortunes of the new nation. However, he also contended that those were not the only incentives that impelled them to create the new government. The larger cultural and religious background of the founders had more to do with their political choices than their economic self-interest. More generally, Kirk found that an excessive concern for economics was neither in accord with conservative principles nor historically accurate: "Most people in the long run are not content with getting and spending. . . . Life isn't like that."[14]

To articulate what would satisfy people, Kirk looked to the imagination, for its persuasive power and for its substantive use, to construct actual solutions to real problems. As Gleaves Whitney has written, Kirk believed that political imagination should be used primarily to explore how individuals can live and prosper together in a community. The careful calibrations of a multitude of individual and communal interests would provide a more acceptable set of po-

13. *CM*, 369; *PP*, 156–71. For a response to what he called Kirk's "vitriolic essay," see Tom G. Palmer, "Myths of Individualism," 1.
14. *CC*, 49–62. The quote is from Person, *Kirk: A Critical Biography*, 202.

litical solutions than a reliance on a preestablished ideology. Like politicians, entrepreneurs and business leaders need imagination to lift them out of the cycle of production and consumption and to elevate economics to a humane discipline.

The political figures Kirk wrote about favorably give some sense of his scale of political principles. He was a fan of the liberal Eugene McCarthy, whom he called one of the "most interestingly complex" and intellectually astute senators of the twentieth century and who won Kirk's vote in 1976.[15] Kirk also spoke approvingly of the socialist Norman Thomas, whom he debated and with whom he shared a memorable trip in the rain after a 1961 debate. Thomas, though blind to the ultimate result of socialism, was nevertheless a stout defender of civil liberties. In a later book, *The Politics of Prudence*, Kirk identified Theodore Roosevelt as an exemplary conservative. In contrast to many conservatives, Kirk also had a favorable opinion of Woodrow Wilson. Kirk commended Wilson in *The Conservative Mind* for being a disciple of Burke, despite the president's "maze of contradictions." Wilson was a conservative president, "born into a liberal era, [and] the political vocabulary of his time was that of the liberals." Wilson the natural conservative became the rhetorical liberal. "A man's words can master him; phrases can intimidate; and uttering the slogans of liberalism that were fashionable in Washington, Wilson presently came to act on liberal abstractions."[16] Nonetheless, Kirk thought Wilson presented a conservative example to the world following the First World War. What failures occurred resulted from Wilson's espousal of liberal abstractions such as "national self-determination" and passion for what now would be termed *nation building*.

Kirk's mixed feelings for Wilson were echoed in his reflections on Herbert Hoover. The latter once considered naming Kirk to head the eponymous institution he was establishing, and Kirk recounted a breakfast he had with Hoover to discuss the proposal. Although a learned and honest man, Hoover lacked, as did other "better liberals in their nineteenth-century heyday and their twentieth-century decline," sufficient imagination for the times.[17] Hoover retained an

15. *SI*, 324–28.
16. *SI*, 315–19; *PP*, 72; *CM*, 417; *EPT*, 182–91.
17. *SI*, 309–14; the quote is at 311.

Enlightenment faith in large-scale international social programs and the goodness of human nature, and Kirk counted his refusal to countenance a return of the Habsburgs to Hungary in 1919 as a failure of his historical and political imagination.

Most significantly, Kirk's opinions on Abraham Lincoln did not sit well with some conservatives. Because of the internecine struggles that opinions about Lincoln aroused in some conservative circles, particularly in the 1980s, Kirk's views on the matter were circumspect. Kirk respected the Great Emancipator's gifts of language and leadership, and he was not afraid to call Lincoln a conservative thinker. In *The Roots of American Order,* Kirk described Lincoln as possessing all the Roman virtues: *pietas,* gravitas, and a sense of duty. To Kirk, Lincoln represented in his native prudence and tragic sense of life, a Christian religious sensibility conditioned by the environment of America's democratic frontier. In this, Kirk explicitly contrasted Lincoln with Robert E. Lee, who epitomized the older American tradition of reconciling freedom and order. President Lincoln was a new type of leader: "for the first time, we see a man from the common clay as defender of order." While Kirk did not endorse Reconstruction and lamented the loss of aspects of the South's traditional culture of civility and deference, he believed that Lincoln represented an acceptable interpretation of conservative defense of political order. Indeed, Kirk criticized Weaver for being "needlessly anxious" to include Lincoln as a conservative in his book, *The Ethics of Rhetoric.*[18] Such opinions belie the portrait of Kirk as a southern conservative, for whom Lincoln represented a turning point from an agrarian republic to an industrial empire.

In his own lifetime, Kirk was active in national politics, and one presidential campaign, in particular, was of primary interest to him: Barry Goldwater's in the 1960s. He first met Goldwater at a "council of war" in Florida in January 1962 and, subsequently, became an occasional speechwriter and active campaigner for him, both in articles and in debates across the country.[19] Although he was not as closely connected to the Reagan campaigns as he was to those of Goldwater—taking, as he said, "next to no part" in Reagan's elec-

18. *RAO,* 449–57 (the quote is at 450); *BDA,* 85.
19. *SI,* 254–60, 285–88, 293–303.

tion bids—Kirk did strongly support Reagan, against Ford in the 1976 presidential primaries, and against Carter in 1980. He was later offered posts in both Reagan administrations.[20]

During the 1980s and early 1990s, Kirk, while sought after as a speaker at conservative events, was not among the inner circle of policy advisers of the Reagan or Bush administrations. As Wesley McDonald noted, Kirk was "[l]argely ignored by the Washington-based Republican establishment, [and] his opinions on public-policy issues were seldom solicited. His anti-modernist traditionalism, combined with his characteristically unfashionable attire, seemed out of place among the button-down Republicans of the Reagan era."[21] Kirk's views began to separate him from the "conservative establishment," although some major conservative policy institutions, such as the Heritage Foundation, continued to host numerous lectures by Kirk. In particular, Kirk had little regard for foreign policy issues, and his growing criticisms of capitalism did not sit well with libertarians or business supporters of conservatism. Never fully at home with the big business conservatives who were his allies in the Republican Party of the 1950s, Kirk continued to spar with their global democratic capitalist heirs through the 1990s. In an essay on neoconservatives, originally presented as a Heritage lecture, while generally praising their talents and entry into the conservative fold, Kirk criticized the work of Michael Novak and Irving Kristol for promoting democratic capitalism as the "American ideology."[22] While Kirk may have judged the neoconservatives too harshly—in that some at the time held opinions similar to Kirk's about the fragility of transporting cultural traditions and the cultural context of democracy and capitalism in the West—nevertheless such opinions reduced Kirk's influence throughout the 1980s.

Relatedly, he lodged a number of attacks against "democratic capitalism," because "the phrase is a contradiction in terms; for capitalism is not democratic, nor should it be, nor can it be." In his opinion, the free market is not the same as universal suffrage or democratic government, and the two need not occur together. More important, Kirk argued that because it is in the nature of an ideology to be abstract and limitless in its claims—as it is not bounded by history, cus-

20. Ibid., 44–50, 450–52.
21. McDonald, "The Sacred Garden," 29.
22. *PP,* 172, 183.

tom, or geography—ideology will lead to an internationalism of the worst sort; one that is not only ineffective but also unprincipled. "To expect that all the world should, and must, adopt the peculiar political institutions of the United States—which often do not work very well even at home—is to indulge in the most unrealistic of visions." Kirk wondered whether Republican neoconservatives were in fact different from the liberal globalizers under Johnson. Kirk concluded, "I am saying that a quasi-religion of Democratic Capitalism cannot do duty for imagination and right reason and prescriptive wisdom, in domestic policies or foreign relations."[23]

Kirk came out strongly in the 1980s for reducing America's interests abroad. He found the conservative embrace of "democratic capitalism" reductive and tending toward a right-wing image of communism. He thought that America should not spread its culture across the world merely because it had the power to do so. Culture for Kirk could not be so easily commodified into "a way of life," endlessly repeatable as a set of prefabricated solutions and policies. Instead, Kirk championed the rights of people to form their own "little platoons" and to have the freedom to create through compromise a workable social, political, and economic system. Intellectually, this position is descended from Burke's position on British India and has personal roots in Kirk's wide travels. An imperial power has the responsibility not to exercise its power to turn all subsidiary local cultures to its will. This respect for a pluralist conception of a good society was balanced by a desire to bring out the values inherent in American culture, derived from the Western tradition, to their fullest.[24]

In 1992, Kirk supported Patrick J. Buchanan as the Republican candidate for president. As he had with his first vote in 1936, Kirk switched his support to Buchanan on the basis of foreign policy. Specifically, Kirk had voiced strong disagreement with the first President Bush's decision to commit American forces in the Persian Gulf against Iraq. Six years later, again speaking of the Middle East, Kirk criticized the interventionist policies of the Republican Party. Invoking Orwell's 1984, Kirk condemned the American "perpetual war for perpetual peace," which "comes to pass in an era of righteousness—that is, national or ideological self-righteousness in which the pub-

23. Ibid., 183–84, 186.
24. *RAO,* 469.

lic is persuaded that 'God is on our side.'" Kirk had expressed his views on these issues as early as 1985, when he decried the lack of "diplomatic imagination" that caused politicians to "fancy that an American paradise of civil rights could be fixed upon embattled Vietnam, or that American money and technology could westernize Iran."[25] His intransigence on this point anticipated the full-scale break that has occurred among conservatives over the invasions of Afghanistan and Iraq.

The Statesman

Kirk approached political questions by exploring the boundaries between statesmanship and party, in order to strike a balance between these competing needs. A party represents principle over time; the statesman provides energy and leadership for the moment. Kirk identified several varieties of statesman, the character of each appropriate for a different set of political circumstances": "There are statesmen whose talent it is to manage, like Walpole; and statesmen whose talent it is to rebuild, like Sully; and statesmen whose talent it is to forge, like Cavour; and statesmen whose talent it is to criticize, like Burke."[26] Because the responsibilities of the moment cannot be predicted, no "science of politics," understood as a uniform system regulating political conduct, can be developed, and Kirk approved of maintaining a sense of mystery about the character of the leader of a party. In a pair of reviews published for the *Kenyon Review* in the mid-1960s, Kirk used the example of eighteenth-century politics to lay out his understanding of that boundary and its relevance in a democratic age.

Bolingbroke and Burke, in these essays, each represented a conservative reaction to the upheavals of the eighteenth century. In an early review of the first edition of *The Conservative Mind*, Harvey Wheeler asked "whether more than that one tradition cannot be justly identified with the Anglo-American conservative mind," naming Bolingbroke, in particular, among others, as conservatives seemingly inexplicably omitted by Kirk.[27] It would take Kirk another decade

25. Kirk, "Political Errors at the End of the Twentieth Century, Part I: Republican Errors," 7; Kirk, "Can We Wake Political Imagination?" 24–27.
26. *JRR*, 220.
27. Wheeler, "Russell Kirk and the New Conservatism," 23.

to explain why Bolingbroke, though admirable, was not a conservative for the times. Kirk had initially excluded Bolingbroke from the conservative ranks in *The Conservative Mind* on the grounds of Bolingbroke's nontheism.[28] But this rationale was unpersuasive because other nontheists were included, and at the time of the first edition, Kirk's own religious affiliations were undefined.

The examples of Bolingbroke, Burke, and Thomas Paine illuminated what Kirk saw as the three divergent approaches of modern politics. The relationship between Bolingbroke and Burke expressed the fundamental tension between thinkers who sought leaders who would rise above "faction" to lead the nation and those who sought to develop responsible parties that would outlast any particular leader. Both Bolingbroke and Burke were remnants of an earlier era, but Burke was prescient enough to see the way of the modern age inaugurated by the great revolutionary movements. Bolingbroke, for his part, was too tied to the premodern forms of political life, and his solutions were therefore necessarily incomplete. Paine, for Kirk, represented the new democratic politics that came to dominate the twentieth century. Bolingbroke sought to establish government "led by grand patriotic gentlemen." Burke instead proposed a "politics conducted by well-organized prudential parties."[29] With the dissolution of the aristocratic politics of the mid-eighteenth century, Burke saw that a substitute must be devised to avoid both arbitrary rule or mob government. The solution Burke struck upon was party government—that is, rule by a combination of classes and interests that channels the force of the charismatic leader and the energies of the populace.

In contrast, Bolingbroke attempted to further the cause of the great leader, who combined aristocratic privilege with the traditional skills of a gentleman. This approach was doomed to failure because the social conditions that had rewarded lineage of birth no longer existed in the emergent democratic age. Kirk gives a number of reasons for the end of the premodern aristocratic age: military innovations, the industrial revolution, increased literacy, and similar factors. In short, the rise of modernity made such premodern strategies of politics obsolete. "Burke labored to bring into being a rep-

28. Kirk, "Rhetoricians and Politicians," 764; Kirk, "Bolingbroke, Burke, and the Statesman," 426
29. Kirk, "Bolingbroke, Burke, and the Statesman" 426.

utable party because the rising popular interests of his time simply would submit no longer to the ascendancy of court factions or aristocratic virtue: responsible party was the alternative to arbitrary rule or the revels of which Lord George Gordon was master." As Bruce Frohnen notes, for Burke party government was the means not only to stable governance but also to political independence for the statesman.[30]

Thomas Paine represents the third and (for Kirk) least respectable path of modern politics. Paine's embrace of French theories of liberty and the natural "rights of man," shorn of any attachment to tradition or custom, proved too much for his former friend Burke—and, later, for Kirk as well. Kirk saw Paine as popularizing that modern view, taken ultimately from Rousseau, against the more traditional position of Burke. Kirk incorporated Burke's view that natural rights are political rights and that the former cannot so easily be segregated from the latter. Kirk therefore avoided what Mary Ann Glendon famously described as "rights talk," except insofar as the rights themselves emerge from a common recognition of the members of the society itself.[31] This position is the avenue by which Kirk was able to praise Burke for his defense of the traditional cultures and customs of India against the aggressions of Britain. Although Burke based his attack against Warren Hastings, the governor general of Bengal, on the principles of natural law, Kirk believed that Burke's position was not one of rationalist domination either through rationalist planning or winner-take-all materialism. Instead, Burke's defense of prescriptive rights demanded that the different customs of India be respected. "Hasting's acts, that is, amounted to a kind of treason against the 'chartered rights of men' (something very different from Thomas Paine's *Rights of Man*). Every society develops such rights through its historic experience; the form of such rights will vary from one people to another."[32] It was through his violation of these historically grounded rights, and his substitution of the rights of the conqueror, that Hastings had "dehumanized" the Indians.

A more detailed examination of Kirk's understanding of rights is

<hr>

30. Ibid., 430; Frohnen, *Virtue and the Promise of Conservatism*, 80–81. For a study of Bolingbroke on party, see Isaac Kramnick, *Bolingbroke and His Circle*, 153–63.

31. Glendon, *Rights Talk: The Impoverishment of Political Discourse*.

32. *EB*, 114.

included in the next chapter, but for our purposes here it should be noted that Kirk contended that rights emerge from political society and exist before or outside of political society only to a limited degree. Louis Dupré argued that the conception of political society as one whose function it is to protect individual rights against the polity, as opposed to the conception that the polity itself creates and maintains rights, is a modern development, which began with Hobbes. In contrast to the classical and medieval understanding of rights, which "acquired a normative status only in and through the legal structure," the modern tradition understood the legal system as "protecting rights that precede law."[33]

In summarizing the views of Burke and Burke's American counterpart, John Randolph of Roanoke, Kirk maintained that Burke and Randolph believed that "rights, in short, are not mysterious gifts deduced from a priori postulates; they are opportunities or advantages which the stability of a just society bestows upon its members."[34] David Bromwich noted that for Burke the application of reason to human affairs to discover a "true human nature" is a futile task: the limits to our self-knowledge can never overcome the layers of culture and custom that structure that self-knowledge. Bromwich also asserted that according to Burke, "All those habits, customs and local superstitions . . . just *are* human nature."[35] Indeed, applied specifically to Kirk, Guroian argued, "A Burkean or Kirkian would say that cultural facts and circumstances are not accidents of place and time, but grow out of human nature itself."[36] The Enlightenment habit of separating "human nature" with its concomitant assemblage of prepolitical rights is contrary to the actual historical experience of human nature. The view Burke expressed anticipated Alasdair MacIntyre's influential counter-Enlightenment contention that a tradition itself embodies philosophical inquiry and is not necessarily separate from it.[37]

Given this limited understanding of the provenance and elaboration of rights, the role of language—which creates the political struc-

33. Dupré, *The Passage to Modernity*, 141–42.

34. *JRR*, 63.

35. Bromwich, *A Choice of Inheritance: Self and Community from Edmund Burke to Robert Frost*, 44–46.

36. Guroian, *Rallying the Really Permanent Things*, 75.

37. This point is brought out most fully, perhaps, in MacIntyre, *Three Rival Versions of Moral Inquiry*.

ture in which society operates—assumes great importance for Kirk. Language is the means through which politics is communicated, and that language can change. Paine and Burke, for example, were both skillful at bringing their positions to life through powerful language, although ultimately Kirk thought Paine's rhetoric lacked staying power, because of its attraction to passing ideological fancies. Burke, in contrast, "reasoned in metaphor. Evoking images, Burke sought to persuade by his appeal to the moral imagination—not by setting his own abstractions against the abstractions of the *philosophes*."[38] Conor Cruise O'Brien, agreeing with Kirk on this point, called this characteristic Burke's "Jacobite" style, which was "both Gothic and pathetic."[39]

Paine ultimately lacked the ability to create sustaining and compelling images to shape political reality, which led in part to his downfall. Not that his language was without power, but its straightforward "simplicity makes Paine's pamphlets shallow nowadays."[40] Almost all varieties of modern political thought share this weakness with Paine. Seeking rational schemes, they fail to move the heart, which for Kirk is where political society begins. Thus Burke evokes through Marie Antoinette the entire history and pageantry of Europe, by which Western society has been created, sustained, and enriched. In response, Paine offers in response only the retort that Burke pities the plumage but forgets the dying bird. While memorable, for Kirk it cannot substitute for the vision contained in Burke's words.

This emphasis on language and rhetoric has several consequences for Kirk. First, like every exercise of the imagination, rhetoric must be tied to ethical ends. If these ends are lacking, language will decay into set phrases or coercive instruments. This was, in a way, Woodrow Wilson's undoing: his concession to liberal language eroded his conservative outlook. Richard Weaver's book on rhetoric—which Kirk praised—presented a particular challenge to Kirk because it concluded that universal a priori assumptions lay behind ethical rhetoric. This was the basis for Weaver's distinction between Lincoln, who he said "argued from definition," and Burke, who he said "argued from circumstance." This overstates the case, Kirk ar-

38. Kirk, "Rhetoricians and Politicians," 765.
39. O'Brien, "Introduction," in Burke, *Reflections*, 43.
40. Kirk, "Rhetoricians and Politicians," 764.

gued: Burke had no problem arguing from principles, for example during the prosecution of Hastings, and Lincoln, by his very position as head of state during wartime, was required to argue from circumstance.[41]

Moreover, rhetoric concerns the nature of the audience and the dispersal of political ideas. In the coming democratic age that was shaped by Paine, a "coherent aristocracy of culture" will no longer exist to whom a "twentieth-century leader of party" can address imaginative political rhetoric.[42] Recognizing the cultural fracturing brought about by the political and economic upheavals of modernity, Kirk thought that the traditional rhetoric of Burke could be fused with the new political circumstances. While Kirk saw a distinction (as postmodern thought generally does not) between a "high" culture and a "low," or popular, culture, that barrier for Kirk is permeable.

Burke crafted narratives for those members of society who were interested in and qualified for public affairs and designed for long-term impact.[43] Rather than exemplifying an unwarranted elitism, however, this approach diffused narratives throughout all levels of society, just not at once and not through narratives that were identical to one another. His message was ultimately transferred, through other media and metaphor, to all classes of society. In an extended discussion of Burke's 1770 pamphlet, *Thoughts on the Cause of the Present Discontents*, James Boulton argues that Burke's imaginative rhetoric does not make an unfavorable comparison between the elites and "the people." While there is no doubt that the intended audience for *Thoughts* was the educated classes,

> Burke does not distinguish between the cultured and the vulgar either in his general references to the people or in the language he uses to refer to different social strata. This is not to pretend that Burke, like Paine, was writing for a "popular audience"—he strongly implies that he is not writing "merely to please the popular palate"—but to insist that, while writing for predominantly upper-class readers, he does not score cheap hits by jibing at the vulgar.

41. *BDA*, 85.
42. Kirk, "Rhetoricians and Politicians," 766.
43. Ibid., 765.

Boulton cites this "humanity and generosity" as a mark of Burke's political language.[44] As Kirk notes, "The *Reflections* sold by the tens of thousands of copies, during the 1790s, but the *Waverly* novels carried Burke's ideas to a multitude which never could have been reached by pamphlets." The multiplicity of narratives necessary to convey a political message both respects the differing sensibilities of the people as well as restricts demagogic appeal. Indeed, Kirk describes the intended effects of his *The Conservative Mind* in exactly these terms of diffusion.[45]

Paine oversimplified his "people," and in doing so he reduced his influence by ignoring all the concrete traditions, social customs, and individual habits that make up communities. Kirk, while conceding that Burke spoke to a "natural aristocracy," which composed the initial audience, nevertheless thought that his message, precisely because it took such things as the differing customs and capabilities of the varied audiences in the political sphere seriously, represented the better and more democratic tradition of political rhetoric. With the passing of the British traditions of political rhetoric in America, Kirk saw neither the brilliant metaphors of Burke nor the striking arguments of Paine as characterizing American political oratory. Instead, he found, "The cliches of daily journalism, unrelieved by wit, are the sum and substance of most political oratory and pamphleteering in this hour."[46]

But there is another meaning behind Kirk's emphasis on rhetoric, which is seen not only in his work on Burke, but also in his writings on other political writers such as Randolph and Orestes Brownson. Kirk contended that rhetoric is not just a mask, covering up a "true" state of affairs with vivid language. Rather, as with his thought on the role of narrative in creating tradition, rhetoric is constitutive of that true state of affairs. For politicans, every word is a moral choice. With words, a statesman participates in the creation of political reality. Thus, Kirk condemned the devolution of "democracy" from what he (quoting Brownson) termed *territorial democracy*, rooted in a particular locality and embedded within local narratives, into an ideological term connoting a set of political absolutes to be imposed throughout the world.[47] Changes in language bring about real ef-

44. Boulton, *The Language of Politics in the Age of Wilkes and Burke*, 71–72.
45. *CM*, 119; *SI*, 152.
46. Kirk, "Rhetoricians and Politicians," 766.
47. *PP*, 277–79.

fects. Ideology negates the multiple crosscurrents and eddies of compromise, history, circumstance, custom, and structure that make up a political culture. This critique Kirk applied both to the liberal centralizers as well as to the conservative democratic globalizers. Both groups are heirs to the misleading political absolutism of the Enlightenment.

Kirk adapted his convictions about the relationship between a statesman and party and the role of rhetoric in politics to the American political scene with some difficulty. Kirk was subjected to criticism for even trying to find in the United States the trails of a Burkean conservatism. Nevertheless, Kirk thought he saw connections, although he conceded that America had a severe dearth of political leaders who could master the rhetoric of either Burke or Paine, and he instead settled for a watered-down language that has been further coarsened by polls and the influence of the mass media. He lamented, "Very rarely did truly imaginative candidates win office in twentieth-century America."[48]

Nevertheless, Kirk discovered figures in American political life who embodied the ideals that he thought important to the practice of politics. The first of these in the chronology of Kirk's own writings was John Randolph of Roanoke, the subject of Kirk's master's thesis at Duke. Randolph was more of an idiosyncratic thinker than a man of party, and in that respect Kirk thought he had not fully followed Burke's lead. Randolph was in every other respect, however, an exemplar for Kirk's first major study. Randolph was opposed to both the Francophile liberal Jefferson and the Anglophile conservative Adamses. He was also a practical politician whose work reflected deep reading on the first principles of politics, whose defense of those principles rested on the defense of a particular social structure and tradition, and who was a master of language. Also appealing to Kirk was Randolph's funereal countenance and reputation, which echoed Kirk's own Gothic inclinations.

Kirk's most famous essay on a contemporary political leader is his "The Mind of Barry Goldwater," which was published in *National Review* in August 1963.[49] Written in support of Goldwater's presidential candidacy, Kirk outlined several qualities that he thought

---

48. *SI,* 306.
49. In addition to those cited in text and elsewhere in these notes, see Kirk, "The Enduring Achievement of Sen. John East," D3; "A Vote for Ford," 681; "The Case for Nixon," 16.

made Goldwater a "political mind" equipped to face the challenges of the day. Kirk did not stress Goldwater's rhetorical ability. Instead, he preferred to discuss the sense of authority Goldwater provided to a party seeking a new direction and concurred in the opinion of Hans Morgenthau—voiced in a debate with Kirk—that Goldwater was more honest and decent than his opponent Johnson.[50]

The only other major political figure to whom he devoted a book was Senator Robert A. Taft. In *The Political Principles of Robert A. Taft*, the book-length study of the Ohio senator that Kirk wrote with James McClellan in 1967, Kirk painted a figure that, though perhaps sympathetic and in some ways admirable, did not fire the imagination. Indeed, in introducing his subject, Kirk spent more time focusing on what Taft was *not*—orator, crowd-pleaser, possessor of Theodore Roosevelt's "magnetism," or FDR's "beguiling public charm."[51] Kirk's Taft was a statesman suited to resist rather than create. According to Kirk, Taft resisted the ideological fervor of the Roosevelt era that extended into the immediate postwar period by resorting to his intelligence and passion for details. And while Kirk attributed to Taft's legacy many positive results—such as the maintenance of a proper sense of party, as shown below—Kirk did not find in him the imaginative leader.

Similarly, Nixon was a more "realistic" candidate than Kennedy. Nixon would be better able to resist communism than Kennedy's "wooly, Leftward-drifting 'idealism,'" which, to Kirk, was equivalent to ideology. Kirk recounts the curious story of a meeting with Nixon at the White House, during which he recommended that the president read Eliot's *Notes toward the Definition of Culture* for a diagnosis of contemporary ills. While Kirk found Nixon to be a sharp and astute politician, able to succeed in a democratic age, he ultimately saw him as a tragic figure, possessing "not much imagination." About Eisenhower, Kirk also concludes, it "would be difficult to discover a public man less imaginative."[52]

While Kirk tried to situate these politicians into the political framework of American government, it is clear that Kirk did not believe them to be strong proponents of the conservative political imagination. These were the statesmen of a mass democratic age, whose role,

50. *SI*, 300.
51. Kirk and McClellan, *The Political Principles of Robert A. Taft*, 3.
52. Kirk, "Case for Nixon," 115; *SI*, 141, 328–36; Kirk, "Vote for Ford," 381.

Kirk thought, was one of rear-guard preservation, just as the "popular" or average conservative was practical and had little imagination.[53] None was really equipped with the imaginative gifts to counter fully the rise of the modern state and modern mass political culture.

Ronald Reagan, with his gift for language and metaphor, came closest among contemporary American politicians to Kirk's idea of a creative and imaginative political leader, though Kirk did not agree with his full political program. Reagan was "American confidence incarnate," who "really was the Western hero of romance . . . audacious, dauntless, cheerful, honest—and skilled at shooting from the hip." In a time that needed imagination, Reagan the former actor could be relied upon to supply the proper imagery necessary to move a nation. Indeed, it was precisely that ability that made Reagan so effective and that is reminiscent of William Butler Yeats, who "tells us that everyone ought to make a mask for himself, and wear it, and become what the mask represents. Ronald Reagan put on the mask of the Western hero . . . and truly lived the part, and became the Western hero."[54] Recognition of Reagan's rhetorical power was not limited to Kirk: in a critical analysis of post-1960s conservatism, Lawrence Grossberg wrote that Reagan "consciously placed himself within the popular, not only rhetorically (in terms of his appeals to popular narratives and fantasies) but also socially." He and his advisers recognized that "the visual images were more affective than the words because the images pointed to Reagan's affective investment, his caring, the fact that these things mattered to him."[55] While Kirk was at times perhaps too generous in his praise of Reagan—explaining away his "blunders," he nevertheless saw in the former actor's ability at "self-creation" a talent reminiscent of political imagination.

This assumption of a role was as important a political attribute as knowledge of the intricacies of the federal bureaucracy, indeed perhaps more important. And, as discussed with reference to Kirk's own donning of a mask, this understanding of political character itself parallels postmodern understandings of the self. Roberto Unger, for example, places the development of a "self" that combines the

53. *PP,* 152.
54. Ibid., 151; see also *SI,* 448–54.
55. Grossberg, *We Gotta Get Out of This Place: Popular Conservatism and Postmodern Culture,* 268–69.

historically contingent nature of the individual human life with the commonalities of a universal human nature at the center of his critique of the liberal theory of personality.[56]

The Role of Party

Kirk maintained that the existence and growth of political parties were natural effects of the constitutional structure and, although not explicitly set forth in the text, the political party was one of the institutions of the "unwritten" constitution that enabled the America federal system to function. In addition to their political responsibilities, parties provide a narrative for adherents and a mode of entering into the political and social life of a nation with a particular language, symbols, heroes, and institutional supports. Large parties emerged in the nineteenth century as a result of the growth of mass democracy. Although Kirk's friend Albert Jay Nock once grumbled that it was the typical American party rally that convinced him *not* to become involved with politics, for Kirk the party remained the core structural support for representative government.

Because a party stands in part outside the demands of those who brought it into being, it can, according to Kirk, be "more devoted to the national interest than to the immediate advantage of the party's stalwart members." When it is in power, it holds that power in trust for the nation, restraining the energetic leader. When out of power, a party serves as a check to those in power. David Bromwich has written that Burke's sense of party, by which Kirk was deeply influenced, "denoted a voluntary association bound by principles and loyalty, which could serve as a counterweight to ministerial or monarchical authority and at the same time curb the egotism of day-to-day political bargaining."[57] So too in a modern commercial democracy, Kirk thought that parties had value. They blunted the grasping of interest groups and at their best would allow true statesmanship to emerge. Further, parties inspired loyalty that temporary political advantage could not.

However, the party system is always in danger of decay. Parties

56. Unger, *Knowledge and Politics*, 222–26.
57. Kirk and McClellan, *Political Principles of Taft*, 50; Bromwich, in Burke, *On Empire, Liberty, and Reform: Speeches and Letters*, 8.

face the temptation of surrendering principle for electoral success (to which Kirk thought the Republicans were particularly susceptible) or of considering political principles as rigid ideology, which must be imposed upon the entire nation (a path Kirk thought more often taken by the Democrats). Indeed, in 1985, writing in the wake of Ronald Reagan's large victory in 1984, Kirk warned that expectations of the death of the Democratic Party were unrealistic and, indeed, undesirable. "Constitutional representative governments cannot well function without the existence of at least two parties; and by nature a party in opposition to a party in power always arises." What the Democrats had suffered from in 1984, and the Republicans at other times, was a failure of imagination; they had transformed their living tradition into a rigid ideology called "liberalism," which, Kirk thought, was long outmoded. If reconstituted, however, the party could once again speak for a majority of voters, a result so desirable that Kirk thought "we ought to wish long life to such a reconstituted Democratic party."[58]

In *The Political Principles of Robert A. Taft*, Kirk provides his longest explanation of what he means by party government in a chapter entitled "The Struggle for Responsible Party." Kirk places party government squarely in the center of the American political structure: "if parties were lacking," he argues, "true representative government would be impossible, and democracy on a national scale a sham." The alternatives to such responsible party government are tyranny or mob rule. He encourages parties to rise above self-interest or office-seeking, but not above the notion of party itself. Kirk casts Taft as trying to craft a "responsible and imaginative Republican criticism of the New Deal," rather than merely accepting its premises and promising only—as Kirk alleges Dewey, Willkie, and Eisenhower to have done—to administer its programs better.[59] Instead, Kirk uses Taft's opposition to the Roosevelt administration as a basis for elaborating on Taft's theory of party.

Party government is not the same as government by interest group; the role of a party, by contrast, is to reduce and limit power, even its own, through attachment to principle. "The function of party was more than simply providing for an orderly transfer of power, or of merely consolidating public opinion. A political party must

58. Kirk, "The Future of America's Political Parties," 22.
59. Kirk and McClellan, *Political Principles of Taft*, 40, 48.

stand . . . upon the principles which brought it into being, even at the risk—or the certitude of defeat at the polls."[60] Kirk's view of party, therefore, has a tragic element, and it implies that a party should not take power merely for the sake of having it, unless it can retain its principles as well.

Kirk contended that the dissolution of party as the driving force in politics began during Taft's lifetime. Parties were replaced by numerous individual "pressure groups," which were "more determined than the old amorphous parties, unrelated to the old political constituencies, and alien to the American Constitution."[61] This was the real difficulty with the New Deal and, indeed, most large-scale government actions. Governmental programs create beneficiaries, who then form pressure groups. These groups, bound by self-interest rather than principle, agitate for further largesse from the state at the expense of others. This new arrangement shifted power from large parties, who in order to succeed need to represent principles with which a large number of people across the nation can agree, to small, organized groups, who seek advantages only for themselves. In this context, therefore, it matters little who is in power, or what they stand for, so long as pressure can be applied to gain advantage for the particular group. Interest-group government also increases the process of centralization, since it is easier for pressure groups to influence policy from one national center rather than from fifty state capitals. Such a centralized system is helpful to liberal and conservative ideologues alike.

Interest-group government transforms representatives of the people into delegates for a particular set of "issues." The latter must answer to their supporters and cannot readily refuse their commands. The former, however, in the general practice of American politics, which Kirk derives from the British custom, and specifically from Burke's speech to the electors of Bristol, is broader. An elected representative is not beholden to his electorate except in the sense that all representatives serve the nation as a whole. Representative government allows historic governmental institutions, such as the states, to enter into the political scene. It also, ideally, permits representatives the freedom to consider national interests over those of their electorate. Government by interest group is instead a modern

60. Ibid., 50.
61. Ibid., 49.

notion based on principles that Kirk thought incompatible with real democracy.[62]

There are nuances in this view of party government, however, that are not fully addressed. While Kirk commends the existence of national parties of permanence and of change, he does not offer any detailed critiques of when he considers one should prevail over the other. Nor does he fully explore the relationship between a statesman who leads a national party with the fractured federal system, where each party has fifty state and innumerable local outposts, which Kirk prefers for America. Kirk argues that the problems of Michigan, for example, are not those of Ohio, and so Michigan's problems need to be solved in Michigan rather than by a national party leader, whose support may conflict with a desire for a national platform. Indeed, Kirk wrote in 1964 that most of the functions of society were more properly managed at the local or state levels.[63] While Kirk staunchly defends federalism, he tends to discuss only national leaders, though he does note that in a federal system power should be diffused through substate government such as small towns.[64]

Thus, for example, Kirk does not spell out a theory of representation that would account both for his localism and for his affection for party government. A localist conception of representative governance would, presumably, argue that local representatives should identify with the interests of their constituents. Indeed, that is roughly the sort of representation argued for by the Antifederalists during the battles over the ratification of the Constitution. Yet Kirk, in his discussion of Burke's speech to the electors of Bristol, firmly sides with Burke, calling the speech "the most moving and persuasive speech Burke ever uttered."[65] Kirk rejects the notion of representation as mere "delegation," a position advanced by Bristol, and finds that those "members of Congress—who still make up their minds little influenced by special interests, lobbyists, and the popular infatuation of the moment . . . may be heartened even today by Burke's intrepidity" in refusing to represent only the interests of Bristol rather than the nation as a whole.[66] Nevertheless, his defense of localism does not completely fit with his defense of party, which works

62. *ABC*, 56–58.
63. Kirk, "Is Washington Too Powerful?" 22.
64. Kirk, "Ruminations on Small Towns," 485.
65. *EB*, 84.
66. Ibid., 87.

more successfully in a unitary state such as Great Britain than in the fragmented American federal system.

Federalism and Territorial Democracy

In *Roots of American Order*, Kirk argued that federalism was the founders' answer to the problem of reconciling order and freedom. Arising from the ruins of the Articles of Confederation, the new political structure of the United States needed to "provide a general government with sufficient power to ensure" its proper objectives. Among these objectives Kirk identified providing a common defense, promoting the general welfare, and conducting diplomacy. However, this structure also needed to "provide for the survival and vigor of the several state governments, including the free and relatively democratic forms of local government, which had developed first in the colonies then in the states."

Federalism rests upon the "autonomy of the narrower communities" and preserves the widest scope of authority for them. It "divides practical power between a general government and territorial governments, with the aim of safeguarding local liberties and choices while securing national interests." Federalism should allow the widest scope for local liberty, even where the national government has the primary responsibility for a particular area. Provocatively, Kirk used the example of national security to support local autonomy and federalism. National security, of course, is one of the areas vouchsafed to the national government in the Constitution. In advocating federalism even here, Kirk was not arguing that each state provide its own army or independently decide issues of security. Rather, he believed that the states and localities were closer to their citizens and security risks than a central government. Therefore, they could better contribute to national defense from their own resources, needing only guidelines from the national government. "If there has been negligence," he wrote, "the fault has lain with the very general government upon which the centralizers would load fresh responsibilities."[67] Merely because the central government has authority over an area such as defense, in other words, does not necessarily mean that it should usurp state or local governments where

67. *RAO*, 421, 423; Kirk, "Prospects for Territorial Democracy in America," 52.

the latter could do a better job in effectuating the national government's objectives.

Kirk is often thought of as a defender of states' rights and is sometimes joined to groups of pre–World War II conservatives such as the Southern Agrarians or their contemporary heirs, the "paleoconservatives." With respect to federalism, though, his interpretation is different from the southern tradition. Importantly, Kirk argued that the Constitution created a *new* system of government that was *national* in scope. *Federalism* is not an adequate term to describe the current government under the Constitution, though it may once have been sufficient. The Constitution changed the very meaning of the word *federal*, from a government in which the central authority possesses no power apart from its constituent parts, and merely serves as the administrator of an alliance of states (a "confederated" state), to one in which the federal authority is separate from and above the subordinate governments (in other words, a "national" state). "The structure created at Philadelphia amounted to a new pattern of government, not truly 'federal' in the old sense," as in "league," but rather the Constitution abandoned the plan of a confederacy, and substituted that of a single nation. This "altered the very usage of the word 'federalism,' which no longer is generally taken to mean a simple league of sovereign states."[68]

The states, in other words, did not have authority, or "rights," apart from their being part of the general government. The Civil War shattered that arrangement, and its aftermath opened up a new role for the national government. "Whether or not the people of America so intended it, sovereignty passed to the general government of the United States, not long after the Constitution was ratified. . . . The 'federal' system created by the Constitution established a true general government—which, nevertheless, was not a centralized, unitary, absolute government." The war also affected the interpretation of rights and, along with Reconstruction, damaged territorial democracy and "confused and obscured the distinction between a unitary, centralized system and the voluntary associations of territorial democracies into states and a republic."[69] The question the Civil War and its aftermath raised for Kirk was how to reconcile the contingencies of the nation-state with local liberties.

68. *RAO*, 422.
69. Ibid., 423.

In Kirk's distinction between a general government and territorial governments in *Roots,* we see his debt to the American thinker and political theorist Orestes Brownson (1803–1876). Kirk adopted Brownson as one of his personal heroes early in his career and promoted him in a number of books and articles. Brownson himself occupies a unique place in American intellectual history. Born in Vermont of Protestant parents, Brownson moved through most of the varied sects of nineteenth-century America, including transcendentalism (he was a founding member, with Ralph Waldo Emerson, of the Transcendentalist Club), until he converted to Catholicism in 1844. His most famous book-length work is probably the political treatise *The American Republic,* published in 1865 at the close of the Civil War. Arthur Schlesinger Jr. and Woodrow Wilson are among those who considered him one of the few true political thinkers America has produced.

The burden of *The American Republic* was to explain American government in terms of political theory in light of the Civil War. For Brownson (who wrote against both the northern abolitionist and the southern secessionist movements and opposed both slavery and the Civil War), the states were neither preexisting nations that "contracted" with one another to form a more perfect Union, nor mere provinces of a general government. According to Brownson, the former contradicted principles of sovereignty; the latter equated the federal system with the centralized democracy of Jacobin France.

Rather, the states were sovereign in their own spheres, but that sovereignty existed only because they were part of a nation. Territorial democracy is based in the conviction that political power must be centered on a geographic unity within which all people participate in governance. Power, in other words, is not portable by a person or class; it inheres only within the society that grants it. Sovereignty is expressed, therefore, through the states only as they exist as units within the United States. This is what Brownson meant by territorial democracy; "not territorial because the majority of the people are agriculturists or landholders, but because all political rights, powers, or franchises are territorial." The United States shares sovereignty over a territory with the state in that particular territory. "The American States are all sovereign States united, but, disunited, are not States at all. The rights and powers of the States are not derived from the United States, nor are the rights and powers of the United States derived from the States."[70] This judgment led Brownson to sometimes-odd conclusions, such as that the states did not have the authority to secede, but they did have the authority to cease being states, in which case they would revert to territories of the Union.

To explain the American constitutional system, Brownson joined territorial democracy with another interpretive tool, the "unwritten constitution," which supplements and preexists the written constitution. The unwritten constitution includes all the mores, customs, and ways of life that together form the American political culture and support the written constitution. The latter could not exist without the former, because the unwritten constitution is a more nuanced and complete reflection of a people's political experience.

Kirk adopted Brownson's views on sovereignty and the unwritten constitution to explain how local democracy could be protected within a republican nation. As he explained, "no matter how admirable a constitution may look upon paper, it will be ineffectual unless the unwritten constitution, the web of custom and convention, affirms an enduring moral order of obligation and personal responsibility."[71] Political structures must be supported by social traditions, the same argument Burke made at the close of the eighteenth century, just adapted for American circumstances.

Relying on the work of Felix Morley, whose book *Freedom and Federalism* appeared in 1959, Kirk argued that the unwritten constitution of these localities in turn supported good—and moral—government at the national level. The states have a different function. If localities express local democratic sentiment, the states act as buffers between the national government and the localities and also represent, in a corporate fashion, state, regional, and territorial interests. Kirk explained Brownson's thoughts in a 1990 collection of the latter's essays: "Brownson distinguishes between the old American territorial democracy founded upon local rights and common interests of the several states and smaller organs of society, and the pure democracy of [Jean-Jacques] Rousseau, which later writers call 'totalitarian democracy.'"[72] This pure democracy of Rousseau is char-

70. Brownson, *The American Republic*, 191, 142.
71. Kirk, *Rights and Duties*, 260.
72. Kirk, "Introduction," in Brownson, *Orestes Brownson: Selected Political Writings*, 8.

acterized by centralized administration in the name of an abstract "people," with little authority or freedom at the local level. For Kirk, this meant the dissolution of true democracy. This assessment owes obvious debts to Tocqueville and his celebration of the township, an insight into the local roots of self-governance that has engendered its own body of scholarship.[73]

The conversation Kirk envisions among the democratic localities, indirectly democratic states, and a representative national government is the genius of the American system. Federalism is a necessary instrument to protect that conversation. "If the federal character of American government decays badly, then American democracy also must decline terribly, until nothing remains of it but a name; and the new 'democrats' may be economic and social levellers, indeed, but they will give popular government short shrift."[74] As he argues in "The Prospects for Territorial Democracy in America," even for the new western states, whose boundaries were set by fiat rather than by culture or history, territorial democracy can give "Montana and Arizona and Kansas, say, some distinct and peculiar character as political territories, by fixing loyalties and forming an enduring structure of political administration."[75]

Kirk identifies a number of problems that threaten the existence of territorial democracy. For example, the mere size of the nation creates problems of efficiency and scale. Ideas or programs that might work for one state, or even for a small country, cannot easily be adapted to a nation as large and as diverse as the United States. Also, the burdening of Washington with additional duties only hampers its ability to effectively act upon its constitutionally derived responsibilities. The most interesting of the problems a centralized system poses is in the development of a class of leaders. The nation's decentralized structure prevents a national elite from forming even as it nurtures local leadership. The United States, Kirk argues, "accustomed to territorial democracy ha[d] no class of leaders and administrators competent" to oversee so large a nation.[76] While Kirk maintains that such an elite class might work for smaller nations accustomed to such a class system (Kirk has the United Kingdom in mind), it is probably unlikely to succeed here. A centralized govern-

73. Filippo Sabetti, "Local Roots of Constitutionalism," 70–78.
74. *EPT,* 239–40.
75. Kirk, "Prospects for Territorial Democracy," 43.
76. Idid., 60.

ment cannot sustain the leadership class necessary to make it function effectively or as a body truly representative of the people. In fact,
as we have seen, Kirk expresses his general disappointment with the
quality of the leaders America had produced, of whatever party.

In this context, however, Kirk was not entirely correct. A cadre of
administrators, lobbyists, corporate executives, and others has in
fact arisen to govern the nation. Later in his career, Kirk criticized the
development of this "New Elite," which he described as being made
up of "bureaucrats, scientists, technicians, trade-union organizers,
publicity experts, sociologists, teachers, journalists, and professional politicians," but Kirk only partially integrated consideration of
this class into his critique. This class lacked the foundations of place
and sentiment that Kirk thought important for representative government. As a result, they were themselves at the mercy of the forces
they attempted to control. They "are not socialists . . . they do not resemble Norman Thomas or Clement Atlee; they are the new elite,
though they constitute no aristocracy of birth or of nature. They are
at once jailers and jailed."[77] More familiar with global corporations
or K Street lobbyists, this class has lost the sense of place and the sentiments of loyalty between localities and their leaders.

Although local control has long been rooted in the American tradition, in law Kirk's doctrine of territorial democracy is hard to find.
American law accords little protection to units of government other
than states, and state governments can generally abolish or modify
localities within their borders. However, in several different contexts
the Supreme Court has recognized that localities represent the values and concerns of their constituents and therefore should be giv-
en some degree of legal autonomy in order to affect those concerns.
For example, in 1926, the Court held in *Euclid v. Ambler Realty Corp.*
that localities have broad control over land use within their boundaries. The Court has upheld local restrictions on "adult" businesses
and occupancy restrictions.[78] More recently, in *Lopez,* the Court
made positive references to local control, which many legal observers thought would herald a new era of federalism.[79]

---

77. *CM*, 468.
78. *Euclid v. Ambler Realty Corp.,* 272 U.S. 365 (1926); *Barnes v. Glen Theatre, Inc.,*
501 U.S. 560 (1991); *Village of Belle Terre v. Boraas,* 416 U.S. 1 (1974).
79. *United States v. Lopez,* 514 U.S. 549 (1995).

The Limits of Politics

Because of Kirk's doubts about the capacity of human knowledge, and the temptation to power inherent in human affairs, he did not trust political or economic solutions that promised to solve problems in a definitive manner. Kirk's politics was defined by recognition of limits. He preferred to define the powers of economics or politics narrowly, leaving to the individual choices and custom the real work of society.

The centrality of limits was the result of a series of interlocking principles in Kirk's thinking, which conditioned his understanding of the practical effects of political or economic reform. First, there were the limits of language. Although Kirk valued the power of the rhetor highly in forming political values, he also understood that the powers of language could be exhausted or misused. Words are tools that break in the hand, he often said, and can never be trusted to fully encapsulate the speaker's meaning, or be fully understood by the audience. And, moreover, language can be deliberately misused, for short-term gain or ideological posturing. At its most limited, language is only an instrument of force, to be used by "the streamlined men who think in slogans and talk in bullets," in a phrase of Orwell's that Kirk often invoked.[80] Kirk believed that the statesman's role was to transform the tendency of language to be used as an instrument of force to one of imaginative persuasion.

The second limit arose from Kirk's understanding of the Christian doctrine of original sin, which prevented any political motive from being completely pure and separate from hopes of gain, either for self or for party. Not that Kirk thought this necessarily a disadvantage, as self-interest could be a spur to action. However, the presence of such self-interest, combined with political power, could have a corrupting effect. While Kirk did not think that those who seek or hold political office should be considered "plaster saints" or need be a President Galahad, nevertheless, Kirk believed that those to whom great power is given should be watched carefully, lest the power to lead transform itself into the power to control. Private character— the capacity for good or evil—did have an impact in the public sphere, Kirk wrote in 1988.[81] What people do in private and the

80. *JRR*, 105; *PP*, 181.
81. Kirk, Symposium, *Policy Review* (Spring 1988): 29. For an earlier account

promises made in public were at least in part connected, according to Kirk, and that connection should also warn the public against entrusting too much power to those who seek it. Thus Kirk's reliance upon party served a second function. A great leader will be able to embody and further the principles of the party, and the party, in turn, will be able to limit and restrain the power of the leader.

The line between the strictures of private conduct and the action required in political affairs was one Kirk treaded carefully. While Kirk clearly identified the United States with its Judeo-Christian heritage, and believed in norms governing conduct, he warned against the injection of purely religious concerns into politics. If one interprets a religious commitment to mean "that a self-righteous politicized Christendom could remedy in short order all the alleged injustices of life in community—why, then we are back with the Fifth Monarchy Men and their cry, 'The second coming of Christ, and the heads upon the gates!'"[82] Religion becomes merely an ideology, with the same destructive tendencies as any other. While religion does have a political component, for Kirk that component was expressed largely through individual acts that may result in a larger impact, and not through wholesale imposition upon others. In this way, the religious impulse is not a "master narrative," constructed in opposition to real life, but rather an innumerable number of acts of grace that together would work a transformation. Indeed, Kirk thought that the most extreme of the "Christian activists" to be as afflicted with the modern *libido dominandi* as any secular ideologue.

In this system, prudence becomes the overriding virtue of the statesman, as the opposite of ideological action. The political leader must know how to reconcile principle with politics and when to compromise. In such circumstances, ideology is a poor guide to solving the intricate and shifting public policies of a large nation. Kirk sought what Brian Anderson has called "the recovery of the political," meaning the complex of customs and traditions that constitute political practices, against the reductionism of ideology.[83] The reconstruction of political language is vital to this task, in order to reinject historical experience, persuasive force, and prudential considerations for culture and the limits of possible action. In short, Kirk

---

of corruption, in the context of Watergate, see Kirk, "The Persistence of Political Corruption," 2.

82. Kirk, "Promises and Perils of a 'Christian Politics,'" 13, 14.

83. See Anderson, *Raymond Aron: The Recovery of the Political.*

advocated an *imaginative* politics against what he saw as a growing tendency toward an *ideological* politics.[84]

Taken together, these principles explain why Kirk so preferred an array of structural limits on political power. Kirk spoke little on theoretical issues, so long as "power itself remained allocated." As will be discussed in the next chapter, Kirk much favored a common law system of piecemeal action rather than large legislative enactments. He condemned, borrowing language from Randolph, the "legislative maggot" that served private interest in the name of the public good. Legislation is often written in broad strokes or aspirational terms, leaving the more difficult tasks of interpretation and implementation to unelected officials in administrative agencies or undemocratic courts, each of which assumes, in their differing ways, the "prophetic afflatus." Kirk thought this process largely a ruse to gain points with the interest groups that favored the legislation, while avoiding responsibility for its implementation. Thus, in reviewing Taft's legislative achievements, Kirk concluded that the Taft-Hartley Act was a legitimate legislative measure, because it served to check the expansive prolabor legislation that had been passed in previous years. It restored balance, and despite his conclusion that the act "conferred new rights—and not merely upon employers, but upon employees" as well, Kirk nevertheless thought the act worthy of praise.[85]

Even when the legislatures acted forthrightly Kirk saw danger. The Constitution limited the power of the temporary majority; it was "a shield of minorities." To acknowledge that some immediate need could trump the basic structure of limitations was to render all equally unsafe, for any "interest, state, or section, no matter how mighty, is liable one day to find itself a minority." In politics, in fact, Kirk in his later years rejected Tocqueville's notion of the "tyranny of the majority," instead finding that American political culture lay under the tyranny of minority pressure groups, who end up controlling whoever is in office.[86]

Place, as noted earlier, was a core feature in Kirk's thinking, and especially in reference to politics. While there is a need for national

---

84. See also Frohnen, *Virtue and the Promise of Conservatism*, 76–80; Person, *Kirk: A Critical Biography*, 49–51.
85. *JRR*, 89; Kirk and McClellan, *Political Principles of Taft*, 125.
86. *JRR*, 108; *PP*, 146–47

structures, these should be limited in scope and power, not because government power, per se, is a bad thing, but because the farther it is distanced from the people whom it affects the less control there can be over it. As scholars have argued, localities in recent years have become more involved with a range of issues that previously would not have concerned them. Indeed, Kirk's essay on territorial democracy can serve as a summary of his political thinking. First, Kirk commended the federal system for its protection of "multiplicity in unity," allowing a number of versions of political life to flourish, so that in the American system, variety itself becomes a component of that system. Second, Kirk raised the importance of political language. While Kirk thought that most persons would not prefer a unitary national government to a federal system, he also believed that people might get carried away by "incantations" that would lead to results opposite to their intentions. Political terms, such as *democracy* or *the people,* should be used carefully, because such words can have powerful effects. Indeed, Kirk maintained that political rhetoric is so powerful that it can overcome even the normal self-interest expected in the political arena.[87]

Despite the tendency toward centralization, the ties of locality still provide a sufficient countercurrent worth preserving. Always suspicious of those who would assume total knowledge or expertise, Kirk thought that centralization would lead to government by "professional administrators," who would empty "democracy" of any real meaning. It is precisely the nation's decentralized structure that has prevented a national elite from forming, and so a centralized government would not have the leadership class necessary to make it work. While Kirk believed that such an elite class might work for smaller nations accustomed to such a class system, it was probably unlikely to succeed in the United States. In any event, if the nation were moving to a more centralized nation, the lack of imagination and reflection in that evolution bothered Kirk. "If the federal system is obsolete, then we ought to prepare the leaders of a new order, and to define the character of that domination, novel to us."[88]

87. Kirk, "Prospects for Territorial Democracy," 49–50.
88. Ibid., 58, 60, 64.

Economics and the Social Order

John Bliese places Kirk at the beginning of an American conservative body of thought opposing what Bliese calls the "ideology of growth." Bliese argues that Kirk (along with Weaver, Roepke, and others) valued a free market for reasons of personal freedom and would be appalled at the devotion to growth for its own sake.[89] As economist John Attarian discusses, Kirk rejected both the economic utopianism of the Left as well as the economic anarchism of the Right. As early as *Confessions of a Bohemian Tory*, Kirk was defining his conservatism in opposition to the "bourgeois fad and fable." Indeed, Kirk condemned both for the same failing: "Whenever we go about looking for a solution to some great social problem, we rarely recur to the first principles of human nature and society. Instead, we turn back to Benthamite dogmas. 'Efficiency,' 'progress,' and 'economic security' are our god-terms, as they are those of the Soviets."[90] Although written in 1957, Kirk was to echo these themes throughout his writings on economics.

While Kirk in general approved of capitalism—a word, he often noted, coined by Marxists—it was with reservations. A free economy was beneficial, perhaps most important, because it limited the power of government and provided yet another barrier to state control of individual freedom. In contrast, an economic system that enshrined government as the primary actor reduced the play of individual acts, both those in self-interest and those for philanthropic purposes. As with politics, however, an economic system could become an ideology, a self-sufficient master narrative that would usurp all other principles. Kirk was just as much a critic of capitalist or free-market excesses as he was of socialist excesses, perhaps even more so because the former was so much more prominent in America.

Extreme proponents of capitalism shared with extreme proponents of socialism an Enlightenment mentality that considered social arrangements, custom, and politics subordinate to economics. They lacked the "social imagination" to consider other forms of life and other values in addition to economic values. "The ideology of capitalism and socialism are two sides of a counterfeit coin," Kirk wrote, both trapped in outdated conceptions of human nature and

---

89. Bliese, "Conservatism and the Ideology of 'Growth,'" 117–25.
90. Kirk, "Ideology and Political Economy," 390.

particular assumptions about human society. Against the Left's "utopia of statism," Kirk concluded that such a position ignored the self-interest and motivations of real individuals, including the motivation of charity. Similarly, Kirk opposed the Right's "utopia of affluence," which enshrined avarice as a cultural value.[91] As one reviewer noted, Kirk thought that both "[i]ndividualistic ideology and socialist ideology are branches" of the same modern flaws. Kirk concluded that both socialism and capitalism were the barren results of nineteenth-century rationalism, reliance on which "terribly damages communal existence [and] also produces an unquestioning confidence" in the competitive market economy and leads to a heartless individualism.[92] His discussion of Santayana in *The Conservative Mind* revolved around the Spanish writer's attack on "industrial liberalism," in which "Materialism, confused with tradition, is turned into a sort of religion, and more and more America inclines toward a universal crusade on behalf of this credo of mechanized production and mass consumption."[93]

Kirk appealed to the political and social imagination to resolve these imagined tensions between private property and community need, free trade and state activity.[94] "It is freedom of spirit that produces a free economy, among other things—not the other way around."[95] Indeed, like political beliefs, economic values are open-ended until given voice and a purpose. Otherwise, Kirk saw a poor future for America's economic system, because its ideology of endless growth and consumption created, on the one hand, a proletariate unable to do anything but consume and, on the other, a small enclosed elite that consolidated economic power to itself.[96]

Kirk's insights into economic life are set out mostly in piecemeal form, through his essays. His most extended treatment of economics is in his 1989 textbook, *Economics: Work and Prosperity*, which was all but ignored when it first appeared and which has not been given extended analysis by commentators on Kirk's thought. Admittedly, *Economics* is a quirky textbook, and the form is not indicative of

91. Attarian, "Russell Kirk's Political Economy," 190, 192. For a shorter analysis, see William F. Campbell, "An Economist's Tribute to Russell Kirk."
92. Dwight D. Murphy, review of *RAO* and *BDA*, 458, 462; *PP*, 118–19.
93. *CM*, 451–52.
94. Kirk, "Capitalism," 18–20.
95. Kirk, "Perishing for Want of Imagery," 9.
96. *PP*, 111–12.

Kirk's strengths as a writer. Kirk, of course, was not an economist, and the book is peppered with poems, anecdotes, historical examples, and illustrations drawn from his own experiences that take it far afield from the usual text. Actual economic principles are presented, but in a context widely different from the usual format. Kirk presents a different angle from which to view economics and to create an alternate framework for economic insights that rejects the commonplaces of the past.

At the very beginning of *Economics*, Kirk acknowledges the benefits of the free market system as "the most complex and productive economy that has ever existed." But that economy did not come into being ex nihilo, but by "the hard and intelligent work of many people." His first chapter, on the Pilgrims, illustrates this theme of the interdependence between theory and fact, action and result. The themes of the remainder of the text are present in the first few pages: prosperity exists and is obtainable, but only through work; chance has a large role to play in success or failure; and the values that surround an economic system are as important as abstract economic "laws" that govern behavior, although Kirk does indicate his acceptance of the general "laws" of economics. Material prosperity, he asserts, "depends upon moral convictions and moral dealings."[97] This is of course as true of individuals as of entire societies.

Kirk did not favor collectivist economic systems for a number of reasons, including their dismal historical record, but also because they are invariably imposed from above rather than emerging out of historical experience. Moreover, the group that is imposing such an economic system more often than not, as in many postcolonial societies in the Third World, has something to gain by the timely announcement and implementation of socialist plans. Generally, the system is opposed to historical and traditional economic thinking and behavior and for that reason is doomed to fail. On the other hand, Kirk thought "democratic capitalism" was similarly misguided. He condemned those who would offer the national parks or the post office for sale in the name of an abstract "freedom of contract" or assets in the global marketplace. He condemned the consumer society "insatiably devouring minerals and forests and the very soil . . . to gratify the appetites of the present tenants of the country." In 1962, Kirk was already defending small-scale localist economies, not

97. Kirk, *Economics: Work and Prosperity,* 4–5, 25, 365.

against excessive state action, but against the "gigantic corporation [and] the gigantic union,"[98] which were threats to freedom.

As far as Kirk was concerned, "planned society" or "rational apparatus" were never abstract. They become visible in the very physicality of existence. This belief that ideals are, and must be, reflected in concrete social and physical realities explains Kirk's lifelong concern for architecture and the physical representation of societal ideals. Just as language can alter our perception of reality, so too can the buildings in which we choose to live and to work. The rationalistic mentality that creates ideology also produces the "architecture of servitude and boredom." This "colossal architecture" is perfectly suited to our "colossal state of unparalleled uniformity," argued Kirk, and is a stark reminder of Tocqueville's democratic despotism. This "colossalism" represents not a new democratic form of construction, nor even Charles Jencks's postmodern mixture of old and new, but the aspirations of the masters of what Kirk saw as a new technological and bureaucratic order.[99]

However, Kirk was not a reactionary in his economic thinking. In discussing Adam Smith, for example, Kirk sheds no tears for the traditional nail-making industry of Kirkaldy in Scotland, which was surpassed by the new more efficient nail-works of Carron. Rather, while acknowledging the free market's successes, as well as its role as a solvent of culture and custom, Kirk attempts to create out of that dynamism a new sort of economic thinking that is not bound to modern notions of progress or production. Thus, in addition to the general statements against collectivism or statist policies throughout his textbook, Kirk does not hesitate to condemn the extreme acquisitiveness or random destruction generated by a full market economy. Indeed, a few pages after highlighting the example of Smith and his insights into the division of labor, Kirk introduces a section entitled "The Limits of Economics," in which Kirk states quite clearly that economics is concerned with only a limited part of human life: it "is simply the study of producing, distributing and consuming goods."[100] To expand the reach of economics beyond those limited boundaries will draw attention away from other values in life.

Although he credited entrepreneurs for their diligence, intelli-

---

98. *PC*, 81; Kirk, "Little Shops and Socialist Capitalism," 317.
99. *RT*, 98.
100. Kirk, *Economics*, 32–33, 39.

gence, and imagination, he also decried the economics-obsessed American as the "Inhumane Businessman,"[101] because the businessman has been deprived of any standard of value other than that of the marketplace. Producing, acquiring, and spending become the whole of existence. While technology may make industry more efficient, only imagination can fully attune economic production with human needs and other societal values. In this context, Kirk quoted approvingly Tocqueville's passage expressing astonishment at the attachment of Americans to consumer goods and their substitution of material prosperity for any other kind. This drive to equate material with social or spiritual success has become more visible during the seemingly immense gains of the stock market during the 1990s and the concomitant explosion of consumer goods.[102] While Kirk often spoke of the importance of a leisure class that was able to reflect upon issues of governance or the social order, he also criticized the idle rich, or the "Wealthy American Bum."[103] A governing class is not the same as being governed by "the business class." In 1956, Kirk rejected the equation of economic success and political imagination. "One of the principles of conservatism is the protection of private property and private industry. . . . Yet respect for the rights and duties of business does not mean that industrialists ought to write our laws and direct our state policies." Here again he emphasized his conclusion that politics, to be conservative, must rise above interest and seek to "conserve something larger."[104]

Kirk's efforts in economics engage the distinction between what Winifred Barr Rothenberg has called the "marketplace" economy and the "market" economy.[105] While both systems regulate the exchange of goods in a competitive environment, the former does so by operating within a "thick" social context of norms, customs, habits, and ways of doing business. The latter, in contrast, is based on what Kirk would call the ideology of capitalism. The sole motive is profit, and the entire social or government structure is designed to further that motive.

101. Kirk, "The Inhumane Businessman," 160.
102. See David Brooks, *On Paradise Drive: The Way We Live Now (and Always Have) in the Future Tense;* Virginia Postrel, *The Future and Its Enemies.*
103. Kirk, "The Wealthy American Bum," 198.
104. *BDA,* 41–42.
105. Rothenberg, *From Market-Places to a Market Economy;* see also Gordon Wood, "Was America Born Capitalist?"

The confluence of economics and ideology reached its height for Kirk during his controversies with the neoconservatives during the late 1980s and 1990s. Kirk's criticism of the neoconservative positions centered exactly on the modernist transformation of economics into an ideology of "democratic capitalism," which is the conservative counterpart to socialism's deification of the state. Kirk rejected the call made by some neoconservatives for an ideology to counter that of the Soviets and called "democratic capitalism" a contradiction in terms. Kirk would not have agreed with neoconservatives such as Kristol that "bourgeois capitalism" represented the true American tradition nor that "economic growth" was a necessary ingredient for political stability. For example, Kirk found that during the Great Depression, America's worst economic crisis, the threat of radicalism was less than it was supposed: Americans had binding ties other than prosperity that provided resources to resist radicalism. Similarly, in the libertarians Kirk discovered the doctrinaire heirs to Paine, who would take the notion of economic freedom to absurd lengths.[106]

Kirk and Postmodern Politics

A central part of postmodern political criticism has been the unlocking of "hierarchies of power," the structures that cause one group or class to dominate over others. The political theorist Roberto Unger, for example, in his 1988 work *Politics*, developed the notion of a "superliberal" society, which is dedicated to the endless destruction of structures of domination and control, with no definite social arrangements permitted to last. This has its conservative variant, too, in the paeans to "creative destruction" that has from time to time emerged from the economic Right.

One result of that criticism, as noted in earlier chapters, has been to reveal the Enlightenment pretense to objectivity as just that—a pretense used for political and cultural control. As Stanley Fish recently argued in an energetic book, almost every liberal theory of tolerance that has emerged in the last few years inevitably turns to enforcing the theory's own prejudices, and conspicuously has no place for those who do not already agree with the theory's premises—most specifically, religious believers.[107]

106. *PP*, 185–87, 156.
107. Fish, *The Trouble with Principle*.

Writing in 1980, Kirk thought that conservative insights into the need for rhetoric and the power of imagination in politics would become more important in the postmodern age. "The statesman of the Post-Modern Age must be skilled equally at making bold decisions and at the art of pleasing the volatile public. Thus, the qualities of actor, rhetorician, and poet may count for more than ever before in the American experience." Kirk explicitly rejected the advocacy of a conservative "program" to replace the liberal one, in the wake of Ronald Reagan's first victory in 1980. Conservatives, he wrote, "would be foolish to try to promulgate a 'dynamic democratic capitalism' ideology in the Post-Modern Age, which is beginning to transcend ideologies."[108] Rather, Kirk recognized the emergence of a more fluid set of narratives that were replacing both the liberal progressivism or the conservative counterparts, one of which he hoped would be imaginative conservatism.

As the modern age passed into the Age of Sentiment, Kirk became more concerned over the dissolution of the foundations of American political life. As Bernard Yack noted, American constitutionalism, far from being a completely modern project, contains little of that restless transformation and rejection of authority that characterized, for example, the European experience of the modern age. Kirk held a similar position, and he never accepted that America was the culmination of "the modern project." Kirk shared Yack's sentiment that "Whatever experience of transitoriness Americans may pick up in the marketplace, the workplace, or in their cultural lives develops alongside from, and for the most part, unquestioned expectations of political stability."[109] Despite the overwhelming emphasis on the "newness" of the American political experiment, which was even defended by conservative scholars, Kirk never fully accepted that the United States was the culmination of the Enlightenment or the political science of Locke and Hobbes; for Kirk, that narrow view from the top obscured the deeper continuities in the American experience.

As the nation-state has receded in importance in favor of the global economy and the international economic units that make up its power structure, the placement of individuals, their communities, and their values has become the new problem facing social thinkers.

108. Kirk, "Imagination against Ideology," 1576, 1578–79.
109. Yack, *Fetishism of Modernities*, 91.

Steven Connor notes that "the means to orientate one spatially may be precisely what are missing from the postmodern world." Various strategies have been devised to overcome this seeming "placelessness."[110] While for some postmodern thinkers seeking to replace society has involved radical politics or invoking the example of marginal subcultures, for Kirk it involved an imaginative reaching back—first to the eighteenth century and the emergence of democratic political culture, then farther back into the past of the West. Political demagoguery and ideological language were to be fought intellectually with multifaceted rhetoric and the prudence of the party leader, and through the institutions of federalism, the separation of powers, and more generally a respect for the customs and conventions of localities. Kirk found in Burke the nuance and hierarchy that he thought political rhetoric required. However, in the more democratic United States, "the least poetic of nations," Kirk was unable, for the most part, to find statesmen who were able to transform a Burkean rhetoric to the democratic idiom. Indeed, in general Kirk agreed with Oakeshott that the best of the Western tradition treats politics as a "poetic" rather than a "scientific" discipline. Unpoetic politics must be politics without imagination—or, at best, to be illuminated only by the impractical idyllic imagination, to be followed by the grisly diabolic imagination. The moral imagination, therefore, is not a mere ornament to a society, but one of its bulwarks.

110. Connor, *Postmodernist Culture*, 229–30.

4

The Jurisprudence of Russell Kirk

Conservative constitutional theory might be interesting, but it isn't.

Mark Tushnet, "Conservative Constitutional Theory"

The Natural Law as a Guide for Individual Action

As the liberal rights-based theory of law undergoes a slow collapse, there has been a marked increase in "natural law" as an alternative approach and its implications for modern legal systems.[1]
As Robert George of Princeton has noted, however, while the idea of
natural law as the basis of the Anglo-American legal system has
wide currency, among both conservatives and liberals, the theoretical basis and the substantive results it leads to vary widely.[2] Kirk too
participated in this debate, but his hesitancy toward discussing anything "theoretical" led him to construe the reach of natural law in the
legal realm quite narrowly.

In fact, Kirk did not repair to the natural law as a ground for the

1. The modern literature on natural law is varied and wide-ranging. For a bibliography, see James V. Schall, S.J., "A Natural Law Bibliography."
2. George, "Natural Law, the Constitution, and the Theory and Practice of Judicial Review," 151.

formal legal order in his earlier works. As Peter Stanlis has pointed out, Kirk did not at first explicitly rest his conservative defense of prescription in natural law concepts. "Only later did [Kirk] learn that Burke's principle of legal prescription was itself a derivative principle, originating from natural law."[3] The first edition of *The Conservative Mind* lists as a conservative canon the "belief that a divine intent rules society as well as conscience." Later editions replace this with "belief in a transcendent order, or natural law."[4] Kirk's definition remained at this comfortable level of generality.

Kirk indicated how strictly he would hold lawmakers to clear legal principles rather than disputed questions of natural law in his examination of the Higher Law controversy of the 1850s. In March of 1850, Senator William Seward made a speech on the Senate floor declaring, "there is a higher law than the Constitution," referring to the justice of proposals on the emancipation of slaves. The polemicist Orestes Brownson argued in response, in his essay, "The Higher Law," published in January 1851, that while Seward was correct in stating that there is a higher law than the Constitution—the law of God—nevertheless, he was not justified in appealing to his own interpretation of that higher law to overturn the concrete written law by which he held his authority. In other words, private appeals to a law superior to that which actually governs the state will eventually lead to anarchy.[5]

Kirk draws from this controversy a lesson on the relationship between higher, or natural, law and positive human law. Recourse to natural law, especially when that law is interpreted by an individual or small group, should not normally take precedence over legally constituted authority in settling conflicting claims.[6] Kirk is suspicious of so-called natural law principles being used as the basis for governing the body politic without being first incorporated into the social customs of the people. Where every individual is free to determine the status and force of legal norms, civil society collapses.[7] Natural law provides the authority for positive law, not an alterna-

3. Stanlis, "Russell Kirk and the Roots of American Order," 5.

4. W. Wesley McDonald, "The Conservative Mind of Russell Kirk: 'The Permanent Things' in an Age of Ideology," 98; *CM*, 8.

5. For a discussion of this controversy, see Person, *Kirk: A Critical Biography*, 101–2.

6. Kirk, "Natural Law and the Constitution of the United States," 1041.

7. For a discussion of the *Casey* decision, see Russell Hittinger, "Government by Dissent: A Note on Our Judicial Sovereigns," 379–81.

tive to it, and natural law principles are effected through properly enacted laws.[8] As Charles Kesler frames the issue, "The natural law remains lower than the constitutional law in the important sense that the [American] people have not consented to be ruled by natural law in the abstract; they have consented only to be ruled by the Constitution."[9] However, the two are not entirely separate. Kirk rejects the argument that because the Constitution does not explicitly mention natural law, natural law has no place in American constitutional law.

While the Constitution is "not a philosophical treatise, but instead a practical instrument of government," it is a product of the natural law tradition of the Anglican divines and legal thinkers, particularly Blackstone. Therefore, the natural law is not set up as a "check" upon the Constitution, to be employed by judges when they believe the constitutional structures have erred; it should already inhere in the constitutional and statutory structures themselves. Any employment by judges of natural law concepts should be based in the materials they have on hand rather than their private judgment. While Kirk does not provide his opinion as to which branch of government is entrusted with expounding on the natural law—a question that has vexed a number of natural law thinkers—it is clear that he rejects the theory that "private interpretation of natural law should be the means by which conflicting claims are settled."[10]

For Kirk, a modern counterpart to the Higher Law controversy is the jurisprudence relating to church and state. Entire government-sponsored programs have been struck down, despite having strong community support and lacking any discernible harm, because they violated an understanding of the "wall of separation"[11] that was based on a particular view of historical circumstances. The basic law of the nation, Kirk argues, had too often been left to the "impulses, prejudices and ideological dogmata of the nine Justices of the Supreme Court"[12]—and to many lesser judges besides. Reliance on

8. Kirk, "Natural Law," 1047.
9. Kesler, "Natural Law and the Constitution," 558.
10. RD, 129–30, 135–37.
11. Terry Eastland, ed., Religious Liberty in the Supreme Court, 382. The Court, however, has seemed to retreat from its earlier extreme views; see Agostini v. Felton, 521 U.S. 203 (1997), which upheld portions of a modified New York program.
12. Kirk, The Conservative Constitution, 12 (hereafter cited as CC). For examples of Kirk's encounters with the judiciary in this area, see his "Shelton College and State Licensing of Religious Schools: An Educator's View of the Interface be-

private revelation transforms truths into ideology, a tendency to which natural law is particularly susceptible.[13]

Natural law, then, according to Kirk, should not be used as a supervening authority to trump a carefully crafted legislative and judicial structure, except in the most desperate of circumstances. This position reveals Kirk's deep-seated anxiety that invocation of natural law will serve as a cover for abuse of the legal and political system. This worry parallels the contention of certain postmodern legal writers that the Enlightenment, or "classical," conception of law, based on the universality and rationality of legal principles that are discovered and applied by judges, masks an oppressive or restrictive culture. While Kirk may not have gone as far as to contend that all such principles are covers for oppression, he does argue that some judges, imbued with a sense of private revelation, use their position to advance their own versions of constitutional law, which is obscured by their surface obedience to the constitutional text.

For this reason, Kirk finds the meaning of natural law primarily in the guidance of individuals, not as a plan for society or the legal system. Application of the natural law to society as a whole is an exercise in prudence. Statute and common law, supported by custom, are generally enough to keep the peace; indeed, Kirk states clearly that both natural law and positive law are subverted by private impositions of supposed normative principles. As the results of Higher Law controversy show, that way can lead to violence. In this, Kirk seems to approve of the position taken by Brownson concerning the constitutionality of the Fugitive Slave Law. The law was undoubtedly constitutional and should have been obeyed, in the interest of avoiding war.[14] It is interesting to compare this controversy with Kirk's defense of the attempted assassination of Adolf Hitler. The assassins "being law abiding, in defense of true law were prepared to slay the chief of state [who was] a perverter of the laws of man's nature."[15] According to Kirk, direct application of natural law is only for a last resort, but this begs the question. The abolitionists and Higher Law advocates surely thought, as did the would-be assassins, that they were at a last resort in ending a great evil.

---

tween the Establishment and Free Exercise Clauses," 169; and *Reclaiming a Patrimony: A Collection of Lectures*, 5.

13. Yves Simon, *The Tradition of Natural Law*, 16, 23.

14. Kirk, "Natural Law," 1043–44.

15. Kirk, "The Case for and against Natural Law," 3, 5.

Kirk, in one of his last writings on the subject, defines natural law as "a loosely knit body of rules of action prescribed by an authority superior to the state."[16] What is important in Kirk's approach to the natural law is his reluctance to describe its functions or characteristics in any detail. When Kirk does venture a definition of natural law, he hedges it with qualifications and limitations. The natural law in this instance seems to serve as a backstop for tradition, to keep it from veering too far from its internal goals, a strategy similar to that taken by MacIntyre. MacIntyre employs the concept of "epistemological crisis" to explain those circumstances when a tradition would be wrenched from its former path through a process of self-evaluation as against another tradition, what John Tate has called MacIntyre's "hermeneutic leap."[17] The natural law may have the same sort of function for Kirk, as a counterpoise to tradition unmoored from its sources or ends.

Kirk fears the modern temptation to establish the state or some component thereof as the only source of normative principles. The state, when legitimate, is indeed an authority, but there are other authorities with which it may conflict, such as those of conscience or church. When there exists a conflict between authorities, "the conscientious man endeavors, according to what light is given him, to determine which representatives of authority have claimed too much." The reluctance to believe that the natural law, when applied by state power, can, or indeed should, solve every human ill follows an important strand in natural law thinking. As Ernest Fortin has written, "because of its very generality, the natural law does not provide a sufficient guide to action and must be supplemented by the human law." The Anglican divine Richard Hooker, whose *Laws of Ecclesiastical Polity* was an important influence upon Kirk, echoes this sentiment, as does the twentieth-century natural law theorist A. P. d'Entrèves.[18]

For lawmakers, the natural law has a specific function: "to guide the sovereign; the chief of state; the legislator; the public prosecutor; the judge—to guide you and me, indeed, there endures the natural law, which in essence is man's endeavor to maintain a moral or-

---

16. Ibid., 1.

17. MacIntyre quoted in Tate, "The Hermeneutic Circle vs. the Enlightenment," 9, 27–29.

18. *EPT*, 283; Fortin, "Natural Law and Social Justice," 17; d'Entrèves, *Natural Law: An Introduction to Legal Philosophy*, 76.

der."[19] And again, "Natural law is not a harsh code that we thrust upon other people: rather it is an ethical knowledge" that we employ to restrain will and appetite in our ordinary lives.[20] It is a mistake to conceive of the natural law as a ready-made body of rules to which the positive law must conform.[21] Kirk recognizes that many cultures have developed similar moral precepts, based in the natural law and expressed in proverb, maxim, and injunction, but he seems to hold that the actual number of governing principles of natural law are few in number. Whatever their number, however, these are generally not the proper materials for a comprehensive legal code. Instead, Kirk sees the appearance of these patterns of belief in many cultures as evidence of a common literary and imaginative tradition of justice.[22] The development of a legal code is a work of reason, which relies on, but does not adopt wholesale, the imaginative tradition of the natural law and adapts its teachings to particular circumstances.

Apprehension of the Natural Law: Reason and Intuition

Kirk, therefore, advocated a natural law whose primary purpose is to guide individual conduct. Natural law principles will most likely find their way into the formal legal institutions of a society, primarily through many individual decisions and court cases that reflect the settled convictions of the people involved in those decisions and cases. Invocation of natural law by a constitutional authority that will bind the entire nation should be a rare event, occurring only in dire circumstances. This understanding of the role of natural law diminishes the force of the will and appetite and allows for the operation of prudence in shaping the principles of this normative external order to concrete circumstances.[23]

How, then, do we know what the natural law requires? The fluidity with which Kirk sometimes discusses natural law and the role it plays seems to conflict with his contention that a natural, definable order exists. Wesley McDonald has criticized Kirk's understanding of natural law for being overly "intuitive": Kirk places too great an

19. Kirk, "Natural Law," 1046.
20. Kirk, "The Case for and against Natural Law," 3.
21. Russell Hittinger, "Introduction," in Simon, *Tradition of Natural Law*, xxvii.
22. *RAO*, 44–45.
23. Kirk, "The Meaning of 'Justice,'" 7.

"emphasis on the moral imagination as an immediate, intuitive grasp of the good [and] appears to unduly depreciate the role of reason in preference to . . . the intuition." Kirk has likewise been faulted for not providing a proper "philosophic" defense of his moral and legal thought, and according to McDonald, his "intuitional" system makes conceptual philosophy almost useless.[24] In his book-length study of Kirk, McDonald drops that precise argument, but he maintains more generally that Kirk's intuitional defense of the "Permanent Things" does not sit well with one understanding of the natural law tradition of St. Thomas Aquinas and the medieval schoolmen. The main tradition of natural law, McDonald asserts, conceives of the good "as static and predefined because the precepts of natural law are viewed as unchanging and universal." Because Kirk mistrusted universal abstractions, therefore, he "could not accept a natural law that predefines the good for all time and formulates a code that transcends all other codes."[25] Judged by these standards, Kirk's connection with the natural law tradition has been called into question for being "unsatisfactory and confusing."[26]

McDonald's argument is valid, insofar as Kirk believes that the imaginative or poetic modes of thought permit an apprehension of the good as effectively as that achieved through what the Enlightenment called reason; indeed, Kirk states that "properly understood, the law of nature is the moral imagination." But Kirk does speak well of the Scholastic tradition of natural law, comparing it favorably to that of the medieval nominalists, who did away with universals entirely. Further, Kirk defends Montesquieu as a legitimate exponent of natural law "that had come down from Plato and Cicero and Aquinas and Hooker." Law, Kirk argues, "has its roots in general truths," but these truths will be variously applied. In a suggestive passage in *The Roots of American Order*, Kirk defines Cicero's natural law theory as a system of justice that grows out of human recognition of enduring natural laws, a recognition that enables choice between justified and unjustified claims.[27] This process of recognition is an operation of reason, informed by a body of normative imaginative literature and tradition, which is conditional. These sources

24. McDonald, "Reason, Natural Law, and Moral Imagination in the Thought of Russell Kirk," 23.
25. McDonald, *Kirk and the Age of Ideology*, 76.
26. McDonald, "Reason, Natural Law, and Moral Imagination," 22.
27. *RAO*, 112, 209, 352, 111.

can change over time in response to consideration of its claims to authority.[28]

It is also unclear whether the tradition of natural law offered by Aquinas is as sharply rationalistic as McDonald avers. Rather than positing a strict separation between reason and "intuition," the medievals made a distinction between what they termed *ratio* and *intellectus*. As Josef Pieper explains in *Leisure: The Basis of Culture*, "*Ratio* is the power of discursive, logical thought, of searching and examination, of abstraction, of definition and drawing conclusions. *Intellectus*, on the other hand, is the name for the understanding insofar as it is the capacity of *simplex intuitus*, of that simple vision to which truth offers itself like a landscape to the eye." The actual process of knowing consists in the operation of both at once.[29] Reason, therefore, is only the active mode of knowing; it is interpenetrated by *intellectus*, the passive capacity to receive truth that Kirk calls "intuition." As Bruce Frohnen notes, this passive reception of knowledge can come in a variety of forms, such as long-established practices or rules of conduct.[30] Whatever the merits of the version of natural law offered by McDonald, it is not Kirk's, but in part perhaps because Kirk did not bother fully to set out the basis for his conclusions about the natural law.[31]

Intuition is suprarational, a sort of "participation in the simple knowledge which is proper to the higher beings" that speaks to the deeper nature of humanity.[32] "Law is a natural force; it is the mind and reason of the intelligent man, the standard by which Justice and Injustice are to be measured." Imagination is a necessary condition to a rational and humane application of the law, both customary and statutory.[33] In emphasizing both the active and passive aspects of apprehension, Kirk allows for a degree of creative freedom in applying the natural law. His critics have misinterpreted this complex interaction as a cloudy reliance on "intuition"; it is more like the *determinatio* of St. Thomas Aquinas. That is, the natural law would often have an indirect rather than a direct application, which neces-

28. *EPT,* 285–86.
29. Josef Pieper, *Leisure: The Basis of Culture,* 26–27. For a further discussion of this point, see Wolfe, "The Catholic as Conservative," 25, 28–29.
30. Frohnen, *Virtue and the Promise of Conservatism,* 172–73.
31. Pieper, *Leisure,* 27.
32. Ibid.
33. *RAO,* 111–12.

sarily involves a process of determination. So, for example, "the law of nature has it that the evil-doer should be punished, but that he be punished in this or that way, is a determination of the law of nature."[34]

The philosopher Yves Simon has a similar notion of the transmission of natural law, which he calls the "way of inclination," as opposed to the "way of cognition." The former method is the only way, he maintains, to ascertain practical judgments considered concretely. Indeed, Simon goes on to say that the "last word" belongs to inclination. He does not discuss the source of this "inclination" in the same terms as Kirk, but for both there are both rational and suprarational components to the natural law. Knowledge of the natural law can come by way of cognition first, or by way of inclination. This inclination is "not purely intellectual [but] that of the good, honest will."[35]

Kirk's perception of the natural law has a strong historical component. His examples of good behavior or moral excellence are drawn from historical figures. Kirk, however, knows that history is not the final arbiter of value; history is meaningful only insofar as it "reveals the general principles to which men and societies, in all ages, are subject."[36] This hesitation to accord history the final judgment reflects Kirk's recognition of human frailty. At its best, history can teach us only the outlines of general principles, through the "splendor and misery of our condition."[37] Yet, it is this recognition that allows Kirk to use history in the first place; uneasy with the use of principles without foundation, Kirk is always prepared to use historical context to demonstrate the limits of abstractions.

The Need for Order

Although the Anglo-American common law system has long been a resource for conservative thinkers, until his last years it was not a focus of Kirk's own writing. As of 1980, for example, there were barely a dozen items under the entries "Justice" or "Law" in his bibliog-

---

34. Aquinas, *Treatise on Law*, q.95.
35. Simon, *Tradition of Natural Law*, 125–36 (quotes on 129 and 131).
36. Kirk, "Behind the Veil," 468.
37. Kirk, "Introduction"; John Lukacs, *Historical Consciousness*, xii.

raphy.[38] The situation changed dramatically in the subsequent decade and a half before his death. Kirk penned a number of significant articles on the law for both the popular and scholarly press and presented a series of lectures on justice at the Heritage Foundation.

At the root of his discussions on the law is Kirk's concern with maintaining a constitutional structure that would be able to protect individual liberty against arbitrary authority, to provide stability and continuity, to establish a representative system reflective of the national interest, and to combine founding principles with the changing realities of political life.[39] Drawing on the work of Simone Weil, Kirk maintained that order is the first need of society that is only partially captured through a society's laws.[40] Underlying the formal legal system is the web of customs, traditions, and moral norms that allow legal authority to be recognized or exercised in the first place. Law, properly understood, is "at base a knowledge of the ethical norms for the human being."[41] Social order extends beyond the prohibitions and commands imposed by the law to include "the harmonious arrangement of classes and functions which guarantees justice and gives consent to law." Where there is no order, obedience to the law is compelled rather than given: "the policeman supplants . . . the old influence of emulation and the soft but effectual controls of good repute."[42] However, there are few sharp lines. A high degree of individual order is necessary for a tolerable social order; conversely, a decent social order supports the attainment and maintenance of individual order. Order, therefore, suggests a level of cooperation that permits individual freedom and the preservation of social goods without, usually, the necessity of invoking the coercive force of law. As Kirk wrote in *Roots of American Order*, laws generally should arise from an ordered society, rather than used to im-

---

38. Brown, *Kirk: A Bibliography*. The major source for Kirk's writings on the law is the posthumous collection *Rights and Duties*, which incorporates much of the material in his earlier *The Conservative Constitution*, in addition to other previously uncollected essays. Kirk also touched on legal subjects in *Roots of American Order*, *A Program for Conservatives*, and in his studies of John Randolph, Edmund Burke, and Robert A. Taft.

39. CC, 14–15.

40. *RAO*, 3–5.

41. Ibid., 110–11.

42. Both this quote and the one in the preceding sentence are taken from Kirk, *Prospects for Conservatives*, 187, first published as *A Program for Conservatives* in 1954.

pose order on an unruly society. The formal legal order is therefore of a secondary nature, because the determination of legal questions will arise from the other settled norms and customs of a society.

Law is not an ideological blueprint, to which a society is grafted Procrustes-like; rather, the rule of law is a series of compromises and principles that will arise out of the habits and dispositions of the people subject to them. Burke called law the "pride of human intellect"; it is an artificial construct, but one that, ideally, evokes and protects the values of the society that constructs it. Kirk believed, drawing ultimately from Aristotle, that the laws of a society are in part a reflection of the character of its members, hence the need for a stable social order. Kirk's friend, the essayist Albert Jay Nock, expressed this point more cynically: "The law is whatever the people will back up."[43] Those who would create a perfect world by means of legal coercion will end up subverting the very legal order they claim to champion, a result Kirk found in examples from the French Revolution to modern social planning.

As in other areas, narrative and context for Kirk play large roles in construction of the legal environment. Robert Cover, an influential legal theorist, argues, "No set of legal institutions or prescriptions exists apart from the narratives that locate it and give it meaning. For every constitution there is an epic, for each decalogue a scripture. Once understood in the context of the narratives that give it meaning, law becomes not merely a system of rules to be observed, but a world in which we live."[44] Law and the institutions that enforce and explain it must be contextualized and placed within the larger story of that society. Law, by itself, does not create meaning for a society. That is the function of other, what Cover calls "strong," forces, such as religious belief or moral principles. Legal systems merely hold in place the structure of values established by these other forces.

The choice of narrative within which the legal forces will operate, therefore, is of central importance. This choice will not only emphasize certain values and ways of acting within society, but also by necessity cut off other possible alternative narratives. This insight into the role of narrative in the construction of legal meaning has received more attention recently from legal academics. The results of that increased attention, however, have been mixed.[45] Some of these nar-

---

43. Nock, *State of the Union*, 143.
44. Cover, "Nomos and Narrative," 5.
45. David A. Hyman has called the scholarship concerning narrative a "boom

ratives constitute "storytelling" of highly personalized (sometimes bordering on the fictional) and explicitly nonanalytical accounts that are justified by their proponents primarily in terms of their political impact.[46] Some scholars, however, while noting the commonplace use of narrative in legal practice, both academic and professional, nevertheless caution that the turn toward storytelling can reduce the explicative and persuasive power of legal reasoning. For if everyone has an individual story, how do we compare the relative importance of the stories being told?[47]

To Keep the Peace: The Purpose of Law

In contrast to theories advocating law as an agent of social change or as a force in the preservation of free-market mechanisms, Kirk stated quite forcefully in several works that the primary purpose of law is to keep the peace.[48] Indeed, in his early writings, it was virtually the only opinion concerning law that Kirk clearly supported, although he later considered whether positive law had any moral bases. Only if citizens know they are protected by the rule of law from oppression or fraud can they be free to participate in a common culture and exercise their freedom. When this purpose is forgotten or superseded, the rule of law becomes an instrument of injustice and extortion.[49]

Kirk sets out three general characteristics of Anglo-American legal thought: that the law is not an arbitrary system to be used by those in power to punish those in opposition; that no one is above or exempt from the law; and finally that the law primarily arises from custom, tradition, and the decisions of judges.[50] Kirk does not enumerate more specific components of a general "rule of law"; to delve into the peculiarities of a nation's legal system and to pick and

---

industry" ("Lies, Damned Lies, and Narrative," 797). For a larger discussion, see the symposium on "Legal Storytelling," *Michigan Law Review* 87 (1989): 2073.

46. See Mary Coombs, "Outsider Scholarship: The Law Review Stories," 713. One of the most prolific legal storytellers has been Richard Delgado, whose idiosyncratic "Rodrigo's Chronicles" have been published in many of the nation's most prominent law journals. See, for example, his "Rodrigo's Chronicle," 1357.

47. See Daniel A. Farber and Suzanne Sherry, "Telling Stories Out of School: An Essay on Legal Narratives," 807.

48. *ABC*, 29.

49. Kirk, "Christian Postulates of English and American Law," 49.

50. *ABC*, 73–74. See also Arthur M. Hogue, *The Origins of the Common Law*, 190.

choose among its features according to an abstract standard would be an exercise in folly. The rule of law cannot be divined by what Kirk calls "coffeehouse philosophers." Kirk cites as a cautionary example utilitarian philosopher Jeremy Bentham's offer to devise a legal code for the United States, a country he had never visited, by means of an abstract utilitarian calculus.[51] If law is meant to keep the peace, what constitutes "peace" in a given society will influence the structure of the legal system.

The sources of law in the Anglo-American system are precedent, statute, and custom. Precedent is the uncodified collection of opinions by common law courts that supply general rules of justice. It is intended to be flexible and to adapt to the changing factual situations of particular litigants.[52] At the same time, however, the common law is able to retain sufficient certainty for parties to determine the legal boundaries of their actions. Through the centuries, the "common law doctrines have a stable meaning, though expressed in a variety of different ways."[53] In a dispute between X and Y, for example, if X can demonstrate that similar persons in similar situations in the past have prevailed, then, barring any special circumstances, X too will prevail in a common law system.[54]

In his defense of precedent and custom as indispensable bases for the legal system, Kirk follows in the tradition of the school of "historical jurisprudence" begun by Sir Edward Coke, which continued in England through John Selden, Matthew Hale, and William Blackstone to Edmund Burke.[55] Federal judge Richard A. Posner counts Kirk among the "neotraditionalists," who seek to return law to an autonomous discipline, untainted by contact with other areas of knowledge.[56] While not neglecting the use of reason in the legal process, according to Posner, the neotraditionalists recognize the limits of rationalism in the design of a legal system. They turn instead to the "artificial reason" of law, as expressed in customary uses, tradition, and precedent in their efforts to understand the scope and

---

51. *RAO*, 371–72.
52. *ABC*, 30–31.
53. Richard Posner, *The Problems of Jurisprudence*, 246.
54. A detailed account of the development of an Anglo-American "common law thinking" is provided in James R. Stoner Jr., *Common Law and Liberal Theory: Coke, Hobbes and the Origins of American Constitutionalism*.
55. See Berman, "Origins of Historical Jurisprudence," 1651.
56. Posner, *Problems of Jurisprudence*, 442–43.

proper function of a legal system, which Kirk collectively refers to as the unwritten constitution.[57]

In a common law system, the contending parties, the facts of their case, the judge, and the jury all participate in making new law that conforms with precedent. The jury, in particular, was of crucial importance to Kirk because it places part of the creative process of law-making into the hands of the general populace.[58] The common law derives some of its strength from the belief of the English people that the common law was "their" law, the product of their own historical experiences and the result of centuries of common effort. Kirk thought that the founders were greatly influenced by the introduction of the common law to the New World.[59] Only their Protestant Christianity was more influential in the founders' thinking than the common law.

Statutes, too, are part of the legal landscape, and indeed the importance of statutory law and its interpretation has almost eclipsed traditional emphasis in legal training and practice on common law reasoning.[60] Kirk does not discuss codified law often, preferring to concentrate on legal principles generally and the common law, a major exception being the statutory law discussed in his study of Taft. When he does address statutory law, Kirk is generally not complimentary. First, in *The Conservative Mind,* Kirk speaks approvingly of John Randolph's disdain for the "legislative maggot." Legislation is too subject to wholesale revision and enactment based upon improper motives or passing fads. Under a legislation-driven system, "nothing remains settled, every right, every bit of property is endangered."[61] If more responsive at times to the will of the electorate than the common law, legislation often lacks the structure that legal principles give to judicial decisions. In his study of John Randolph, Kirk continues his critique of the dangers of legislation. In particular, he decried the American passion for enacting positive laws to cover every conceivable wrong, rather than waiting for slower methods to reach an appropriate resolution.[62] Public confidence in legislative power is turned instead to personal and class advantage, "so

57. Berman, "Origins of Historical Jurisprudence," 1732–35.
58. *ABC,* 32–33.
59. *RAO,* 190–92.
60. Guido Calabresi, *A Common Law for the Age of Statutes.*
61. *CM,* 159.
62. *JRR,* 210–11.

that government becomes a means for extracting money and rights from one portion of the population" to suit others, an argument to which Kirk later returns.[63]

Second, each party in a typical lawsuit contends against the other, with the judge as arbiter and jury as fact finder and the party that decides the verdict. The power to frame the issues and decide the matter is divided up among the parties, and no one party has a lasting interest in pleasing any of the others. This is not the case with the legislature, the members of which deal with each other, with lobbyists, and with other interested groups on a regular basis. When statutes are necessary, they should be enacted in the face of a concrete need and only to redress an imbalance in the common law, as we saw in Kirk's discussion of the Taft-Hartley Act.[64]

Kirk's account of the common law system can be attacked as too formalistic; indeed, his discussion of how law should be interpreted reveals a number of weaknesses. In the United States, the common law system of precedent and *stare decisis* has been criticized as being a mere cover for political agenda or personal predilection, by writers on the right as well as on the left, and thus judicial interpretation is at bottom no different from the enactment of a statute. The legal realists, for example, did much to expose the weaknesses in traditional judicial reasoning and its reliance on allegedly outmoded canons of law. According to the Realists, the reasons announced for a decision merely disguise the judge's previously held political or social convictions. The study of law, therefore, moves from the belief in a specific set of reasoning skills to the piercing of "real" reasons for judicial pronouncements. Kirk too often takes at face value the justification for the common law system.

There are deeper problems, however, with Kirk's connection between a defense of precedent and underlying traditions and customs. Precedent and tradition are not identical and may in fact serve cross-purposes. As David Luban notes in an important article, recent precedent is usually better than older precedent, and in a common law system, any precedent, no matter how ancient or respected, can be overruled by a court (for example, the highest appellate court in a state) with the authority to do so.[65] Thus, prominent liberal theo-

63. *CM*, 159. See also Kirk's discussion of competing interest groups in *PP*, 46–47.
64. Kirk and McClellan, *Political Principles of Taft*, 124–25.
65. Luban, "Legal Traditionalism," 1035.

rists such as Bruce Ackerman can comfortably defend one understanding of the common law system as the basis for an unlimited expansion of rights, a result Kirk condemns on numerous occasions, while employing the same methods that he praises.[66]

There may be a point here, however, that is more subtle than a simple defense of the common law method. Precedent, both substantively and because of the process by which it is elaborated, is important for a conservative legal theory, not just for its "intrinsic" reasons—that is, the content of the decisions that are considered binding—but also for its "extrinsic" reasons. That is to say, precedent represents concrete remnants of the connections between one generation and the next; past decisions of course affect the present, and present decisions are engaged both in a dialogue with the past and in forming precedent for the future. It is this sensitivity to the distinction between past and present, and to the authority the past has over the present simply because it is past, that Anthony Kronman finds the "truly foreign" element in a precedent-based legal system.[67] Even when there is a departure from precedent, the departure is usually explained in terms of the precedent itself.

This defense of precedent is tied to Kirk's conservative individualism. While precedent is of course generally binding on subsequent courts, the system reduces the threat of capture by parties interested in the result. Among other things, prior cases themselves become cultural artifacts subject to argument and adjudication by future parties whose circumstances will differ.[68] In contrast, legislation creates blanket rules that are applicable to everyone in the same way. Their power is amplified especially when it is joined to quasi-judicial bodies such as administrative agencies, which make rules and are in part insulated from judicial review. Because courts consider cases on an individual basis and a decision is most strongly binding only on the parties before it, combined with the even more flexible powers granted to a court of equity, whose decisions in the traditional understanding are not precedential, the common law system for Kirk represents the proper combination of stability and change.

Common law and statute are supported by custom, the "unwritten law" that furnishes cohesiveness to the written law. Custom pro-

---

66. Ackerman, "The Common Law Constitution of John Marshall Harlan," 23.
67. Kronman, "Precedent and Tradition," 1037.
68. James Boyd White, *Heracles' Bow: Essays on the Rhetoric and Poetics of the Law*, 55–56.

vides the crucial "narrative" background for Kirk and a brake to the unlimited use of the "artificial reason" of the law, by specifying which results are within and without its scope. This unwritten code is a collection of political compromises, conventions, habits, and ways of living in a social order that have developed among a people over time.[69] Kirk cites political parties, the presidential cabinet, and presidential primary elections as examples of unwritten conventions that undergird our written constitution. Custom, according to this view, is safer than "command," from either a judge or a legislature, because custom exists for a long period before the particular case, as well as supplying a critical democratic element to the development of the law.[70]

These conventions reflect Kirk's contentions that the governing text of a nation embodies only a portion of the "constitution," or constitutional meaning, of that nation. The remainder will be supplied by the ambient culture, which will serve also as a check upon both judges following their own private muse and legislatures pressed into hasty action. Kirk's vision of the surrounding culture is described in *Roots of American Order* and *America's British Culture.* In both of these works he places the United States squarely in the British common law story. With particular reference to the law, elements of the surrounding narrative might include the education of lawyers; the structure of the bar, both nationally and within each state; the influence of particular members of the bar; the relationship of practicing attorneys with members of the bench; and the stature of the judiciary.

In his two terms as a justice of the peace in a rural county in Michigan, Kirk exemplified his understanding of the connections between the sources of law in supporting order. Faced with a boundary dispute or some other controversy, Justice of the Peace Kirk did not resort to abstract notions of "right" or "the rule of law" to decide the issues before him. Nor did he pause to determine according to his own lights who was more "entitled" to judgment. He turned instead to previous judicial decisions, the statute books, local custom, and the records in the county commissioner's office.[71] Although this example is drawn from Kirk's actual experience, nearly two decades before he had made

69. CC, 4.
70. See John P. Reid, *Constitutional History of the American Revolution,* 4–8.
71. Kirk, "The Case for and against Natural Law," 5.

a more general point on the propriety of seldom applying abstract concepts when adjudicating concrete disputes.[72] Adjudication necessarily involves interpretation of precedent and other authority, and Kirk made his decisions within a framework of conventions, norms, and the accepted ways of acting within his community.

His example of the small-town peace officer encompasses all the features of the law that Kirk finds important: continuity, authority, order, and prudence combined—it should be noted—with trust in the individual decision maker, a trust based on the belief that the decision maker will resort to sources understood as binding upon the parties rather than to private judgment alone. Without these supports, the "fundamental law would crumble for lack of an enduring consensus; and every faction or interest would feel free, or perhaps obliged, to pursue its own objects in disregard of the general public interest."[73] Where there are recognizable common law or statutory provisions available as grounds for legal decisions, the rule of law is subverted by private appeals to justice. Those with primary responsibility for upholding and defending the legal system—judges and legislators—have a duty to abide by stated legal principles, not to substitute their own private opinions of justice, lest the rule of law seem irrational and uncertain. The legal profession as a whole is likewise charged with preserving the stability and fairness of the legal system, which entails a particular set of habits and attitudes. This understanding of the legitimacy of legal rules is an internal one, judged in reference to what the law itself provides, rather than by comparison with an abstract justice.

Yet this understanding is only derivatively internal, and for Kirk, it arises out of the decisions of individuals and communities that, as described below, can have recourse to an external set of norms or "natural law," which is generated from a reflection upon historical experience. Because of Kirk's belief in the emergence of legal rules from decisions involving individual participants and his distaste for legislation, he implicitly rejects the view of the legal positivists, who treat as valid only those laws issued as commands of a sovereign. Kirk also departs from the contention that there is no necessary connection between law and morals.[74] While some scholars have stated

---

72. Kirk, "Bentham, Burke, and the Law," 164–65.
73. CC, 102.
74. Positivism as a legal philosophy is generally traced to the legal writings of

that the articulation of the separability thesis was a theoretical move rather than an empirical description,[75] for Kirk, this abstraction would be meaningless. Law, to be authentic and effective, must reflect the underlying morality of those subject to it.

In an essay entitled "The Original—Intent Controversy," Kirk discusses the possibility of changing the Constitution. As "the body of basic laws," such change should come slowly.[76] Given his belief that legislatures or executives are too often swayed by temporary passions, Kirk favors letting judges alter the law "by degrees" rather than permitting change by executive or legislative fiat. Common law judges should be allowed to "interpret precedents in the light of altered social circumstances, and so in effect [to] establish fresh precedents more suited to a different era." The gradual change of legal principles "by vigorous action and prudent reform" is sufficient to bring about the additions and subtractions to the body of legal principles necessary for an active society.[77] Kirk believes this to be the safest way to protect established liberties.

In that essay and elsewhere, however, Kirk indicates that the judiciary has in recent years overstepped its bounds and has led the nation to the brink of "archonocracy," the rule of judges. Thus, the societal trust in judicial decision making becomes suspect, which is a strong blow to civil order. For example, in a lengthy essay on the Supreme Court's pornography jurisprudence, Kirk draws several lessons from the Court's involvement in this field since the 1940s:

> One thing demonstrated is the imprudence of translating a Bill of Rights protection of the several states against Congress into an unlimited license for the Supreme Court to meddle with states' jurisdictions in such concerns. Another lesson is the inefficacy of substituting personal and shifting value judgments of nine justices —who can form no consensus among themselves—for enduring moral standards derived from religion, philosophy, and a people's customs and conventions. A third profitable reflection is this: in a self-righteous endeavor to guarantee an extreme of liberty to

Jeremy Bentham and John Austin; the latter's *The Province of Jurisprudence Determined*, first published in 1832, remains the classic work. For a recent discussion of positivism, see Brian Bix, "Positively Positivism," 889.

75. See, for example, Frederick Schauer, "Positivism as Pariah," in Robert P. George, ed., *The Autonomy of Law: Essays on Legal Positivism*, 31–56.

76. CC, 3.

77. Ibid., 109; *RAO*, 188; *EPT* 286.

"emancipated" individuals, the judicial branch of government may work sorry harm—possibly irreparable damage—upon the body social.[78]

Kirk also notes that this activity by the Court was largely at its own behest; neither the larger public nor the legislatures were the impetus for most of its pornography decisions. With the pornography cases, his objection lay primarily in the Court's transformation of the First Amendment into a weapon against traditional understandings of the state police power and "soft" social norms that defined decent behavior. As James Stoner argues, under the common law, in the absence of an argument to the contrary, tradition was authoritative and needed to be proven incorrect or unjust in some way. In contrast, the pornography decisions, as in other areas, use the fact of a tradition as a "prejudice" against its legality.[79]

Defining the intent of the legislature in construing their actions is a difficult business, and liberal theorists such as Ackerman, no less than conservatives, also appeal to history and intent.[80] The doctrine of *stare decisis* may be weakened by a written constitution, which is an authority greater than any cases decided under it. Because an authoritative text exists, judges may appeal directly to it to overturn otherwise-authoritative precedent. It is unclear under what circumstances Kirk would permit judges to contravene the founders or a decision of the legislature. Kirk does not indicate, for example, how courts are to assess whether a legislative act is invalid except where it clearly contravenes the constitutional text. Nor does he discuss at length the many canons of construction that are intended to place a presumption of validity upon legislative acts.

Constitutional Law

American conservatives have commented on the Constitution and the American federal system almost as long as there has been conservative thought in America. Conservatives have supported their attacks on a liberal view of the constitutional structure in a variety

78. *RD*, 208.
79. Stoner, "Is Tradition Activist? The Common Law of the Family in the Liberal Constitutional World," 1291, 1294.
80. Kirk's discussion on this topic can be found in *CC*, 99–115.

of ways. Some have sought an answer in southern constitutional thought, for example, that of John C. Calhoun and his theory of "concurrent majorities." Others have found refuge in the Ninth Amendment. Still others have advocated a radical decentralization of power, along the lines contemplated by the original Articles of Confederation. These conservative approaches have been complemented by a renewed interest in the wider historical and social context of the Constitution across the interpretive spectrum. Movements such as the "new federalism" or the revived interest in classical republicanism that has characterized much recent legal scholarship illustrate this trend. The debate revolves around the sources of constitutional authority and is taking place within a wider philosophical discussion over the collapse of liberalism mentioned in previous chapters.

While the recent political efforts to oppose what conservatives denounced as the "activism" of the judiciary, particularly that of the Warren Court, are interesting, even more fascinating are the intellectual bases for such opposition. Several points guide Kirk's understanding of the Constitution: his usual distaste for theory of almost any sort, which would derive from the constitutional text results measured against some abstract standard (an aversion coupled with a suspicion of those who claim to have special insight into the requirements of justice); a belief that in most cases the intentions of the founders can be discovered (though he distinguishes that question from whether they would decide an issue in the same way as we would now); and a conviction that historical experience and development, even with its recognized flaws, is a surer safeguard of liberty than an appeal to vague or expansive "rights." Subsequent interpretation of that constitution must recognize its continued reliance upon these factors, even if they are not given specific legal weight. This is constitutional law developed "from the bottom up," in which legal norms are recognized through custom, usage, and underlying beliefs as much as (if not more than) from formal judicial pronouncements.

A formal, written constitution is only the top layer of the larger constitutional edifice. Like "some great tree," America's founding document has extensive roots in Anglo-American political and legal practice that remain important to elucidate in order to understand the constitutional text. Thus, Kirk admits that the creation of the federal system's tripartite division of powers was largely an original invention of the founders, without any clear Burkean precedents and based in part of the "new political science" expounded by Hamilton and Madison in *The Federalist*. Nevertheless, he argues that the actual workings of the system, at both the federal and state levels, retained much from their British models. Kirk does not directly address, however, the argument made by some conservative theorists that the vision of the individual presented in the constitutional documents, and contemporaneous publications such as *The Federalist*, represented a new vision of the human person as a political entity. Thus, for example, Mark Henrie has questioned whether Kirk adequately explained the relationship between normative principles and concrete traditions, especially with regard to the American founding.[81]

Similarly, Kirk was never persuaded by the arguments of some conservative thinkers that the Declaration of Independence, adopting language from John Locke, imported new notions of "equality" into the colonial, and then newly independent, American structure. The promise of equality, on this view, was part of the fabric of American constitutionalism, but it was a promise not fulfilled until Lincoln. In arguing that even the early radicals among the founding generation turned rather to their colonial and British heritages, Kirk concluded, "For novel abstract theories of human nature and society, most of the men who subscribed to the Declaration and the Constitution had no relish."[82] However, Kirk's neglect of this argument tends to undermine his defense of constitutional tradition.

For Kirk, nevertheless, every written constitution is "conservative," in that it attempts to preserve a political order. Indeed, that is why written constitutions are proposed in the first instance. In the epilogue to *Rights and Duties*, "The Constitution and the Antagonist World," Kirk wrote, "no matter how admirable a constitution may look upon paper, it will be ineffectual unless the unwritten constitution, the web of custom and convention, affirms an enduring moral order of obligation and personal responsibility."[83] A "conservative" position that adheres rigidly to the constitutional text may cause results neither intended by the founders nor congruent with underlying principles, yet not explicitly prohibited by the text.

Professor Russell Hittinger uses the example of property rights to

81. *RD*, 3; Henrie, "Russell Kirk's Unfounded America," 55–57
82. *RAO*, 401.
83. *RD*, 260.

illustrate this point. The Constitution, in its only use of the word *right* outside the amendments, provides that the national government can protect the rights of persons to profit from their "Writings and Discoveries" through the issuance of patents.[84] Yet this provision does not address whether the Congress should so protect the inventor (for example) of a suicide machine or a severely addictive narcotic. The unwritten constitution, however, employs a different logic and different criteria than the written. It should be relied on to assist legislators and judges in deciding those questions. Without it, such choices are left either to the reigning majorities or to judges, and the constitutional order is reduced, according to Hittinger, to an "operational positivism," that diminishes the legal theory about the Constitution to "the problem of judicial conduct and theories about it."[85]

These questions have assumed greater importance in recent years, as the debate over the role of the Supreme Court in the constitutional order has increased.[86] The current controversy centers on the identity of the American constitutional government itself, on "the very meaning and nature of the Constitution," in the sense that the judiciary is now widely assumed—not least by the judges themselves—as the only proper forum for constitutional disputes. These conservative commentators see in the Supreme Court's *Casey* decision a departure from the admittedly already wide understanding of judicial authority. In particular, they focus on a central passage of that decision, in which the Court states,

> To all who would be so tested by following, the Court implicitly undertakes to remain steadfast lest in the end a price be paid for nothing. . . . So, indeed, must be the character of a Nation of people who, aspire to live according to the rule of law. Their belief in themselves as such a people is not readily separable from their understanding of the Court invested with the authority to decide their constitutional cases and speak before all others for their constitutional ideals.[87]

These are astounding claims, as Justice Scalia notes in an acerbic dissent. The *Casey* decision is an example of what Kirk feared would

---

84. United States Constitution, art. 1, sec. 8.
85. Hittinger, "Introduction," *RD*, xxi.
86. See Mitchell S. Muncy, ed., *The End of Democracy? The Judicial Usurpation of Politics;* and *The End of Democracy II: A Crisis of Legitimacy.*
87. *Planned Parenthood v. Casey,* 505 U.S. 833, 868 (1992).

come to pass. The Constitution should not be a template for "politico-religious dogmata,"[88] expounding on the meaning of existence and guaranteeing a panoply of freedoms that have but a tenuous connection with the historical understanding of those freedoms. Such constitutions are fragile instruments, as a comparison of the endurance of the American Constitution with constitutions established in the Third World or in former Communist nations attest. To burden a constitution with furthering vaguely defined theories of justice that can change at the whims of the governing classes will divert a constitution from the central task of assisting in the governance of the nation, a problem that even liberal theorists are now beginning to recognize.[89] Conversely, however, the calls for the Supreme Court to follow a higher law on the abortion issue may have discomfited Kirk, as much as Seward's call did to Brownson on the issue of slavery.

In his introduction to *Rights and Duties*, Hittinger compares the jurisprudence of the late Justice William J. Brennan Jr. with that of Kirk to highlight their differing conceptions of the role of moral reasoning in constitutional interpretation. Kirk and Brennan shared a belief that the Constitution represented a "complex interplay between written and unwritten norms, including certain transcendental principles of right." Justice Brennan understood constitutional rights as protection for the individual against community coercion and thought that the Constitution needed to be interpreted in order to guarantee individuals emancipation from societal control.

Kirk, in contrast, although he recognized the protection of rights as a constitutional responsibility, did not separate individual rights from community norms so starkly. Rather, he believed that the rights of individuals can be understood and maintained only in community, particularly communities whose members share similar beliefs as to what constitutes a right. Once a community accedes to every individual claim of right, with no thought as to how those rights can be preserved or integrated with others, the community will collapse. As Kirk noted in his study of Randolph, there may be a right to self-defense and therefore a right to some sort of weapon. However, if the person with the weapon becomes dangerous or mentally disabled, the community has the power, and in some cases the obligation, to

88. *RD*, 62.
89. Tushnet, *Taking the Constitution Away from the Courts*.

remove the weapon and the means to exercise the right. Indeed, Kirk essentially rejected the idea of "human rights" as improperly descended from the dangerous abstractions of the French Revolution. He distinguished "human rights" from both the dignity afforded each individual that he found in the natural law and "civil rights," those practical immunities and privileges developed in every concrete legal system.[90] If there were any human rights, moreover, their number was limited and their scope restricted.

This principle has a converse: every right preserved within a community has a concomitant duty. The Constitution, in part, protects individual rights by allowing a space for codifying community standards of morality; that is to say, it protects rights by announcing the duties the members of a given community have to one another. This defense of community, however, does not aim at simply guaranteeing whatever the majority considers a right, because often those "rights" will coincide merely with the majority's wishes. According to Kirk, individual rights will be preserved by the extreme split of power that a common law and federalist system provides. Indeed, Kirk thought that conservatism was impossible without "the spirit of particularism, the idea of local associations and local rights."[91] While American law generally accords little protection to units of government other than the state governments, in several different contexts the Supreme Court has recognized that localities represent the values and concerns of their constituents, and so should be given some legal autonomy in order to effect those concerns.

In his attention to the American tradition of self-government and constitutional democracy and his emphasis on the role of prudence and legal in constitutional interpretation, Kirk anticipates in some ways the efforts to reconcile theory with "practical reason," an approach that has characterized an increasingly influential school of legal thinkers.[92] Practical reason posits that law has its own internal logic that cannot be justified by extralegal norms (for example, literary theory or economics). His use of traditional sources such as Story and Blackstone indicate Kirk's understanding that the law has an

90. *RD,* xxii, 44, 74, 231–32.
91. *CM,* 164.
92. The foremost proponent of this view is Dennis Patterson, *Law and Truth.* For a defense of practical reason as reflecting a return to traditional legal analysis using postmodern principles, see Michael A. Livingston, "Postmodernism Meets Practical Reason," 1125.

internal logic of its own, which must be respected when trying to come to a decision in legal terms.

Kirk stressed that the cultural and social atmosphere that surrounded the founders was more influential on their understanding of constitutionalism than Enlightenment theories of government. Several of Kirk's essays (under the general heading "Revolutionaries and Framers") sketch the intellectual background of the Revolutionary era and its more important members. These include a pair of important essays on the relative influence of John Locke and Edmund Burke on the founding generation. Kirk contended that Burke, as a defender of the British constitutional system as it evolved from the Glorious Revolution of 1688, was a greater source of America's constitutional heritage than John Locke. Burke was a political man, and he appealed far more to the practical instincts of the founders than did any other theorist; Burke's influence could be found throughout the writings of many of the founders, such as John Dickinson and Rufus King, as well as those of other prominent figures such as John Marshall. Kirk found Locke, in contrast, to be of relatively minor importance, when compared with the weight of Christian and common law tradition, his presumed influence on the Constitution the result largely of misguided scholarship.[93] "The Americans would make use of Locke," Kirk wrote in *Roots of American Order*, "but they would not worship him."[94]

This summary obscures some complexity of Kirk's view of Locke, and Kirk's changing view of Locke's importance. In 1956, as part of a series of classics produced by the conservative publishing house Regnery, Kirk provided the introduction to Locke's *Essay Concerning Human Understanding*, first published in 1690. In that introduction, Kirk praised Locke for his "lucidity," in particular his defense of language: "Locke has enduring meaning of us when he denounces the deliberate obscurity of pedants," such as "certain Marxist thinkers," who believe words are a means to further ideology.[95] Indeed, Kirk thought that in the collectivist West of the 1950s, Lockean man "had his virtues, and among those merits was a good understanding of the significance of words, and a critical talent for examining lan-

93. *RD*, 112, 95. Judge Edith Jones, of the Eighth Circuit Court of Appeals, for example, refers to Kirk's arguments approvingly in her "The Nature of Man According to the Supreme Court," 237.
94. *RAO*, 291.
95. Locke, *Essay Concerning Human Understanding*, x–xi.

guage which saved him, much of the time, from what Mr. Richard Weaver calls 'god terms' and 'devil terms.'"[96]

Locke's flaw, Kirk found in 1956, was that his thought lacked any sense of the transcendent, and so his "intellectual atomism" ultimately would not hold together. This is the strand of the critique Kirk developed in *Roots of American Order*, almost two decades later. Gone are the references to Locke's laudable defense of language or the virtues of Lockean man. Instead, Kirk noted that Locke's commonwealth of empirical reason has no affinity with Burke's "spiritual continuity," and that the founders were more indebted to the Christian moralist Thomas Browne than to Locke.[97] Three years later, Kirk was even to move away from the conviction that words could fully capture reality, referring to them instead as tools that break in the hand.

Kirk finds four traces of Burke in the founding. First, "the Constitution did not break with established institutions and customs of the American people," tracing back to the seventeenth century. Second, "the Constitution recognized and incorporated a body of experience far older than the North American colonies: the constitutional development of England," Third, "the Constitution rejected *a priori* theories of government," in particular those set out in the Declaration, which "retired into the background." And fourth, "the Constitution put strong restraints upon arbitrary power, distinctly limiting the operations of the federal government. It preserved state powers for the most part, avoiding the curse of centralization for which Burke was to reproach the French revolutionaries."[98] This last was to be a consistent theme in Kirk's defense of federalism and "territorial democracy."

Locke, in contrast, had been interpolated into the American founding by both liberals and conservatives, to a degree that was out of proportion to his actual influence. Kirk especially singled out philosophers John Rawls, the author of *A Theory of Justice*, and Robert Nozick, the author of *Anarchy, State, and Utopia*. "These writers, though disagreeing in much, both take as the fundamental premise of their whole argument John Locke's hypothesis of a 'state of nature' for mankind out of which arose the social contract." This was

96. Kirk, "Introduction," ix.
97. *RAO*, 293.
98. *RD*, 119–20.

the height of abstraction for Kirk, as he did not accept as a proper basis for decision an imaginary social contract that never existed and from which one could suppose a "social contract." Society was a contract, perhaps, but one joined first and foremost by sentiment, loyalty, and love, binding the generations in reciprocal rights and duties. In opposing Burke to Locke, Kirk contended, "In defense of social harmony, Burke appealed to what Locke had ignored: the love of neighbor and the sense of duty."[99] These things could not be supplied by rationalism, but only by the bonds of sentiment and imagination.

In several essays, Kirk explored the place of property in the constitutional system. Perhaps surprisingly, Kirk stated flatly that the Constitutional Convention of 1787 was motivated by economic necessity. Yet economics was not the sole criterion by which the founders judged their design for a constitutional order, and Kirk, following the constitutional principles of Burke, contended that economic prosperity alone does not maintain order.[100] In an essay on the economic interests of the founders, Kirk argued that although questions of property and economics were of great concern, they were not the only, or even the primary, motivation for the founders' crafting of the Constitution, even for the ones most interested in such questions. Similarly, Kirk, relying on the historian Forrest McDonald, found Charles Beard's economic interpretation of the Constitution incomplete, because it did not take into account the noneconomic motivations of the founders.

Kirk, although respectful of "property rights," did not think that a right to property (nor, indeed, any right) was absolute. To elevate the corporation as an intangible instrument for acquiring property and distributing wealth would lend legal support for institutionalized greed and concentrate power in the hands of a few, while pretending to "democratize" wealth through ownership of stock. Such rights need to be curtailed for the common good. Indeed, while generally supportive of the judicial protection of property before the New Deal, Kirk expressed concern that the focus on private property "reinforced the materialism and obsession with wealth" noted by Tocqueville and Brownson. Not that Kirk invariably opposed the

99. Ibid., 98, 102.
100. Ibid., 80. See Stephen B. Presser, "What Would Burke Think of Law and Economics?" 417; *RD*, 89–90, 84–85.

idea of a corporate person, so long as that "person" was understood in some sense as furthering the public good. He spoke approvingly, for example, of Disraeli's attempts to retain corporate representation in parliament after passage of the Reform Bill in 1832. He also approved of the important Supreme Court case of *Santa Clara County v. Southern Pacific Railroad*, which held that a corporation was a "person" within the meaning of the Fourteenth Amendment. However, Kirk never retreated from his position that corporate charters should remain subject to the control of the legislatures that grant them. Kirk even argued that the celebrated *Dartmouth College* case, which increased protections for corporations from state governments, was not to the contrary.[101]

Kirk instead advanced a more subtle argument based on an older understanding of corporate charters as privileges granted by the state rather than as bundles of private contracts. As Gregory Alexander, following the work of Carol Rose, noted, the early American understanding of property balanced between the notion of "property as commodity" and "property as propriety."[102] The former notion restricted property to its economic usefulness in a market context. The latter conception presumes a richer relationship between the ownership of property and the participation in the civic life of the nation. In his qualified respect for property, Kirk was at odds with the southern conservative thinker Richard Weaver, who contended that there was an "absolute" right to property. Indeed, Weaver thought that property was "the first metaphysical right" remaining in the world.[103] Although both in general were opposed to a society based solely on "invisible" property such as stocks, which separated individuals from actual possession, Kirk did not oppose all forms of expressing corporate property. Rather, Kirk understood property as "propriety," not in the sense of *proprietas* ("one's own") as used by Weaver, but rather in the sense of a flexible understanding that almost anything "owned" is recognized as such by law, custom, and tradition, and only insofar as it can contribute to the larger public good, and not in the sense of having a basis in a static metaphysics.

When circumstances warranted, Kirk approved of the modifica-

101. *RD*, 242–43, 131–32, 240, 219–20; *CM*, 131–32; *Dartmouth College v. Woodward*, 17 U.S. 518 (1819).

102. Alexander, *Commodity and Propriety: Competing Visions of Property in American Legal Thought, 1776–1910*.

103. Weaver, *Ideas Have Consequences*, 131; *RD*, 242.

tions the federal courts have applied from time to time to the rights of property, in light of changing population densities and living arrangements. On the other hand, however, when the modifications to property proceed too far, in the name of a vague "public interest," then the courts should step in to redress the balance, a step Kirk found the courts, in recent years, had been unwilling to take.[104] In particular, Kirk argued that "industrial firms" seeking profit have combined with persons who have an ideological interest in "reform" to deprive individuals of modest means of their property rights in the name of (for example) "urban renewal." However, there remained a frustrating ambiguity in his work at times as to which circumstances dictated which course of action.

The role of government in economic structure and development is a complex one, and one that extended beyond merely setting the "rules of the game" within which individuals would compete. The structure of the game itself in part determines its scope and the values it promotes. If legislatures intended to scrutinize more carefully the activities of corporations, or to condition granting corporate charters on provisions protecting the "public interest," there would obviously be a greater role for government in economic development. Indeed, Kirk stated bluntly that American economic prosperity "could not survive for a single year, without the protections extended by government at its several levels."[105] Ideally, however, that intervention would be countered by a judicial sensitivity to the rights of property, as well as to the maintenance of order.[106]

Conclusion

Determining the proper scope of relevant traditions is crucial in providing the basis for legitimate judicial or legislative decisions. From suggestions in his work, Kirk might have found an answer in the connection between federalism and the unwritten constitution. The states, presumably, will have more detailed traditions and customs upon which to draw—and localities even more so—than the nation as a whole, which may have to rely upon more abstract prin-

104. *RD*, 243, 247.
105. *PP*, 161.
106. Stephen M. Bainbridge, "Community and Statism: A Conservative Contractarian Critique of Progressive Corporate Law Scholarship."

ciples. When the two conflict, Kirk might have argued, the former should in most cases prevail, to protect the diversity of practice that was clearly part of the constitutional plan.

It is unlikely Kirk would have laid out any grand plan or general theory if his planned book on the law had been written. However, extrapolating from his existing work, there are clear continuities in his thinking. Kirk's reluctance to base political and legal change on abstract notions of "right" are as evident in 1976 as they are in 1993, and his reflections on the sources of the common law's strength can be traced as far back as the first edition of *The Roots of American Order*. Most of the changes are ones of emphasis. Kirk's focus in his discussions of law are concerned with the tension between abstract right and prudent action: Brownson and Seward, Burke and Hastings, Hitler and his assassins. This study of historical examples confirmed Kirk's innate wariness concerning the use of abstract principles and led him to consider natural law as either a poetic and a spiritual insight into the moral order, or else a carefully nuanced application of basic principles of justice to concrete problems.

Yet even with those caveats, Kirk's thought may provide the beginnings of an answer to Tushnet's low opinion of conservative legal thought, quoted in the epigraph to this chapter, and demonstrates that conservative thinking on the law might be very interesting indeed.[107] Contrary to its critics, conservative legal thought need not be rigidly doctrinaire nor oblivious to social change. Its reluctance to cede excessive power to any one authority, or to any group of persons within government who have the ability to enforce uniformity, allows the "jurisgenitive" nature of law to occur, so as to become an outgrowth of actual lived experience.

---

107. For an effort to trace the Burkean legacy in the American judiciary, see James G. Wilson, "Justice Diffused: A Comparison of Edmund Burke's Conservatism with the Views of Five Conservative Academic Judges."

5

Conservatism, Modernity, and the Postmodern

> Disintegration is the defining experience of the cul-
> ture of modernity.
>
> Roberto Unger, *Knowledge and Politics*.

An Alternative Conservative Genealogy

Postmodernism—its definitions, future, and possible merits—seems to have little to do with Kirk and his traditionalist conservatism. Further, it is, as Hans Bertens has written, an "exasperating term," which has been used to describe everything from high culture to low kitsch, from art to restaurants, from shopping malls to politics. But it nevertheless is a term not completely without meaning, and, as the foregoing chapters have tried to show, it can help. At its core, postmodernism takes as its starting point a dissatisfaction with modernity. "If there is a common denominator to all these postmodernisms, it is that of a crisis of representation: a deeply felt loss of faith in our ability to represent the real, in the widest sense. No matter whether they are aesthetic, epistemological, moral, or political in nature, the representations that we used to rely on can no longer be taken for granted." While the emergence of postmodernism has resulted in much trendy criticism and empty theorizing, Bertens sees positive consequences as well, not the least of which is a "return to history." Freed from the modern conception of progress, Bertens argues, postmodernists must return to the past "in order to illuminate the present."

Theodor Adorno and Max Horkheimer, in their influential book, *The Dialectic of Enlightenment,* define the essential nature of modernity for later postmodern thinkers: "For the Enlightenment, whatever does not conform to computation and utility is suspect."[1] Kirk himself defined the Enlightenment in a similar manner:

> The strong intellectual tendency towards doctrines of progress, rationality, secularism and political reform. . . . At the heart of the Enlightenment mentality was an enormous confidence in the reason of the individual human being. . . . If properly cultivated, every man's private rationality could emancipate him from the delusion of sin, from ways of violence and fraud, from confusion and fear. This dream ended in the French Revolution.

In his earlier works Kirk found a second Enlightenment in another set of thinkers, whom he favored: Burke, of course, but also Montesquieu, Hume, and Blackstone.[2] In later works, however, Kirk lessened his emphasis on this "other" Enlightenment and claimed that whatever his Enlightenment influences, Burke was in fact engaged in protecting "the Gothic edifice of European civilization" rather than primarily defending a tempered modernity. Ultimately, however, Kirk was less interested in describing a sharp shift between Enlightenment and pre- or post-Enlightenment thought than with outlining the characteristics of a "modern" outlook.

Chronologically, postmodernism emerged most prominently during the 1960s and 1970s as a response to a perceived collapse in modernism in the arts. Charles Jencks first used the term *postmodern* in this way in 1977. Later, in his 1982 work *Current Architecture,* he applied it to buildings, noting that a "post-modern building is double-coded—part Modern and part something else: vernacular, revivalist, local, commercial, metaphorical, or contextual." Such a "something else" has two presumed audiences: it speaks not only to

1. Bertens, *The Idea of the Postmodern: A History,* 3, 11; Joseph Natoli and Linda Hutcheon, eds., *A Postmodern Reader,* 25–71; Adorno and Horkheimer, *Dialectic of Enlightenment.* For a collection, see Andrew Arato and Eike Gebhardt, eds., *The Essential Frankfurt School Reader.*
    2. *RAO,* 349.

the elite, who understand the coded language of the building, but also to "the inhabitants, users, or passersby, who want only to understand and enjoy it." This postmodern perception was soon applied to philosophy and social and cultural theory, but it focused more on elites and decoding messages in social symbols to the detriment of postmodernism's larger social goals. New philosophic approaches—such as linguistic theory and structuralism—made postmodernism seem intellectually formidable, while political events, especially in France, supplied an external proof to the conviction that a world was ending.[3]

But is joining postmodernism with conservatism helpful in assessing whether Kirk speaks to contemporary conservatives? Conservative analyses have found the term useful, if at all, only as a "devil-term."[4] Postmodern thought, in any variety, is on the usual conservative view "a cultural contagion" that "destroys not only our cultural health but our ability even to perceive its decline."[5] For them, postmodernism has no diagnostic or empirical value; it is at best a noxious remnant of liberalism. Conservatism has already won the battle, politically at least, first against communism, then against liberalism. For these conservatives, the only remaining issues concern watching out for threats to the "totality of the project of conservative governance."[6]

Nor have liberal commentators on conservatism seen much of a connection. Standard interpretations of conservative thought have come in one of two varieties. Conservatism is considered either an ancillary support for liberalism or an unwelcome mutation caused by social stress. The first assessment is at least as old as Emerson, who wrote, "The cast which conservatism is set to defend, is the actual state of things, good and bad." Beyond a defense of the status quo, Emerson's formulation deprives conservatism of any substance. Karl Mannheim's essay "Conservative Thought" adds a layer of apparent sociological rigor to this opinion. In Mannheim's account, conservatism emerges only when confronted by massive

3. Jencks, *The Language of Post-Modern Architecture*; Gabardi, *Negotiating Postmodernism*, 4.

4. For example, see Kopff, *The Devil Knows Latin*, 115–25. Longer treatments are given in Peter A. Lawler, *Postmodernism Rightly Understood: The Return of Realism in American Thought*; and in Thomas Pangle, *The Ennobling of Democracy: The Challenge of the Postmodern Era*.

5. Arthur Pontynen, "Art, Science, and Postmodern Society," *American Outlook* (November/December 2000).

6. Editorial, "Conservatism at Century's End," 6.

social change. Specifically, "In a word—traditionalism can only become conservatism in a society in which change occurs through the medium of class conflict—in a class society. This is the sociological background of modern conservatism."[7] In a 1957 article, "Conservatism as an Ideology," Samuel P. Huntington took Mannheim one step further and identified a type of conservatism as *situational*, which is "that system of ideas employed to justify any established social order . . . against any fundamental challenge to its nature or being."[8] Huntington concluded that only the situational form of conservatism could have any lasting power. He found that a true conservatism appears "only when the challengers to . . . established institutions reject the fundamentals" of those institutions. Once the threat disappears, conservatism will as well, until the next "situation" brings it into existence again.

The second school of thought descends from Richard Hofstadter's characterization of conservatism as a "paranoid style." In *The Paranoid Style in American Politics*, published in 1965, Hofstadter famously described conservatives as afflicted with status anxiety. The "ultraconservatives" or, somewhat paradoxically, "pseudo-conservatives," he said, were animated by "a rather profound if largely unconscious hatred of our society and its ways" and characterized by a "restlessness, suspicion and fear."[9] In contrast to the Mannheim/Huntington model, which viewed conservatives as at best a necessary but temporary evil, Hofstadter's conservatives were dangerous to the social order.

Hofstadter's study is only the best known of a number of analyses from the 1960s that trace conservatism to an "authoritarian personality" that is inherently irrational. Contemporary reviews of *The Conservative Mind* echo this perception of conservatism. Gordon Lewis, for example, describes Kirk's "impassioned nostalgia for a dead society and a clever contempt for all the schools of political thought" other than his own. Conservatism is a sort of mental defect, hostile to the modern world and holding on to lost certainties as a psychological salve without any basis to do so. According to Harvey Wheeler, *The Conservative Mind* "soothes [the] pent-up injury, forlornness and frustration" for those conservatives left behind

<hr/>

7. Ralph Waldo Emerson, "The Conservative," 275.
8. Huntington, "Conservatism as an Ideology," 454–55.
9. Hofstadter, *The Paranoid Style in American Politics, and Other Essays*, 44–45.

by contemporary life. This strand of critique, too, continues today. One recent example is the 2003 Berkeley study that concludes that conservatism is associated with "fear and aggression," "dogmatism," and other negative traits. Rogers Smith, of Yale University, argues that the liberal interpretation of history should be replaced with "a multiple-traditions thesis." The figures who developed the conservative intellectual tradition since the Second World War go unnoticed. Instead, American nonliberal traditions are represented by the "Racial, nativist, and religious tensions [that] are also prominent in American life, as the [Patrick] Buchanan and [David] Duke campaigns, the Christian Coalition, the Los Angeles riots, the English-only agitation . . . [and] renewed patterns of racial segregation" purportedly show. Along with the radical left, such traditions are "so irreparably different and dangerous that they do not merit equal status in the political community." Although the title of Smith's essay implies that his analysis "goes beyond Hartz" and is separate from the Hartzian thesis, the assumption that liberalism somehow represents a mainstream tradition still inheres in his argument.[10]

But it was, in fact, a conservative, who was among the first even to use the term *postmodernism* as a description of an age emerging from the collapse of Enlightenment rationality. In 1926, an Episcopal priest named Bernard Iddings Bell published a slim volume of lectures entitled *Postmodernism and Other Essays*. As a young man, Kirk became friendly with Bell and credited him with providing "a direct opening to literary circles" for the young conservative.[11] Bell reviewed Kirk's books favorably and introduced Kirk to his friend Albert Jay Nock, a right-wing anarchist and living link to the Old Right whose thought Kirk would graft onto the Burkean tradition he was introducing to America in the 1950s and 1960s.

Bell was no trendy literature professor, however, but an active conservative polemicist. It is said, for example, that Bell left St. Stephens, where he was president, when the students stopped rising from their seats when the professor arrived. And Bell's classic analysis of mass society, *Crowd Culture*, remains a conservative must-read. In *Post-*

10. Lewis, "Metaphysics of Conservatism," 735; Wheeler, "Russell Kirk and the New Conservatism," 23; Kathleen Maclay, "Researchers Help Define What Makes a Political Conservative," http://www.berkeley.edu/news/media/releases/2003/07/22_politics.shtml; Smith, "Beyond Tocqueville, Myrdal, and Hartz: The Multiple Traditions in America," 549, 563.
11. *SI*, 170.

modernism, Bell laid out an early version of the critique of modernity that reappears in conservative polemics, including Kirk's, over the next half-century.

According to Bell, the modern age had gone astray by believing in the wrong things. After the Reformation, belief in a cultural whole called "Christendom" that personified universal values was no longer possible. The religious wars had left the Protestant West with two beliefs: the inerrancy of the Bible and the "sufficiency of the individual intellect." The Scripture scholarship of the eighteenth and nineteenth centuries, which applied historical and archaeological research to the Bible, destroyed what many believed was the inerrancy of the Bible's literal meaning. What remained was autonomous intellect. Bell phrased the challenge of modernity as follows:

> But every religious system, including Liberalism . . . must be based upon some assumption or other in which men can put their trust. Since the Modernist has no infallible Bible, to what can he turn, to what does he turn, as a basis for authority? He still has one faith, usually as yet undisturbed. Protestantism, as we have said, had two, faith in the infallible book, and faith in the competence of the individual intellect. The Modernist has lost the former of these, but not the latter. He still puts his trust in the sufficiency of his own mind.[12]

This confidence in the sufficiency of the individual mind coincided with the rise of science, through which the individual intellect could perceive the infallible laws of nature and divine the form and structure of the universe and, eventually, principles of society and moral conduct. An unerring mind met the mathematically precise rules of physical observation, and the book of nature became the new Bible. But science, as Bell shows, operates only within the frame of the physical and measurable; it cannot answer "why" anything is, which Bell takes to be the basic, philosophical question for society.

To answer this question, Bell called for a return to religion. This new evangelization would not be of the fundamentalist variety, nor mere credulity or fear of scientific hubris. Rather, in a postmodern world, "The time would seem to be at hand for a new school of religious aspirants, one in accord not with the prejudices of scientists of

12. Bell, *Postmodernism and Other Essays,* 9.

a generation ago, but rather consonant with the convictions of scientists today. Fundamentalism is hopelessly outdated. Modernism has ceased to be modern. We are ready for some sort of Postmodernism."[13] The six principles of this postmodern religious school are grounded in the Incarnation of Jesus Christ and a belief that reality cannot be completely known according to either the scientific principles of the twentieth century or the theological principles of the sixteenth. A reception to "miracles," or the mystery of existence, was needed.

Bell's critique of the limits of scientific knowledge speaks directly to Kirk's argument against "scientism." Scientism assumed that there were no limits to human knowledge, and that the absence of limits became an article of faith. Kirk found this overconfidence in scientific reasoning troubling and misleading. First, he contended that there was a "law for man and a law for thing." That is, scientific principles should be reserved for the subjects to which they were best suited: physical objects and processes. The moral and ethical and imaginative realms should be left to other thinkers. Like Bell, Kirk believed that science as it was understood by the general public and used in public affairs was different from that understood by the scientists themselves. "Only science rescued from the clutch of scientism, the pseudo-religion of latter-day positivists, can be animated by the moral imagination. Only scientists able to wonder at creation can emancipate us from the archaic clutch of mechanism and determinism."[14] Kirk contrasted this "wonder" with the rigid application of mechanical rules to natural, and later moral or social, phenomena. Not only were these rules inappropriate to nonscientific subjects, even contemporary science has rejected them.

This argument also accords in some ways with that proposed in the influential book, *The Postmodern Condition: A Report on Knowledge*, by Jean-François Lyotard, which asserts that postmodernism involves, in some sense, a "crisis of narratives."[15] Specifically, Lyotard contrasts a "scientific" with a "narrative" approach to knowledge and social institutions. A "metanarrative," in Lyotard's terminology, is a way in which existing social arrangements and institutions are

13. Ibid., 53–54.

14. Kirk, "Scientistic Ideology vs. Christian Realism," 396.

15. Lyotard, *The Postmodern Condition: A Report on Knowledge*, xxiii. In *The Postmodern Explained: Correspondence 1982–1985*, Lyotard modified his strong position on the role of narratives but remained convinced of their importance.

"legitimated," such as the Enlightenment reliance upon rationality to justify its epistemology and individualism. The two meta-narratives that are the focus of Lyotard's critique are the liberation of humanity, inspired by the French Revolution, and the theoretical unity of all knowledge in a systemic fashion, which was the goal of the Hegelian tradition of philosophy. The patterns of narrative knowledge allow a culture always to be reintegrating its past into its present. Lyotard summarizes this process as "a collectivity that takes narrative as its key form of competence has no need to remember its past. It finds the raw material for its social bond not only in the meaning of the narratives it recounts, but also in the act of reciting them. The narrative's referents may seem to belong to the past, but in reality it is always contemporaneous with the act of recitation.[16]

The philosopher José Ortega y Gasset, no postmodernist, made a similar point two decades earlier, when he contrasted "pure physico-mathematical reason" with "narrative reason." Narrative knowledge represents a way of thinking about the world that constantly reincorporates the past within itself, and which places the legitimacy of a practice on its being practiced in the past. Lyotard attributed the postmodern condition of doubt as a lament that "knowledge is no longer principally narrative."[17] This postmodern emphasis on narrative is analogous to the "participant history" Kirk learned from Lukacs and Eliot. Telling stories is in part how history becomes transformed into memory and tradition.

Scientific knowledge, on the other hand, introduces the notions of proof and falsifiability—that is, a proposition is not considered true unless it accords with scientifically imposed standards of truth. "The scientist questions the validity of narrative statements and concludes that they are never subject to argumentation or proof. He classifies them as belonging to a different mentality: savage, primitive, undeveloped, backward. . . . Narratives are fables, myths [and] legends" and are best discarded in a scientific society.[18] Thus, scientific knowledge becomes a narrative defined by the extension of scientific modes of thought into every area of human life. This understanding of scientific knowledge lends itself to harsh breaks with the

16. Lyotard, *Postmodern Condition*, 31–33, 22.
17. Ortega y Gasset, *History as a System*, 214; Lyotard, *Postmodern Condition*, 26. For a critique of Lyotard, see Connor, *Postmodernist Culture*, 27–43.
18. Lyotard, *Postmodern Condition*, 27.

past, when the "proofs" for an earlier worldview are shown to be incompatible with the scientific method. The most famous of these, perhaps, are the overthrow of the classical astronomy by Copernicus and Galileo and the move from Newtonian physics to the theory of relativity proposed by Einstein.

Since the Enlightenment, scientific knowledge has been accorded a privileged place, but the contemporary triumph of the scientific approach over competing forms of knowledge has come at great political and social cost. Liberation of humanity in the name of progress has too often been accompanied by terror and slaughter, and the quest for the unification of knowledge has led to the crushing of local stories and the peculiarities of history and geography. The assessment of all things by the standard of scientific reason divorced from other concerns was not an unalloyed good. As the historian Christopher Dawson noted in 1929, the modern fascination with reason was transformed during the period between Descartes and Spencer from a belief in the godlike powers of man to a conception of humanity locked in a Darwinian struggle. Reason became only an evolutionary accident: "Cartesian Reason, which had entered so triumphantly on its career of explaining nature and man to itself by its own unaided power, ended in a kind of rational suicide by explaining itself away." In the postwar years, however, unease over the dangers of an overreliance on scientific experts increased along with confidence in science's abilities, and its message of liberation from "superstition" began to sound hollow.[19]

Kirk thought what was being presented as scientific was actually only a debased and antiquated form of scientific reasoning, used as a prop for other ideologies and not "thick" enough to capture the imagination. "Scientism," he wrote, quoting the physicist and theologian Stanley Jaki, embraces the belief that "the empirico-quantitative method was the only reliable access to reality and truth." As a character in one of Canadian writer Robertson Davies's novels stated, science may have replaced religion, but it has "such a miserable vocabulary and a pallid pack of images to offer to us" that "its lack of symbol and metaphor and its zeal for abstraction drive mankind to a barren land of starved imagination." Moreover, scien-

19. Dawson, *Progress and Religion*, 22. For a good discussion of this topic, see Meredith Veldman, *Fantasy, the Bomb, and the Greening of Britain: Romantic Protest, 1945–1980*.

tism assumed that it was "value-free," especially in the social sciences. This was false, as Kirk stated in 1968, at around the same time the postmodernists were also critiquing a "hegemonic" Enlightenment science. "It would be well for scholars in the human sciences . . . to abandon the sterile notion of a 'value-free science.'" Such a pose served often only to hide ideological motives. Thus, for example, the "secularization thesis" of societal development once dominant in anthropology—but which has been criticized in recent anthropological scholarship—posits that societies progress from a simpler, cultural, and sophisticated religious stage to a more complex secular form as technology increases. Kirk's position was not in opposition to "objective" truth; rather, he sought to uncover the roots of the permanent things by removing the falsity that individuals could operate without belief.[20]

Kirk thought scientism used technology for ideological ends and that it replaced inquiry with manipulation.[21] Relying on the work of writers such as Arthur Koestler, as well as recent developments in physics and biology that have cast doubt on the mechanistic science of the nineteenth and early twentieth centuries, Kirk argued for a new science infused with imagination and belief in creativity. Kirk particularly liked to cite Koestler's book *The Roots of Coincidence: An Excursion into Parapsychology:*

> We have heard a whole chorus of Nobel Laureates in physics informing us that matter is dead, causality is dead, determinism is dead. If that is so, let us give them a decent burial, with a requiem of electronic music. It is time for us to draw the lessons from twentieth-century post-mechanistic science, and to get out of the straightjacket which nineteenth-century materialism imposed on our philosophical outlook.[22]

The materialist straightjacket denied the ability of the imagination to transform the physical into a conduit for an appreciation of mystery. Moreover, it was not even in accord with the contemporary science.

20. Kirk, "Scientistic Ideology," 392; Davies, *What's Bred in the Bone,* 16; Kirk, "Prospects for a Conservative Bent in the Human Sciences," 591; Rebecca R. French, "Lamas, Oracles, Channels, and the Law: Reconsidering Religion and Social Theory"; Beer, "Science Genuine and Corrupt," 28.

21. Kirk, "Can We Apprehend Science?" in *The Intemperate Professor,* 63–64.

22. Koestler, *The Roots of Coincidence: An Excursion into Parapsychology,* 138–39.

More recently, quantum physics and the new "chaos" theories have suggested new understandings of reality that are quite at variance with earlier scientific theories, which were inspired, in part, by the Enlightenment opposition to nonempirical reasoning. These new discoveries require an element of imagination to comprehend. As physicist Brian Green argued, physics is now learning that the basic elements of the universe may not be "solid" particles at all, but a singing chorus of oscillating "strings." And in biology, the combinations of genes and the environment are being unraveled in surprising ways. As early as 1931, Ortega y Gasset had identified a similar possibility in modern science. In *The Modern Theme*, Gasset lamented that modern "rationalism" had separated itself from historical existence, and he concluded, "The Cartesian paradox is the foundation of modern physics."[23] Ortega suggested that Einstein's relativity theory could become a way to overthrow the tyranny of reason while at the same time to preserve a concept of objective truth, through Einstein's understanding of perspective, which Ortega thought promised a much more modest and realistic view of rationality.

Many postmodernists took their cue from European Marxists or left-wing intellectuals, but other significant European thinking on the nature of modernity contributed to the formation of a conservative consciousness in America. For example, just after the Second World War, Romano Guardini published *The End of the Modern World*, which was influential among postwar conservatives, especially Catholics. Significantly, it was recently republished with a foreword by Father Richard John Neuhaus, the longtime editor of the journal *First Things*. Neuhaus's own book, *The Catholic Moment*, first published in 1987, bore the subtitle *The Paradox of the Church in the Postmodern World* and has had wide influence on the course of conservative public conversation in America, especially on the place of religion in the public sphere. Even earlier, in 1977, Neuhaus, along with coauthor sociologist Peter L. Berger, argued that the Enlightenment antagonism to "mediating structures" in favor of an abstract "geometry" of rights had been superceded by postmodernist em-

---

23. Green defines his "superstrings" as vibrating particles whose "sound" literally keeps the universe together (*The Elegant Universe* [New York: Norton: 1999]). See also James Shreeve, "Secrets of the Gene," *National Geographic* (October 1999), 41, 48; Ortega y Gasset, *The Modern Theme*, 33, 139–44.

phasis on "tribalism" or the smaller groupings (Burke's "little platoons") of which each individual is a part.[24]

Neuhaus notes that Guardini offers an alternative vision of the future, different from the ones proposed by the modern proponents of progress and the "premodern" conservatives. In a chapter titled "The Dissolution of the Modern World and the World Which Is to Come," Guardini finds three "elements" that are characteristic of the modern world. Each represents a departure from the classical and medieval world. These elements are "a Nature subsisting in itself; an autonomous personality of the human subject; and a culture self-created out of norms intrinsic to its own essence." Guardini distinguishes his analysis from "that cheap disposition which revels always in prophesying collapse or destruction" and from "a longing for a romantically envisioned Middle Ages or with an advance into a glorious utopia of the future." Anticipating a theme of later conservatives, Guardini instead argues that these new understandings of nature, self, and culture will have disastrous effects. He predicts that the future will present a stark choice between the individual merely melting away into the "collective mass," dominated by technology and sophisticated manipulation, or asserting individuality. He also laments the "loss of personality" and that "sense of uniqueness with which man had once viewed his own existence," a view that evokes the postmodern concern over the loss of personality. Or there will be conscious acceptance of the loss of true freedom in order to preserve "at least for a time," a core of existence.[25]

While not every American conservative would come to share Guardini's apocalyptic vision, *The End of the Modern World* fairly illustrates one consistent strand of conservative thought. Guardini joined Bell and others who recounted the collapse of their contemporary circumstances and speculated as to what the future might hold. In the 1930s, Dawson wrote of the "passing of the Liberal-capitalist order of the nineteenth-century" into a newer age whose focus would differ from modernity's materialist assumptions and its economic and political concentration of power. Even in the 1970s, when the postmodern critique in (and of) America began its rise to prominence, some conservatives welcomed it. Traditionalist Burke scholar Francis Canavan, S.J., who had greatly contributed to the re-

24. Guardini, *The End of the Modern World*, x.
25. Ibid., 50–51, 61–63.

vival of Burke as a conservative political figure, had kind words for Roberto Unger's *Knowledge and Politics,* a critical early postmodern critique of liberalism, calling it an "astonishing intellectual performance" that plumbed the root weaknesses of liberal thought. According to Canavan, Unger's work and Thomas A. Spragens's *The Irony of Liberal Reason* together constitute "the definitive critique of liberal rationalism." And Paul Gottfried identified a strain of postmodernism that he characterized as "basic" to the thought of the European New Right in its attacks on Continental liberalism.[26]

Robert Heineman, a political scientist and historian of conservative thought, summarizes the relationship this way:

> Like the traditional conservative, the postmodern thinker has serious doubts about the value of the rationalist Anglo-American tradition that undergirds much of social science. However, in rejecting this tradition, the postmodernist consciously tries to avoid any kind of totalizing ordered explanations of society, while the conservative searches for a broader, deeper concept of rationality that encompasses the actual behavior and beliefs of real people.[27]

Of course, this common suspicion of the "rationalist Anglo-American tradition" does not erase the differing assessments that that suspicion has aroused among postmodernists and conservative thinkers. Where some have found the connection a positive one—or at least worthy of note—others, such as Jürgen Habermas or Bernard Yack, think that both intellectual movements represent a step backward to a "reactionary" position opposed to the next step in the path of modernity.

The foregoing conservative subtext of postmodernism has been subsumed within conservatism for some four decades. When the debate over the future of modernity began to rage among liberals and the communitarians, therefore, some were quick to take note of the coincidence. James Boyle, in a lengthy critique of Robert Bork's *The Tempting of America,* notes that both premodern Burkean conservatism and postmodern thought present similar challenges to "the

26. Christopher Dawson, *Religion and the Modern State,* 153; Canavan, review of *The Irony of Liberal Reason,* 615–17; Canavan, "Knowledge and Politics," 432; Gottfried, *After Liberalism: Mass Democracy in the Managerial State,* 128–30.
    27. Heineman, *Authority and the Liberal Tradition: From Hobbes to Rorty,* 181.

tradition of liberal rationalism." The common elements of this tradition are, first, that facts are knowable by the use of reason, independent of any prejudice or bias; second, that all social institutions and practices can be judged by this standard and that those that fail to meet reason's criteria should be discarded; and third, that values, as opposed to facts, are subjective and personal and therefore can never be used to initiate policy for the society. Postmodernism and conservatism share a skepticism about the limits and powers of reason; a doubt about the "accuracy of political theories built around . . . a rights-holding individual divorced from culture, tradition, language and history"; and a stylistic approach that recreates tradition and history even as it employs them in argument. Bruce Pilbeam adds that conservative thinkers have found postmodernism's "deconstructed notion of the self" to be a fruitful source of reconstructing a "philosophy of modesty" that displaces a rights-bearing sovereign individual with a historically contingent person. Gary Gutting, for example, posits that one alternative to a revivified Enlightenment is a return to tradition, which he describes as the "reactionary" alternative.[28]

A new generation of conservative writers has begun to reinterpret some of the works of the central thinkers of modern conservatism in a postmodern direction, but as Pilbeam notes, the "link between postmodernism and the political right is largely one of implication rather than demonstrated celebration and adoption." David Walsh, in his *Guarded by Mystery: Meaning in a Postmodern Age* attempts to ground postmodern thought in a new understanding of the transcendent, which Walsh argued had been lost—but not rejected—by modernity. And Peter Augustine Lawler, in his recent book *Postmodernism Rightly Understood,* sets out a conservative postmodern tradition that he argues is fully in accord with the tradition of reasoning associated with St. Thomas Aquinas. Lawler concludes that there is a great deal in common among some conservative cultural critics, such as Walker Percy, and some harsh liberal critics of liberalism, such as Christopher Lasch, and postmodernism. Percy, the "stranger in the cosmos," wrote often about a modern world broken and emptied of meaning. Lasch wrote extensively on the false mean-

28. Boyle, "A Process of Denial: Bork and Post-Modern Conservatism," 263, and note 4; Pilbeam, *Conservatism in Crisis? Anglo-American Conservative Ideology after the Cold War,* 158; Gutting, *Pragmatic Liberalism and the Critique of Modernity,* 176.

ings modernity has used in an attempt to fill the emptiness: progress, scientism instead of science, and materialism rather than imagination.[29]

Lawler argues that the abandonment of all attempts to find meaning, such as that advocated by Richard Rorty, is not postmodernism, "rightly understood." In fact, such a position represents only a hypermodernism, "the exaggeration to the point of caricature of the modern impulse to self-creation." Rather, beginning with Tocqueville and continuing through studies of Fukuyama, Allan Bloom, Percy, and Lasch, Lawler sketches a postmodern position that bases its response to the failure of the modern project in a recognition of the limits of philosophy. Using Percy's work as a starting point, Lawler describes postmodernism "rightly understood" as a rejection of "modern rationalism or science, and to some extent rationalism simply, for their futile attempt to eradicate the mystery of being, particularly human being."[30] In contrast, much postmodern thought has committed the same error as the earlier modernists: as Steven Best and Douglas Kellner have noted, for example, most of the prominent postmodern theorists—especially Foucault—have in fact constructed "totalizing" theories as universal and abstract as those of the liberalism they thought to overturn. As Robert Kraynak has written in a recent review of Lawler's book, "conservative postmodernism is premodernism brought up to date." This reformulated conservative position would "show that conservatives need not view the demise of the Enlightenment as a catastrophe to be avoided at all costs," but as a new opportunity for conservative thought to address the remaining dilemmas brought on by modernity.[31]

The division between high and low culture is not as sharp in Kirk's work as some have thought. As a lover of the Gothic who wrote columns and fiction for a popular audience, he could not disdain the popular culture that he so enjoyed and that he sought to enrich. Indeed, through his ghost stories, columns, and other writings, Kirk communicated with and enjoyed all strata of society, as befitted a "bohemian tory." Nor was Kirk above playfully citing popular culture icons. The first quotation in his memoir, for example, is from the

---

29. Pilbeam, *Conservatism in Crisis?* 158. See, for example, Glenn Hughes, ed., *The Politics of the Soul: Eric Voegelin on Religious Experience.*

30. Lawler, *Postmodernism Rightly Understood,* 2, 109.

31. Best and Kellner, *Postmodern Theory: Critical Interrogations,* 280; Kraynak, "Peter Augustine Lawler's Conservative Postmodernism," 304, 305.

cartoon character Popeye, whose motto, "I am what I am," ironical-
ly evokes a modernist conception of the unencumbered self that Kirk
opposed.[32] Kirk "is who he is," as his memoirs make clear, in large
part because of the tradition he has made his own and the persons
and memories that shaped him.

This attitude influenced his conservatism. Conservatives should
endeavor to preserve the "folkways, traditions, and well-rooted beliefs and institutions" in which the majority of Americans participate," and which may be called popular or democratic culture, as
well as "that understanding of culture which champions the cultivation of mind and conscience," that is, high or "aristocratic" culture. Both are necessary and valuable: "it is not a question of conflict
between 'democratic' and 'aristocratic' modes of culture: as T. S Eliot
wrote, in the healthy culture of a people, the differing levels of culture flourish in symbiosis." Further, because the distance between
high and low is so small, the values of the former filter down to the
latter, which in turn contributes vitality and a ready audience. He described such "popular conservatives" as "practical, not very imaginative, patriotic, satisfied for the most part with American society,
traditional in morals, defensive of his family and his property, hopeful, ready for technological and material improvements but suspicious of political tinkering." The breakdown between "high" and
"low," or "popular," culture is another by-product of the postmodern rejection of modern standards of value, with the result that all
products of a culture can be legitimate objects of study.[33]

What Kirk disdained was vulgar culture: popular culture interpreted through the lens of the ideology of the self or of materialism
and transmitted through "somebody else's distant TV camera." With
actual products of the popular mind, such as folk songs or ghost stories, Kirk was more favorably disposed. The modern age had disrupted this natural interaction between high and low cultures
through the rise of a class of people whose skill lay in the manipulation of cultural symbols, but who did not participate in any real popular or "low" culture. Drawing largely on George Orwell, Kirk wrote
that this new class was made up for the most part of "bureaucrats,

---

32. *SI*, xii.

33. *PP*, 192–93, 152. Frederic Jameson, *The Cultural Turn: Selected Writings on
the Postmodern 1983–1998*, 2–3. See also Jameson's major work in this area, *Postmodernism, or, The Cultural Logic of Late Capitalism.*

scientists, technicians, trade-union organizers, publicity experts, sociologists, teachers, journalists, and professional politicians." It had been deprived of all traditional attachments to family, religion, or tradition. As a result, the members of this class were themselves at the mercy of the forces they attempted to control. This new class of administrators, bureaucrats, and functionaries, whether of the left or the right, had neglected the imagination. They were particularly creatures of their era: "produced by the ideas of the nineteenth and twentieth centuries: vulgarized Darwinism, socialism, vulgarized Freudianism, winds of doctrine of yesteryear."[34] In a vicious cycle, the bankrupt imagination of this "higher" class corrupted the more popular or democratic culture, which extinguished the partner that was needed for such a higher culture to flourish.

As Boyle notes, conservatives tend to be "stodgier in sentiment, and more reactionary in political vision" than postmodernists despite their shared characteristics.[35] Yet conservatives can adopt an appreciation of some of the cultural effects of postmodernism, which emphasize the importance Kirk placed on imagination, rhetoric, place, and sentiment. Here, it may be worthwhile to introduce Boyle's distinction between postmodernism as an "earnest epistemology," engaged in a critique of and response to certain themes arising out of modernity, and postmodernism as "arch cultural schtick" that he names "pomo," which is characterized by a much less serious attitude and is less worthy of serious attention. Literary theorist Terry Eagleton employs the word *postmodernity* to define "the more comprehensive, historical or philosophical term," which is a temporal term describing the "end of modernity" and the metanarratives of science, progress, and reason identified with modernity. "Postmodernism," on the other hand, is a "narrow, more cultural aesthetic term" that is simply the form of culture that corresponds to postmodernity.[36] A "pomo" culture, therefore, need not assume only the relativistic form it has up until now assumed. Following up on Lukacs's insight into the participant nature of history, conservative persons interjected into such a culture can change it.

34. *PP,* 153; *CM,* 468; *RT,* 305.

35. Boyle, "Process of Denial," note 4.

36. Boyle, "Anachronism of the Moral Sentiments? Integrity, Postmodernism, and Justice"; Terry Eagleton, *Literary Theory: An Introduction,* 200–201.

The Age of Discussion and the Age of Sentiments:
Kirk's Vision of Postmodernity

The false knowledge of scientism was only one form of modernity against which Kirk thought conservatism should contend. In *The
Conservative Mind*, Kirk identified no fewer than five schools that, in
different ways, manifest what he considered the modern outlook:
the rationalists; the romantic followers of Rousseau; the utilitarians
(whom Kirk almost invariably termed the "Benthamites"); positivists such as Comte and, later, Dewey; and the economic material-
ists of the Marxist school. These schools shared a conception of the
human person that stressed the perfectibility of humanity, held attitudes that ranged from disdain to contempt, and desired political or
social leveling in order to further an abstract principle.[37]

Kirk thought each of these schools demonstrated the same basic
flaw. Each subordinated, or eliminated entirely, the imaginative and
creative aspects of existence, including religious worship, to one abstract idea such as "utility" or "the class struggle." Such an outlook
could not capture the variegated modes of human conduct. For Bentham, Kirk reserved some of his best invective: "Totally deficient in
the higher imagination, unable to grasp the nature of either love or
hate, Bentham ignored spiritual aspirations in man; and, as if to balance the scale, he never spoke of sin." Kirk believed that the system
Bentham and the other utilitarians devised was empty at its core. It
would be filled by worse impulses than the efficiency and the (perhaps misunderstood) humanity Bentham sought to introduce into,
for example, legislation and penal reform. Echoing Burke, Kirk argued, "Utilitarians project long and costly vistas; but at the end of
every avenue, the Romantic spied the gallows."[38]

This was the nub of his conflict with fellow conservative Frank
Meyer. Kirk, because of his experiences as a conscript during World
War II, as an employee for a short time at the Ford automobile plant,
and later as a professor at a large and (to him) featureless university, had come to distrust large-scale planning of any sort. Therefore,
according to Kevin Smant, Kirk concluded, "Most attempts to devise
an integrated 'theory,' such as Meyer's, would result in rigid doctrinaire thinking, which must lead to utopianism and revolution."[39]

37. *CM*, 9–10.
38. Ibid., 115, 124.
39. Smant, *Principles and Heresies: Frank S. Meyer and the Shaping of the American Conservative Movement*, 105–6.

Meyer attempted to join the traditionalist and libertarian wings of conservatism on the basis of a strong commitment to individual liberty. In a long review of Kirk's then-recent books, Meyer argued that Kirk denigrated the individual in favor of a community and represented conservatism, albeit unintentionally, as an ally of collectivism and for the oppression of the individual.[40] Meyer found a "fundamental compatibility" between Kirk's work and liberalism, and he thought the conservative history outlined by Kirk a shaky foundation upon which to build conservative policies. Specifically, Meyer maintained that Kirk's weakness lay in his inability to connect the basic principles of conservative thought to second-order principles that could, through government institutions and "unceasing vigilance," protect those principles. While Meyer agreed with Kirk on according importance to the individual, he thought that Kirk never clearly defined a "second set of principles" that would defend this central idea. These secondary principles Meyer defined as the conclusions that "all value resides in the individual; all social institutions derive their value, and in fact, their very being, from individuals and are justified only to the extent that they serve the needs of individuals."[41] Not that Meyer fully discounted tradition or prescription. Rather, he sought to "fuse" the emphasis on individual liberty that he found central to the political history of the West with the conservative defense of tradition and prescription as defenses against arbitrary power over the individual.[42]

Meyer argued that Kirk held only one form of society acceptable to conservative principles, which Meyer caricatured as "a mixture of . . . eighteenth-century England and medieval Europe—or perhaps, more aptly, . . . Plato's republic with the philosopher-kings replaced by the squire and the vicar." Such a position replaces reason with tradition and prescription and enshrines "whatever is, is right" as the first principle of Kirk's political society. However much Kirk professes to favor individual freedom rather than oppression, what he truly desires is a form of "status society" more congenial to his principles. Thus, Kirk's thought, "stripped of its pretensions, is, sad to say, but another guise for the collectivist spirit of the age." The controversy between Kirk and Meyer continued for some years dur-

40. Meyer, "Collectivism Rebaptized," in *In Defense of Freedom and Related Essays*, 3. Biographical and other background information can be found in John East, *The American Conservative Movement: Philosophical Founders*, 69–104.

41. Meyer, "Collectivism Rebaptized," in *In Defense of Freedom*, 8.

42. See Ibid., 15–17.

ing the 1950s and 1960s. A celebrated exchange of articles published in *National Review* on the thought of John Stuart Mill perhaps best highlights their respective positions. Meyer defended Mill for his defense of the individual against the state and any other pressure to conform. Kirk responded that Mill spoke to an age that is past: "the world of liberal optimism and progress which was Mill's has been dissolving the whole of this century, and no philosopher seems more refuted by the great tendency of things than Mill."[43]

Kirk attacked those, such as John Dewey, who sought to reform society in accordance with an overarching master plan based on abstract conclusions about human conduct. The Columbia University educator, he wrote, was led astray by his belief in the perfection of humanity through the methods of science and a false "objectivity," which ends, according to Kirk, in "pusillanimity." The neglect of the subjective portions of personality, Kirk thought, led not to honest citizens or good men and women but rather to people "[l]acking belief, loyalty, and self-reliance, dependent upon an unattainable perfect objectivity, they are moved only by fad and fable, and are blown about by any wind of doctrine." Looking merely to making things "work," without regard to principle, Kirk wrote, created only unprincipled citizens, not a workable social system. As Jude Dougherty argued, Dewey's pragmatism tended to ignore history and inherited learning in preference for mechanical training and endless "change."[44] Kirk believed this approach toward education and civic life in fact ignored the sources of the democratic virtue Dewey wished to instill.

For Rousseau, Kirk had perhaps the least patience, seeing in him everything opposed to the principles of Burke: hatred of tradition, love of innovation, and exaltation of an invented morality.[45] Both Burke and Rousseau were, in their own way, "modern." Yet against the "era of abstraction" Burke put forth the principles of "experience, duty, old ties, social gradation, [and] the reign of law." Rousseau was the embodiment of the idyllic imagination. In some respects, the contest of the modern age has been between the heirs of Burke and those of Rousseau. Burke stands for the recognition of limits and openness to the transcendent; Rousseau embodies all those who sought limit-

---

43. Ibid., 11, 13. See Kirk, "Mill's 'On Liberty' Reconsidered," 23–24; Meyer, "In Defense of John Stuart Mill," 24, in *In Defense of Freedom*, 164.
44. *EPT*, 158–60; *PP*, 34; Dougherty, *Western Creed, Western Identity*, 81.
45. *CM*, 49–50; 100–101.

less emancipation and the rejection of the past. Kirk saw Rousseau hidden in other figures: "the romantic gaze of Jean Jacques darts out, at intervals, from a variety of masks—the flushed face of Paine, the grim brow of Marx, the pedantic countenance of John Dewey."[46] Kirk found the disdain for the past and the preference for a constructed society to be the common denominator of these descendants of Rousseau.

In opposition to the destructive impulses Kirk saw unleashed by these proponents of liberation, Kirk appealed to those "Obdurate Adversaries of Modernity" who had diagnosed the modern dilemma as its aspiration to "universal domination." In an article outlining his reasons for founding the journal *Modern Age*, Kirk mentioned three writers—none of whom was American—who inspired his thinking about modernity in the 1950s. They were the "French peasant-philosopher" Gustave Thibon, psychologist Charles Baudouin, and the Swiss philosopher Max Picard. These writers uniformly opposed modernity, which for them (and for Kirk) meant "standardization, centralization, effacing of custom and convention, popular shoddiness," and, more generally, the rejection of the past and of religious faith.[47] The now-forgotten Baudouin, for example, was the author of *The Myth of Modernity*, which Kirk specifically identified in his essay. In the course of a chapter defending "eloquence," Baudouin demolished the false objectivity of the modern world:

> There are facts, no doubt; facts, facts, and again facts (or at least, what one has agreed to give the *name* of facts!). . . . To believe what we see is a view of reality is a naivete of which only "modern man" is capable. In short, although they repudiate the superstition of the word, our contemporaries accept without flinching the superstition of the fact, which is no less deceptive.[48]

Kirk had great hope for his journal in the waning years of modernity: "If during the twenty-first century civilization enters upon an imaginative Post-Modern era (rather than a Post-Christian era), *Modern Age* may be remembered for the seed it sowed in lonely fields."[49] By 1987, when this essay was written, Kirk's thought had

46. *EB*, 8–9.
47. Kirk, "Obdurate Adversaries of Modernity," 204.
48. Baudouin, *The Myth of Modernity*, 82
49. Kirk, "Obdurate Adversaries," 203.

developed from its Burkean and Babbittian beginnings. Although McDonald rightly emphasized the importance of Babbitt in Kirk's thought, in his later years Kirk had departed from (if he had ever fully held) the ethical dualism that characterized Babbitt's thinking. For example, Kirk's Christian concept of man's fallen nature and the need for grace is not exactly the same as Babbitt's inner check. The latter has no theological resonance, and Kirk recognized the small but crucial gap, between Babbitt and the rest of the conservative tradition even as early as *The Conservative Mind.* Babbitt, he argued, tried to repair the damage of Rousseau by reasserting ethical standards and the concept of "will." Babbitt did not go as far as his friend and collaborator Paul Elmer More did to associate those standards with the teachings of religion. "He stops short of Burke, therefore, and Hooker, and the Schoolmen," each of whom embraced religious faith as the underpinning of their ethics; and indeed, Babbitt stopped short for Kirk as well.[50]

Significantly, in an early essay, "The Dissolution of Liberalism," Kirk concluded that liberalism was moribund from the beginning "for lack of a higher imagination." Because it didn't have any real narrative power, it could not maintain a hold on the popular imagination for long; liberalism soon "ceased to signify anything, even among its most sincere partisans, [other] than a vague good will."[51] Although written in the 1950s, Kirk's essay anticipated the subsequent scholarly arguments over the content and future of liberalism. Kirk examined the dissolution of the modern age in two prescient essays, one on "the Age of Discussion" and one on "the Age of Sentiments."[52] The Age of Discussion was dominated by the word, by rational argument that ultimately tired of itself. The endless "modernist fatigued and pointless discussion[s]" dictated by outmoded understandings of rationality will, Kirk thought, give way to the Age of Sentiments, which would be dominated by the image.

The Age of Discussion began in the mid-nineteenth century; the phrase itself Kirk borrowed from the English journalist Walter Bagehot. Kirk wrote that he "understood well that during the nineteenth century the old order of things was being effaced—swept away by the nineteenth-century triumph of what Bagehot called Discussion."

50. *CM,* 431.
51. *EPT,* 33, 40.
52. *BDA,* 43; *Wise Men,* 111.

Discussion created democracy, as it did liberalism. Both revolve around the premise that through discourse based on rational principles, social and moral problems could be resolved. Both are based in the same understanding of reason. Discussion emerged with the age of the great eighteenth-century journals of opinion. The Age of Sentiments began with television:

> Into the Age of Sentiments there will survive some serious periodicals, and some decent books, and here and there obscure corners where a few people earnestly discuss some matters that cannot well be swept into oblivion. Yet this remnant of genuine thinkers and talkers may be very small. The immense majority of human beings will *feel* with the projected images they behold upon the television screen; and in those viewers that screen will rouse *sentiments* rather than reflections. Waves of emotion will sweep back and forth, so long as the Age of Sentiments endures. And whether those emotions are low or high must depend upon the folk who determine the tone and temper of television programming.

Kirk admired the old British periodicals, and he was no lover of the Age of Sentiments, but he did not despair over its arrival: "For the most part, the Age of Discussion was an age of shams and posturings."[53] Like its fruit, liberalism, the Age of Discussion lacked "vitality": mired in abstractions, it failed to move hearts. Even Eliot's *Criterion*, closest to Kirk's own cultural attitudes, was a failed defense of Discussion.

Daniel Boorstin, in his book, *The Image*, first published in 1961, contended that in modern America the "language of images is everywhere."[54] Boorstin's book was published just after what was perhaps the most famous presidential debate of the twentieth century, between Richard Nixon and John F. Kennedy. Nixon, by the usual accounts, did not come across well on television but performed better to those who tuned in by radio, and the debate was used to illustrate the emerging power of images and image creation of language. At the same time, media critics such as Marshall McLuhan were discussing the end of the modern age, defined by writing and printing, and the emergence of a new "media" age in the "global village."

53. *RT*, 128–29, 134, 136 (original emphases).
54. Boorstin, *The Image: A Guide to Pseudo-Events in America*, 183.

Kirk was similarly concerned with imagery, which he characterized as "the formation of images by art; a type of general likeness; a
similitude; a descriptive representation; an exhibition of ideal images to the mind; figurative illustration," or more generally, "the formation of images in the mind."[55] Imagery is a central component to
the creation of the individual and society. The process is two-sided.
Images, as the postmodernists never tire of saying, are endlessly presented to individuals, to be emulated, rejected, or repeated. Baudouin argued, "They do not see that even the photograph, the film,
the number, are always merely tokens, just as words are tokens: of
whatever kind is arbitrary, in so far as the moments of reality which
have entered into the texture of the token have been arbitrarily chosen from a multiplicity of others." The danger lay in the creation of
false images, what Boorstin characterized as "pseudo-events."

Kirk was cautiously hopeful that this new age of sentiments and
images would be more amenable to conservative thought than the
last. He believed that "conservatism is sustained by a body of sentiments," albeit of a different sort than those nourished by modernity.[56] However, just as discussions are in danger of degenerating into
empty talk, so too sentiments are threatened by a lapse into shallow
posturing or what Alasdair MacIntyre called "emotivism."[57] Vigen
Guroian commented that for Kirk, sentiment is not the same as emotions or feeling. Rather, Kirk "set out to understand the Age of Sentiments in order to refurbish a moral imagination that might transform and elevate it."[58] To do that returns us to the importance of
images, which for Kirk meant whether the images were true or false.

Both Boorstin and Kirk saw in the proliferation of new media the
increased chance that images will be packaged and presented to a
gullible public without that critical process of discrimination and
judgment being encouraged or engaged. Boorstin stated that the
process of image creation in a modern society is essentially a passive
and synthetic one, that is, the image (of a company, a product, or a
person) is constructed deliberately with a purpose and to encompass
only a limited range of qualities—perhaps even only one quality.
Further the image is passive, in that the "consumer of the image . . .
is also somehow supposed to fit into it."[59]

55. Kirk, "Perishing for Want of Imagery," 9, 10.
56. Kirk, "Preface," in Filler, ed., *Dictionary of American Conservatism*, 6.
57. MacIntyre, *After Virtue*, 11–12.
58. Guroian, *Rallying the Really Permanent Things*, 77.
59. Boorstin, *Image*, 188.

This problem of images, and image creation, has also occupied much postmodern criticism. Because postmodernism is, in one sense, concerned with the production and endless reproduction of cultural symbols, not only in art but in more commonplace forms such as shopping malls and amusement parks, postmodern critics often examine images that have no content in themselves but are only "the shadows we make of other shadows." Kirk similarly argues that "the image often betrays."[60] In other words, the constant array of images provides only superficial form and no substance; it is bereft of real imagination. For Kirk, however, this was not the only path the Age of Sentiments might take. Conservative rhetoric, which was at its best imaginative, could also be suitable for this new age.

In the recovered tradition of Burke and others, there could be found another manner of imagery and image making, which (like its counterpart) evoked sentiment and emotion, but for a different purpose and to different effect. Thus the Age of Sentiments need not be one of unbridled emotionalism, without tradition or authority. As Kirk noted, the Age of Discussion was reserved only for a few; most were content to follow "the doctrines of one faction or another." Sentiments of honor and duty are just as possible as the sentiments espoused by narcissism or materialism. Indeed, "an age moved by high sentiments can be more admirable than an age mired in desiccated discussions."[61]

In light of this sensitivity to the power of images, other traces of a postmodern sensibility appear in Kirk's work. In an essay written for the *National Review* in 1968, Kirk praised "The Pleasures of Williamsburg."[62] In particular, Kirk applauded the reconstruction of the buildings, "painstakingly restored," as a work of "genuine renewal." Similarly, Kirk commended in his memoirs Henry Ford's recreation of artifacts at Greenfield Village, which would otherwise have been destroyed by the mass-production order he had helped inaugurate. Yet sites such as these are problematic from a traditional conservative perspective. These monuments to long-lost worlds are examples of the postmodern clash of symbols and the injection of a modern commercialism into the past. At best, they are reconstructions that interject, by necessity, suppositions about their construction and so are just as much about the present as they are about

60. Ibid., 183; Kirk, "Rediscovery of Mystery," 2.
61. *RT,* 137, 140.
62. Kirk, "The Pleasures of Williamsburg," 860.

the past. Like Baudrillard's "simulacra," these preservation efforts are a representation of reality (even of the reality of the past), rather than reality itself. Kirk seemed to have realized this difficulty, at least in his case of Ford as an antiquary. After all, Ford was responsible, as Kirk recognized, for destroying much of what he had transplanted to his perfect village. Kirk considered them more like imaginative creations rather than accurate representations of a living tradition. Seen from this perspective, the "authentic" re-creations resemble the modern sense of loss more than a return to a premodern tradition.

Kirk's antipathy toward modernity, and his cautious hopefulness toward its end, is of course not the only conservative attitude. Most famously, perhaps, Francis Fukuyama's book, *The End of History*, argues that history itself had reached its end in the form of democratic capitalism. Some conservatives have embraced modernity. Gregory Wolfe, a critic and editor of the arts journal *Image*, for example, has also offered a conservative defense of modernism.[63] While respectful of Kirk, Wolfe ultimately believes Kirk and other conservatives jettisoned modern culture wholesale and retreated from what that culture had to offer, using Eliot as an example.[64] Neoconservative sociologist Peter Berger has opposed "modern" conservatives seeking to defend modernity against the "premodern" conservatives who do not accept modernity. Indeed, one of the early neoconservative influences, Daniel Bell, has argued, as early as 1976, that postmodernism was merely the death-gasp of a modernism at its end: a "porno-pop culture" that is simply destructive.[65]

Two important contributions to this debate have been made by conservative philosophers Roger Scruton and John Kekes, who employ a high level of abstraction to defend their conservative vision. Neither opposes modernity as much as Kirk, and neither Kekes nor Scruton emphasizes religious belief as a component of their conservatism. In books such as *The Meaning of Conservatism*, and the more recent *The West and the Rest*, Scruton tries to lay a foundation for conservative thought by marrying the Enlightenment conception of the nation-state with the Burkean prepolitical loyalties and the recognition of the importance of community and tradition. Kekes, for his part, presents in his *A Case for Conservatism* an "attempt to articulate

63. Wolfe, "Beauty Will Save the World," 31.
64. Wolfe, "I Was a Teenage Conservative," 12.
65. Paul Gottfried, *The Search for Historical Meaning: Hegel and the Postwar American Right*, 119; Bell, *The Cultural Contradictions of Capitalism*, 51.

the basic beliefs of conservatism," to "show that they are true and defend them against criticism" from proponents of "The Enlightenment Faith," which he describes as one of "groundless optimism that substitutes wishes for facts, refuses to face reality, ignores history, and radiates a moralistic fervor that leads the faithful to treat disagreement as a sign of immorality."[66] Both Kekes and Scruton, unlike Kirk, are at home with using modern philosophy to support conservatism.

Like some conservatives, some liberal commentators dismiss the rise of postmodernism as merely another phase of modernity. In his recent book, *The Fetishism of Modernities,* Bernard Yack argues that only a certain form of modernity is ending (or has ended), a form that he contends had held to "the illusion that there are specific forms of cultural and political life that express or complete the distinctive achievements of modern science, technology, and industrial production." Rather than signaling the end of modernity, the transformation to a "post industrial" or postmodern society, in fact, according to Yack, follows from modern principles and is itself a modern phenomenon. Gutting echoes this conclusion by stating, "The postmodern is an impulse of modernity itself."[67]

Kirk was generally less sanguine than Yack about the compatibility of nonmodern forms of life in the modern world. Although aware of their literary and artistic associations, Kirk thought that "modernity" and "modernism" were more often employed as political weapons, on behalf of those who sought to elevate (or, in the postmodern parlance, "privilege") certain ideas over others. Kirk contended that modernity or, more specifically, the modern outlook "is not confined to any especial party, faction, or class; rather it is a cast of mind and character." As a cast of mind, the relevant intellectual characteristics of modernity could arise anywhere, at any time, though they assumed particular cultural and political importance beginning with the end of the eighteenth century. The characteristics Kirk identified as constituent parts of the modern outlook included "neoterism on principle; preference for change over permanence; exaltation of the present era over all previous epochs; hearty approval of material ag-

66. Scruton, *Meaning of Conservatism,* and *The West and the Rest: Globalization and the Terrorist Threat;* Kekes, *A Case for Conservatism,* 3, 211; and his *Against Liberalism.*

67. Yack, *Fetishism of Modernities,* 139, 77; Gutting, *Pragmatic Liberalism,* 176. See also Alex Callinicos, *Against Postmodernism.*

grandizement and relative indifference toward a moral order; positive hostility, often, toward, theism."[68] In these features, Kirk found the modern age to be an heir to the thought of both the positivists and the utilitarians.

For the postmodern, the very idea of periodizing is a holdover from the modernist desire to control reality and bring it under a system by rationalization. Kirk never fully embraced this distinction between premodern and modern, which was adopted by other thinkers (including some of his fellow conservatives), if only because such periodization too often implied a perpetual moving forward to a terrestrial paradise, something Kirk thought impossible. He was writing in the 1950s, against the social planners, that "To think that society can really be reformed by any grandiose program of positive legislation or expenditure of money is itself the grossest of utopian delusions. There is no Grand Design to remedy the ills of the twentieth century—a disappointing statement, perhaps, but ineluctable."[69] Kirk's conclusion then is fully compatible with the postmodern reluctance to condone "metanarratives," precisely because he does not see the two as inextricably linked.

Toward a "Postmodern Conservatism"

The possible connections between these suggestions in Kirk's conservatism and postmodernism are more than a simple enemy-of-my-enemy stance toward liberalism. Given Kirk's dislike for theory of all sorts, postmodern literature, which was heavily influenced by Continental literary theory and Marxism, would not have appealed to him. And Kirk clearly would have rejected the conclusion of most postmodern thinkers that the end of Enlightenment has signaled the need for "radical" political commitments. However, those obvious differences do not by themselves mean that conservatism and postmodernism, a priori, are incompatible. As early as 1982, in an essay for the *National Review*, Kirk suggested that "the Post-Modern imagination stands ready to be captured. And the seemingly novel ideas and sentiments and modes may turn out, after all, to be received truths and institutions, well known to surviving conservatives."

68. *SI*, 192.
69. *BDA*, 185.

With liberalism moribund, it "may be the conservative imagination which is to guide the Post-Modern Age." In the caricatured placidity of the 1950s, Kirk saw disruptions:

> We live, then, in an insecure society, doubtful of its future, an island of comparative but perilous sanctuary in a sea of revolution; and neither the old isolation nor the old received opinions of the mass of men seem likely to hold against the physical force of revolutionary powers and the moral innovations of moral ideologies. This is just such a time as commonly has required and produced, in the course of history, a re-examination of first principles and a considered political philosophy.

Kirk, too, addressed what Bertens called the crisis of representation. How do we perceive the real? As we have seen, Kirk concluded that modern thought was unable to address humanity's deepest longings or to present those longings in a way that was palatable or even comprehensible to most people. Liberalism, as a political or social system, failed because it could not sustain the affections, and it could not sustain the affections because it lacked the capacity to connect individuals to the permanent things. According to Kirk, the imagination, in its various forms, remedied this lack of appeal to the sentiments. The study of history at its best could uncover "the real meanings . . . about the framework of the Logos, if you will: about the significance of human existence: about the splendor and misery of our condition." Literature, especially poetry and myth, provide a path from the fragmented modern world to the permanent things. Kirk's affection for the Gothic tale aptly expresses this conviction: he wrote that such stories "can disclose aspects of human conduct and human longing to which the positivistic psychologist has blinded himself." The great works of literature are not mere pat tales used to reinforce small truths; rather, they "teach human beings their true nature, their dignity, and their rightful place in the scheme of things."[70] Even politics, though at a greater remove, has the task of retaining a view of the "eternal contract" of society through the daily compromises and electioneering. Indeed, all aspects through

70. Kirk, "Conservatism: A Succinct Description," 1080–84, 1104; *BDA*, 18; *RT*, 102; Kirk, "A Cautionary Note on the Ghostly Tale," in *Watchers at the Strait Gate*, x; *EPT*, 41.

which Kirk thought the moral imagination could be employed serve to represent the truth to a bent world.

Kirk shared Lyotard's sensitivity toward the importance and structure of narratives. The scientific approach to human life, when transferred beyond its appropriate sphere, Kirk derided as "defeated rationality." Indeed, in addition to Lyotard, other postmodern or "critical" theorists expressed an appreciation for modes of experiences, such as that in tradition, valued by Kirk. Hans-Georg Gadamer, for example, criticized the modern approach to tradition, in which a person looking at tradition "detaches himself from the continuing action of tradition in which he himself has his historical reality." This approach "flattens" our understanding of tradition. Rather, Gadamer saw tradition as relational, in that a person must maintain "a living relationship to tradition" to understand it fully. In a phrase that could have been lifted from Kirk, Gadamer wrote, "To stand within a tradition does not limit the freedom of knowledge but makes it possible."[71] As Daniel Ritchie noted in a perceptive review of a Burke biography, the Irish statesman shared this understanding of tradition with Gadamer, as did Kirk. Against the revolutionary view of self as an entity abstracted from tradition, for Gadamer as well as for Burke, one always acts from within a "hermeneutical circle," defined by community and tradition.[72] Tradition does not sit outside the individual, as an object of study, nor does it act, as an impersonal force, on passive individuals. To understand tradition, one must enter into it; a process of engagement takes effort. And in understanding that tradition, because it is filtered through an individual consciousness, the tradition itself will be changed.

In line with their critique of modern science, some postmodern writers have concluded that the advances in technology have caused the "end of style, in the sense of the unique and personal." Because individuals now have equal access to almost every conceivable combination of styles and traditions, postmodernists argue that the notion of a "self" that is different from other selves is impossible; all are choosing from the same supermarket of "goods," which are readily available to all. Because of their position that the easy and potentially limitless replication and physical movement of cultural objects has

71. Gadamer, *Truth and Method*, 322–24.
72. Ritchie, "Remembrance of Things Past: Edmund Burke, the Enlightenment, and Postmodernity," 21, 24.

unmoored traditions from their geographic and emotional roots, postmodernists have been fascinated with the interplay of the cultural objects and symbols they continually rework and jumble together. This could mean the end of history, understood as a comprehensible chain of events linking one generation to the next. David Hoeveler, interpreting Frederic Jameson's Marxist-influenced account, asserts, "The experience of history under postmodern conditions loses its depth and feel, becomes ephemerality."[73]

Others draw a different conclusion. Linda Hutcheon has found that this "presence of the past" is one of postmodernism's most important components.[74] Objects of art, for example, cannot be separated from their history and context, nor can their meaning be separated from those who are interpreting them. Even jumbled together, cultural objects retain their residual connections, despite being organized in new ways. There can be no true individualism because every choice is already present; any selection, therefore, involves an element of self-parody.

Such a view does not comport with the strong strain of individualism present in Kirk, and the postmodern ennui about "originality" does not fit with either his optimism or his belief in free will. Kirk himself was an amalgam of different traditions—a Puritan and a Catholic, a midwesterner and a Scot, an American who built himself an Italianate home in the rural woodlands of Michigan. Part of his work was intended to demonstrate how one could reclaim a particular tradition and make it one's own. Kirk argued that Eliot, for example, smashed the nineteenth-century literary world with a perspective that reconstituted tradition even while upholding it. Like Orestes Brownson, he was engaged in an act of recovery as well as creation.[75] Seen in this light, the Italianate house Kirk built for himself in the Michigan woodlands is not mere eccentricity; it represents exactly that kind of jarring juxtaposition that brings the tradition into a new light.

The foregoing chapters have explained the bases of Kirk's opposition to modernity, which rested in part in his opposition to "defecated rationality." The conservative position Kirk adopted from

73. Jameson, *Postmodernism*, 15; Hoeveler. *The Postmodernist Turn*, 175.
74. Natoli and Hutcheon, eds., *A Postmodern Reader*, 244.
75. Robert A. Herrera has commented on Brownson's efforts to reconcile the disparate elements in his background in his *Orestes Brownson: Sign of Contradiction*, 190–91.

Burke and Eliot was grounded in the belief that imagery, narrative, and metaphor are central to society. The conservative function is to preserve them, in their various forms, before any considerations of policy. Conservatism, in Muller's phrase, is constantly presented with a Burkean "choice of inheritance": "conservation of the institutional legacy of the past inevitably involves a selection from among existing traditions and legacies. Conservative theory . . . cannot be applied without judgment."[76] That judgment and process of selection, which Kirk would have called prudence, is enshrined as much in the romantic and literary tradition of conservatism as it is in any other. In using the tradition he found exemplified by the figures he discussed in *The Conservative Mind*, Kirk thought that the criteria for judgment could be derived from the application of imagination to that tradition.

Mark Lilla has illustrated the importance of imagination and rhetoric in his analysis of the liberal and conservative "reactions" in the postwar era. Lilla contrasts the revolution known as the sixties with the Reagan Revolution of the 1980s. Both have assumed dramatic importance in American life:

> These revolutions are quite real, but to the extent that they have become symbols that excite or dull the political imagination they are also imaginary. The cultural revolution has become the predominant imaginative symbol on the American right, fueling a form of cultural reaction; the Reagan revolution has become the corresponding symbol of the left, generating a political-economic form of reaction. The cultural revolution has become the predominant symbol on the American right . . . the Reagan revolution has become the corresponding symbol on the left.[77]

It is important to note that for Lilla, whatever events actually occurred during these revolutions, their *imaginative* importance far outweighs the facts themselves. The rhetorical advantage each of these revolutions has for its opponent has superseded the events themselves.

More strikingly, Lilla posits that "the most surprising phenomenon in postwar American politics [is] that the cultural and Reagan revolutions took place within a single generation, and have proved

76. Muller, ed., *Conservatism*, 31.
77. Lilla, "A Tale of Two Reactions."

to be complementary, not contradictory events." The economic reductionism of the 1980s, in other words, has been comfortably combined with the "lifestyle" revolution that replaced respect for what were considered to be traditional values in the 1960s and 1970s. The combination represents both sides of a "pop Cartesianism" that the Catholic novelist Walker Percy thought constituted the American character. Similarly, left-wing critics such as Thomas Frank and David Rieff, in differing contexts, have noted the compatibility of a right-wing capitalism with left-wing social reforms.[78] This may be liberalism's final mutation, in which the language of personal autonomy combines with those of economic individualism to induce a form Kirk would recognize as the "idyllic imagination."

The renewed emphasis on the power of rhetoric and imagery puts into perspective the anomaly of conservatism in a modern age. Once what Kirk called "the cake of custom" is broken, the conservative loses the ability merely to preserve or rest unreflectively on tradition. Instead, the conservative must formulate a defense to the traditions being dissolved. However, "in becoming self-conscious, he has set himself apart from things. The reasons that he observes for sustaining the myths of society are reasons that he cannot propagate; to propagate his reasons is to instill the world with doubt. Having struggled for articulacy, he must remain silent." Bernard Crick, in a review of *The Conservative Mind,* saw this difficulty five decades ago. Crick thought that Kirk was in an intellectual quandary, because "Having no significant conservative tradition, Americans are put to the unconservative task of inventing one."[79] But invention need not be antithetical to conservatism. From his studies of Burke, Disraeli, Eliot, and others, Kirk believed that tradition always partakes of invention. Facts have no life of their own: it is imagination that makes tradition from history. The narrative of conservative figures he composed was itself an embodiment of the imagination that became the touchstone of his conservatism.

This is Kirk's answer to what both Roger Scruton and Eugene Genovese have found to be the unique dilemma for conservatives. In Genovese's words, "Thoughtful conservatives know that they

78. See Frank, *The Conquest of Cool;* and Rieff, "Multiculturalism's Silent Partner," 62.

79. Scruton, *Meaning of Conservatism,* 191; Crick, "The Strange Quest for an American Conservatism," 359, 365. See also Samuel P. Huntington, "Conservatism as an Ideology," 471–72.

plunge into difficulty whenever they become aware of themselves as conservative." To defend what they thought was worth conserving, conservatives believe that they have to engage liberalism on its own terms, in a "dialectic" mode that presupposes a "collective of propositions, a logic" that is foreign to the rhetorical, didactic, and imaginative modes more amenable to conservative expression.[80] Scruton, for his part, believes that the problem this poses for conservatism, more than other intellectual attitudes, may be "insoluble":

> But the conservative who has risen above the fragments of his inheritance and reflected on the desolation that has been wrought in it cannot return to an innocence which his own thinking has destroyed. . . . He knows what he wants, and he knows the social order that would correspond to it. But in becoming self-conscious he has set himself apart from things. The reasons that he observes for sustaining the myths of society are reasons which he cannot propagate; to propagate his reasons is to instill the world with doubt.[81]

This result, according to James Kalb, has failed to produce any significant defense of conservative thought. Instead, conservatism cannot even present its positions in a persuasive way because conservatives "cannot even talk . . . in language very different from that of triumphant liberalism."[82] Once conservatism concedes in this way, it has no choice but to become either the Huntington situational conservative, defending liberalism, or a reactionary, lamenting a lost (and perhaps nonexistent) world.

Scruton's and Genovese's critiques address head-on the failure of most conservative thinking to endure without appearing to be just like liberalism. Kirk, however, seemed to be trying to overcome that difficulty of articulateness by wrapping his arguments in a protective covering of narrative imagination. To state outright the traditions one wishes to preserve, and the means to do so, succumbs to the dialectical temptation. To cast the same lessons through stories and autobiography leaves enough room for rhetorical life. Rejecting the "dialectical" mode of modern discourse, Kirk found refuge in the

---

80. See Genovese, *The Southern Tradition: The Achievement and Limitations of an American Conservatism*, 20–22, for further discussion in the context of the writers Allen Tate, Weaver, and Bradford.

81. Scruton, *Meaning of Conservatism*, 191.

82. Kalb, "The Tyranny of Liberalism," 241, 245.

premodern rhetorical and imaginative modes, which have emerged again with the death of Lyotard's "grand narratives." The end of the great Enlightenment story has allowed other alternative accounts to emerge, several of which Kirk wove together to form his conservative position. These alternative accounts do not always sit well together. Sometimes the American traditionalist could not also be the displaced Tory, and the chivalrous South was not the same place as midcentury Detroit or Hawthorne's New England. Nevertheless, Kirk located in his different conservative minds common attacks on modernity, which have been echoed, through a very different collection of voices, in postmodern writings.

For example, Kirk's championing of Burke's "little platoons" wherever they are found serves as a warning both to the liberal and conservative proponents of government moralizing. His admiring piece on Donald Davidson's essay on "regionalism" supports localism against both big-business capitalism as well a liberal leviathan. Bill Kauffman, in his essay-polemic *Look Homeward, America*, identifies a "radical reactionary" tradition encompassing Dorothy Day and William Jennings Bryan, Millard Fillmore and 1960s radical Paul Goodman, which rejects both liberal social planning and conservative moralism, big business and big government.[83] This rejection of the universal political or social arrangements, which favors the personal and particular, as we have seen, also fits well with the postmodern critique. In a recent book discussing the "late modern / postmodern transition," Wayne Gabardi suggests in *Negotiating Postmodernism* that the next stage of the modern-postmodern debate will involve increasing attention to "local and microlevel strategies" that resist political or economic aggregation. Roberto Unger elaborates an analysis of what he calls "organic groups" that seeks to avoid the twin errors of liberal political theory, utopianism, and idolatry.

The rise of postmodernism has supplied the possibility of returning conservatism to its more natural mode of discourse. Dialectic, the logical analysis of the human condition according to abstract notions of the individual or society that is characteristic of most forms of liberal modernism, presents, according to its critics, only a "thin" theory of life. In contrast, Kirk's writing was almost defiantly imaginative, frustrating even his admirers for not being sufficiently "an-

---

83. *PP*, 98–113; Kauffman, *Look Homeward, America: In Search of Reactionary Radicals and Front-Porch Anarchists.*

alytic." He concentrated on the formation of images and the cultivation of imagination, for "[w]hether to throw away yesterday's nonsense to embrace tomorrow's nonsense, or whether we find our way out of superficiality into real meaning, must depend in part upon the images which we discover or shape."[84] These traits are peculiarly appropriate to the postmodern age, where excessive self-awareness is reflected in TV commercials, "reality" television, and art exhibits.

In an analysis of postmodern thought, Dale Jamieson finds a certain "poverty" in postmodern theory. Its playfulness toward the ubiquity of cultural symbols available for use sometimes degenerates into mere indifference to their power to influence behavior. Its emphasis on acknowledging difference sometimes cloaks within it a forced, superficial tolerance. And the postmodernist dismissal of the guidelines of logic as modernist relics sometimes makes argument impossible. "What is intended as an argument against postmodernism is swallowed, appropriated, framed, contextualized, or countered—everything but refuted . . . postmodernism coopts criticism rather than confronting it."[85] Because there is no agreed-upon standard of truth, postmodernism transforms counterarguments into mere "juxtapositions" of their own, with neither really able to defeat the other or even to shed light on the controversy at hand.

Kirk mistrusted overarching narratives of any form: Rousseauistic General Will, Hobbesian or Lockean states of nature, Benthamite calculus, Marxist class struggle, or the global marketplace. Kirk opposed the three main variants of the confident materialism, scientism, and progressivism that Paul Berman identified as characteristic of the nineteenth-century exponents of modernity. There are first the "philosophic system builders" such as Hegel or Comte; the "scientific-minded observers" such as Charles Darwin, who found in evolution a map of human development; or the "journalistic nonsystem builders" such as Tocqueville, who described through his careful records, the "universal inevitability" of modernity.

These representatives of the modern age each thought the core of modernity lay in rejection: of sin, of history, or of the limits of human progress. As a Christian Kirk believed in sin; even before his conversion, the reality of evil was clear enough to him. Kirk advocated a reminder of limits, and he called for reinvigoration of "the energy

84. Kirk, "Rediscovery of Mystery," 1, 3.
85. Jamieson, "The Poverty of Postmodernist Theory," 581–82.

and talents of individuals" and a recognition of the "always in-scrutable" work of Providence. Kirk placed the individual and the physical and psychological limits of life against the idealistic dreams of radicals of every stripe—even conservative ones. The statesman, the imaginative entrepreneur, the person at the crossroads of an his-torical moment: this is where the truisms of modernity fail to cap-ture the interstices of life that Kirk relished. In crafting his conser-vative counternarrative, Kirk created "spaces of resistance" against liberalism, pockets of nonmodernity out of which he hoped the imagination could create an alternative future.

Kirk often quoted a phrase adapted from Hamlet, "Nothing is but thinking makes it so," which can serve as a coda to Kirk's own imag-inative restructuring of modernity. Ideas, words, and imagination had consequences; they could change the way individuals and cul-tures experience reality. Kirk tried to construct one such reality from the disintegrating fragments of what he conceived of as a coherent tradition. Against "liquid modernity," to use Zygmunt Bauman's striking term, Kirk thought order could still be created and pre-served. Kirk's religious views on sin and redemption and the exis-tence of evil compelled him to consider a more layered view of is-sues such as progress or the emergence of truth. "Human thought and human actions, unpredictable ordinarily, determine the course of civilizations. Decadence is no more inevitable than progress. Great civilizations commonly experience periods of decay, alternating with periods of renewal."[86] This cautiously optimistic view avoids the disappointment of liberalism when its proposals meet with what Kirk would see as their natural and expected limitations. It also avoids the postmodern despair of meaning, which cannot distin-guish between such things as decadence or progress. It remains to be seen whether that narrow path Kirk navigated can resonate in a world that has chosen a direction different in many respects from that which he advocated.

86. *RT,* 305.

𝔅ibliography

Works by Russell Kirk

Books

The American Cause. Washington, DC: Regnery, 1957.

Beyond the Dreams of Avarice: Essays of a Social Critic. Peru, IL: Sherwood Sugden, 1991.

Confessions of a Bohemian Tory. New York: Fleet, 1963.

The Conservative Constitution. Washington, DC: Regnery, 1990.

The Conservative Mind: From Burke to Eliot. 7th rev. ed. Washington, DC: Regnery Gateway, 1986.

Decadence and Renewal in the Higher Learning. Washington, DC: Gateway Editions, 1978.

Economics: Work and Prosperity. Pensacola, FL: Beka Books, 1980.

Edmund Burke: A Genius Reconsidered. Rev. ed. Wilmington: ISI Books, 1997.

Eliot and His Age: T. S. Eliot's Moral Imagination in the Twenthieth Century. New York: Random House, 1971.

Enemies of the Permanent Things. Peru, IL: Sherwood Sugden, 1988.

The Intemperate Professor and Other Cultural Splenetics. Baton Rouge: Louisiana State University Press, 1965.

John Randolph of Roanoke. Indianapolis: Liberty Fund, 1978.

———, ed. *Orestes Brownson: Selected Political Writings.* New Brunswick, NJ: Transaction Publishers, 1990.

The Politics of Prudence. Wilmington: ISI Books, 1993.

Prospects for Conservatives. Washington, DC: Regnery Gateway, 1989.

Reclaiming a Patrimony: A Collection of Lectures. Washington, DC: Heritage Foundation, 1982.

Redeeming the Time. Wilmington: ISI Books, 1996.

Rights and Duties. Dallas: Spence Publishing, 1997.

The Roots of American Order. Malibu, CA: Open Court, 1974.

St. Andrews. London: Batsford, 1954.

The Sword of Imagination: Memoirs of a Half-Century of Literary Conflict. Grand Rapids, MI: Eerdman's, 1995.

Watchers at the Strait Gate. Sauk City, WI: Arkham House, 1984.

The Wise Men Know What Wicked Things Are Written on the Sky. Washington, DC: Regnery Gateway, 1987.

Articles

"Behind the Veil of History." *Yale Review* 46 (March 1957): 466.

"Bentham, Burke, and the Law." *Great Issues* 9 (Troy, MI: Troy State University, 1976): 153–68.

"Bolingbroke, Burke, and the Statesman." *The Kenyon Review* 28, no. 3 (Summer 1966): 426–32.

"Can We Wake Political Imagination? *Southern Partisan* (Fall 1985): 24–27.

"Capitalism." Symposium on Humane Socialism and Traditional Conservatism, *New Oxford Review* (October 1987): 18–19.

"The Case for and against Natural Law." Heritage Lecture No. 469, Heritage Foundation, Washington, DC, July 15, 1993.

"The Case for Nixon." *New York Times Magazine* (November 6, 1960): 16–19, 114–17.

"Cats, Eliot, and the Dance of Life." *Renascence* 40, no. 3 (Spring 1988): 197–203.

"The Christian Imagination of T. S. Eliot." *Southern Academic Review* (1988): 123–35.

"Christian Postulates of English and American Law." *Journal of Christian Jurisprudence* 1 (1981): 49–75.

"Civilization without Religion?" Heritage Lecture No. 404, Heritage Foundation, Washington, DC, July 24, 1992.

"Conformity and Legislative Committees." *Confluence* 3 (September 1954): 342–53.

"Conservatism: A Succinct Description." *National Review* 34 (September 3, 1982): 1080–84, 1163–64.

"Conservatism Is Not an Ideology." *National Review* 12 (January 30, 1962): 59, 74.

"The Conservative Movement: Then and Now." Heritage Foundation Lecture No. 1, Heritage Foundation, Washington, DC.

"A Conservative Program for a Kinder, Gentler America." Heritage Lecture No. 198, Heritage Foundation, Washington, DC, April 27, 1989.

"Dreamthorp and Linlithgow." *National Review* 13 (August 14, 1962): 102.

"Edmund Burke and the Future of American Politics." *Modern Age* 31, no. 2 (Spring 1987): 107–14.

"Eliot and a Christian Culture." *This World* (Winter 1989): 5–19.

"The Enduring Achievement of Sen. John East." *Washington Times* (July 22, 1986): D3.

"Enlivening the Conservative Mind." *Intercollegiate Review* 21, no. 3 (Spring 1986): 25–28.

"The Federal Budget." *More . . . common sense* 3, no. 2 (Summer–Fall 1990): 2.

"Flannery O'Connor and the Grotesque Face of God." *The World and I* (January 1987): 429–33.

"Foreword." Symposium on Conservatism and History, *Continuity* 4, no. 2 (Spring–Fall 1982): i-iv.

"The Future of America's Political Parties." *Southern Partisan* 5, no. 1 (Winter 1985): 20–23.

"HEW May Get You Too." *National Review* 28 (January 23, 1976): 34.

"The High Achievement of Christopher Dawson." *Chesterton Review* 10 (November 1984): 435–38.

"Historical Consciousness and the Preservation of Culture." *The World and I* (January 1989): 491–501.

"Ideology and Political Economy." *America* 96 (January 5, 1957): 390.

"Imagination against Ideology." *National Review* 32 (December 31, 1980): 1576–78, 1583.

"I Must See the Things, I Must See the Men: One Historian's Recollections of the 1930s and 1940s." *Imprimis* 16, no. 10 (October 1987).

"The Inhumane Businessman." *Fortune* (May 1957): 160–61, 248.

"Is Social Science Scientific?" *New York Times Magazine* (July 23, 1961): 30.

"Is Washington Too Powerful?" *New York Times Magazine* (March 1, 1964): 22, 82.

"Killing with Regulatory Kindness." *National Review* 24 (April 24, 1972): 406.

"May the Rising Generation Redeem the Time?" Heritage Lecture

No. 37, Heritage Foundation, Washington, DC, December 11, 1991.

"The Meaning of 'Justice.'" Heritage Lecture No. 457, Heritage Foundation, Washington, DC, March 4, 1993.

"Mill's 'On Liberty' Reconsidered." *National Review* 1 (January 25, 1956): 23–24.

"The Mind of Barry Goldwater." *National Review* 15 (August 27, 1963): 149–51.

"The Moral Imagination." *Literature and Belief* 1 (1981): 37–49.

"The Myth of Objectivity." *Triumph* 3, no. 9 (September 1968): 35–37.

"Natural Law and the Constitution of the United States." *Notre Dame Law Review* 69 (1994): 1035–48.

"Obdurate Adversaries of Modernity." *Modern Age* 30, no. 1 (Summer / Fall 1987): 203–6.

"Perishing for Want of Imagery." *Modern Age* 20, no. 1 (Winter 1976): 9–10.

"The Persistence of Political Corruption." *Center Magazine* (January / February 1974): 2.

"The Pleasures of Williamsburg." *National Review* 20 (August 27, 1968): 860.

"Political Errors at the End of the Twentieth Century, Part I: Republican Errors." Heritage Lecture No. 321, Heritage Foundation, Washington, DC, February 27, 1991.

"Promises and Perils of a 'Christian Politics.'" *Intercollegiate Review* 18, no. 1 (Fall–Winter 1982): 13–23.

"Prospects for a Conservative Bent in the Human Sciences." *Social Research* 35 (Winter 1968): 580–92.

"The Quickening of Imagination." *Modern Age* 33, no. 3 (Fall 1990): 280–87.

"The Rediscovery of Mystery." *Imprimis* 6, no. 1 (January 1977): 1–6.

"Reinvigorating Culture." *Humanitas* 7, no. 1 (Winter 1994): 27–42.

"Religion in the Civil Social Order." *Modern Age* 27, no. 4 (Fall 1984): 306–9.

"A Republican View of the Democrats." *New York Times Magazine* (July 17, 1960): 7, 49–51.

"Rhetoricians and Politicians." *Kenyon Review* 26, no. 4 (Autumn 1964): 764–68.

"Ruminations on Small Towns." *National Review* 15 (December 3, 1963): 485.

"The Salutary Myth of the Otherworld Journey." *The World and I* (October 1994): 425–37.

"Salvation by Bus." *National Review* 24 (September 29, 1972): 1065.

"Scientistic Ideology vs. Christian Realism." *The World and I* (March 1987): 391–96.

"Shelton College and State Licensing of Religious Schools: An Educator's View of the Interface between the Establishment and Free Exercise Clauses." *Law and Contemporary Problems* 44 (1981): 169–84.

"A Vote for Ford." *Commonweal* (October 22, 1976): 681–83.

"The Wealthy American Bum." *National Review* (March 12, 1963): 198.

"You Can't Trust Perpetual Adolescents." *Cosmopolitan* 172, no. 5 (May 1966): 62.

Essays in Edited Collections

"Introduction." In *Essay Concerning Human Understanding,* by John Locke. Chicago: Regnery Gateway, 1956.

"Prospects for Territorial Democracy in America." In *A Nation of States: Essays on the American Federal System,* edited by Robert A. Goldwin. Chicago: Rand, McNally, 1963.

"There's a Long, Long Trail A-Winding." In *The Color of Evil,* edited by David G. Hartwell, 87. New York: Tor Horror Books, 1987.

Secondary Sources

Books

Adorno, Theodor, and Max Horkheimer. *Dialectic of Enlightenment.* New York: Verso, 1979.

Alexander, Gregory S. *Commodity and Propriety: Competing Visions of Property in American Legal Thought, 1776–1910.* Chicago: University of Chicago Press, 1997.

Allitt, Patrick. *Catholic Intellectuals and Conservative Politics in America, 1950–1985.* Ithaca: Cornell University Press, 1993.

Anderson, Brian C. *Raymond Aron: The Recovery of the Political.* Lanham, MD: Rowman and Littlefield, 1997.

Arato, Andrew, and Eike Gebhardt, eds., *The Essential Frankfurt School Reader.* New York: Continuum, 1995.

Babbitt, Irving. *Democracy and Leadership.* Indianapolis: Liberty Fund, 1979.

Bailyn, Bernard. *The Ideological Origins of the American Revolution.* Cambridge: Harvard University Press, 1967.

Barzun, Jacques. *From Dawn to Decadence.* New York: HarperCollins, 2000.

Baudouin, Charles. *The Myth of Modernity.* London: Allen and Unwin, 1950.

Baudrillard, Jean. *The Gulf War Did Not Take Place.* Bloomington: Indiana University Press, 1995.

Bauman, Zygmunt. *Liquid Modernity.* Malden, MA: Blackwell, 2000.

Bell, Bernard Iddings. *Postmodernism and Other Essays.* Milwaukee: Morehouse Publishing Company, 1926.

Bell, Daniel. *The Cultural Contradictions of Capitalism.* London: Heineman, 1979.

Bertens, Hans. *The Idea of the Postmodern: A History.* London: Routledge, 1996.

Best, Steven, and Douglas Kellner. *Postmodern Theory: Critical Interrogations.* New York: Guilford, 1991.

Boorstin, Daniel J. *The Image: A Guide to Pseudo-Events in America.* New York: Atheneum, 1962.

Boulton, James T. *The Language of Politics in the Age of Wilkes and Burke.* London: Routledge and Kegan Paul, 1963.

Bradford, M. E. *The Reactionary Imperative.* Peru, IL: Sherwood Sugden, 1990.

Brokaw, Tom. *The Greatest Generation.* New York: Random House, 1998.

Bromwich, David. *A Choice of Inheritance: Self and Community from Edmund Burke to Robert Frost.* Cambridge: Harvard University Press, 1989.

Brooks, David. *On Paradise Drive: The Way We Live Now (and Always Have) in the Future Tense.* New York: Simon and Schuster, 2004.

———. ed., *The New Conservative Writing.* New York: Vintage, 1996.

Brown, Charles. *Russell Kirk: A Bibliography.* Grand Rapids: Clarke Memorial Library, 1981.

Brownson, Orestes. *The American Republic.* Wilmington: ISI Books, 2003.

Buchanan, Patrick J. *The Death of the West.* New York: St. Martin's Press, 2002.

Buckley, William F., Jr. *Right Reason.* New York: Doubleday, 1985.

Burke, Edmund. *On Empire, Liberty, and Reform: Speeches and Letters.* Edited by David Bromwich. New Haven: Yale University Press, 2000.

———. *Reflections on the Revolution in France*. Edited by Conor Cruise O'Brien. New York: Penguin, 1986.

Calabresi, Guido. *A Common Law for the Age of Statutes*. Cambridge: Harvard University Press, 1982.

Callinicos, Alex. *Against Postmodernism*. New York: St. Martin's Press, 1990.

Caputo, John D., and Michael J. Scanlon, eds. *God, the Gift, and Postmodernism*. Bloomington: Indiana University Press, 1999.

Carr, David. *Time, Narrative, and History*. Bloomington: Indiana University Press, 1986.

Connor, Steven. *Postmodernist Culture: Introduction to Theories of the Contemporary* London: Blackwells, 1995.

Crunden, Robert. *The Superfluous Men: Conservative Critics of American Culture, 1900–1945*. Wilmington: ISI Books, 1999.

Davies, Robertson. *What's Bred in the Bone*. New York: Viking, 1985.

Dawson, Christopher. *The Dynamics of World History*. New York: Sheed and Ward, 1956.

———. *Progress and Religion*. Peru, IL: Sherwood Sugden and Co., 1994.

———. *Religion and the Modern State*. New York: Sheed and Ward, 1938.

d'Entrèves, A. P. *Natural Law: An Introduction to Legal Philosophy*. New Brunswick, NJ: Transaction Publishers, 1994.

Dillard, Angela D. *Guess Who's Coming to Dinner Now? Multicultural Conservatism in America*. New York: New York University Press, 2001.

Dorrien, Gary J. *The Neoconservative Mind: Politics, Culture, and the War of Ideologies*. Philadelphia: Temple University Press, 1993.

Dougherty, Jude P. *Western Creed, Western Identity*. Washington, DC: Catholic University of America Press, 2000.

Dreher, Rod. *Crunchy Cons*. New York: Crown Forum, 2006.

D'Souza, Dinesh. *What's So Great about America*. Washington, DC: Regnery Gateway, 2002.

Dupré, Louis. *The Passage to Modernity*. New Haven: Yale University Press, 1993.

Eagleton, Terry. *Literary Theory: An Introduction*. Minneapolis: University of Minnesota Press, 1998.

East, John P. *The American Conservative Movement: Philosophical Founders*. Washington, DC: Regnery Gateway 1986.

Eastland, Terry, ed. *Religious Liberty in the Supreme Court*. Washington, DC: Ethics and Public Policy Center, 1993.

Edwards, Lee. *The Conservative Revolution: The Movement that Remade America from Robert Taft to Newt Gingrich.* New York: Free Press, 1999.

———. *Goldwater: The Man Who Made a Revolution.* Washington, DC: Regnery, 1995.

Ehrman, John. *The Rise of Neoconservatism: Intellectuals and Foreign Affairs, 1945–1994.* New Haven: Yale University Press, 1995.

Eliot, T. S. *Christianity and Culture: The Idea of a Christian Society and Notes toward the Definition of Culture.* New York: Harcourt Brace, 1977.

———. *Selected Prose of T. S. Eliot.* Edited by Frank Kermode. New York: Harcourt Brace, 1975.

Emerson, Ralph Waldo. *Essays and Lectures.* Washington, DC: Library of America, 1983.

Feldman, Stephen M. *American Legal Thought from Premodernism to Postmodernism.* Oxford: Oxford University Press, 2000.

Filler, Louis, ed. *The Dictionary of American Conservatism.* Philosophical Library, 1987.

Fish, Stanley. *The Trouble with Principle.* Cambridge: Harvard University Press, 1999.

Francis, Samuel. *Beautiful Losers: Essays on the Failure of American Conservatism.* Columbia: University of Missouri Press, 1993.

Frank, Thomas. *The Conquest of Cool.* Chicago: University of Chicago Press 1997.

Frohnen, Bruce. *Virtue and the Promise of Conservatism: The Legacy of Burke and Tocqueville.* Lawrence: University of Kansas Press, 1993.

Fukuyama, Francis. *The Age of Disruption.* New York: Free Press, 1999.

———. *The End of History and the Last Man.* New York: Avon Books, 1993.

Gabardi, Wayne. *Negotiating Postmodernism.* Minneapolis: University of Minnesota Press, 2001.

Gadamer, Hans-Georg. *Truth and Method.* New York: Continuum, 1975.

Genovese, Eugene. *The Southern Tradition: The Achievement and Limitations of an American Conservatism.* Cambridge: Harvard University Press, 1994.

George, Robert P., ed. *The Autonomy of Law: Essays on Legal Positivism.* Oxford: Oxford University Press, 1996.

Gerson, Mark. *The Neoconservative Vision: From the Cold War to the Culture Wars.* Lanham, MD: Madison Books, 1995.

Glendon, Mary Ann. *Rights Talk: The Impoverishment of Political Discourse.* New York: Free Press, 1993.

Gottfried, Paul. *After Liberalism: Mass Democracy in the Managerial State.* Princeton: Princeton University Press, 1999.

———. *The Conservative Movement: Revised Edition.* New York: Twayne, 1988.

———. *The Search for Historical Meaning: Hegel and the Postwar American Right.* DeKalb: Northern Illinois University Press, 1986.

Grossberg, Lawrence. *We Gotta Get Out of This Place: Popular Conservatism and Postmodern Culture.* London: Routledge, 1992.

Guardini, Romano. *The End of the Modern World.* Wilmington: ISI Books, 1998.

Guroian, Vigen. *Rallying the Really Permanent Things.* Wilmington: ISI Books, 2005.

Gutting, Gary. *Pragmatic Liberalism and the Critique of Modernity.* Cambridge: Cambridge University Press, 1999.

Hamilton, Paul. *Historicism.* London: Routledge, 1996.

Hartz, Louis. *The Liberal Tradition in America.* New York: Harcourt Brace, 1955.

Hassan, Ihab. *The Dismemberment of Orpheus: Toward a Postmodern Literature.* Oxford: Oxford University Press, 1971.

Heineman, Robert. *Authority and the Liberal Tradition: From Hobbes to Rorty.* New Brunswick, NJ: Transaction Publishers, 1994.

Herrera, Robert A. *Orestes Brownson: Sign of Contradiction.* Wilmington: ISI Books, 1999.

Hoeveler, J. David. *The Postmodernist Turn.* Lanham, MD: Rowman and Littlefield 1996.

Hofstadter, Richard. *The Paranoid Style in American Politics, and Other Essays.* New York: Knopf, 1965.

Hogue, Arthur M. *The Origins of the Common Law.* Washington, DC: Regnery, 1985.

Howe, Irving. *A Critic's Notebook: Essays.* New York: Harcourt Brace, 1994.

Hughes, Glenn, ed. *The Politics of the Soul: Eric Voegelin on Religious Experience.* Lanham, MD: Rowman and Littlefield, 1999.

Huntington, Samuel P. *The Clash of Civilizations and the Remaking of World Order.* New York: Simon and Schuster, 1996.

Hutcheon, Linda. *The Politics of Postmodernism*. London: Routledge, 1989.

Iggers, George G. *Historiography in the Twentieth Century: From Scientific Objectivity to the Postmodern Challenge*. Wesleyan: Wesleyan University Press, 1997.

Jameson, Frederic. *The Cultural Turn: Selected Writings on the Postmodern 1983–1998*. New York: Verso, 1998.

———. *Postmodernism, or, The Cultural Logic of Late Capitalism*. Durham: Duke University Press, 1991.

Jencks, Charles. *The Language of Post-Modern Architecture*. London: Academy Editions, 1977.

Kauffman, Bill. *Look Homeward, America: In Search of Reactionary Radicals and Front-Porch Anarchists*. Wilmington: ISI Books, 2006.

Kearney, Richard. *The Wake of Imagination*. London: Routledge, 1988.

Kekes, John. *Against Liberalism*. Ithaca: Cornell University Press, 1997.

———. *A Case for Conservatism*. Ithaca: Cornell University Press, 1998.

Kendall, N. D., ed. *Willmoore Kendall Contra Mundum*. New York: Arlington House, 1971.

Kirk, Russell, and James McClennan. *The Political Principles of Robert A. Taft*. New York: Fleet Press, 1967.

Koestler, Arthur. *The Roots of Coincidence: An Excursion into Parapsychology*. New York: Vintage, 1972.

Kopff, E. Christian. *The Devil Knows Latin*. Wilmington: ISI Books, 1999.

Kramnick, Isaac. *Bolingbroke and His Circle*. Ithaca: Cornell University Press, 1992.

———. *The Rage of Edmund Burke: Portrait of an Ambivalent Conservative*. New York: Basic Books, 1977.

Kristol, Irving. *Neoconservatism: The Autobiography of an Idea*. New York: Free Press, 1995.

Lawler, Peter A. *Postmodernism Rightly Understood: The Return to Realism in American Thought*. Lanham, MD: Rowman and Littlefield 1999.

Locke, John. *Essay Concerning Human Understanding*. Chicago: Regnery Gateway, 1956.

Lukacs, John. *Historical Consciousness: The Remembered Past*. New Brunswick, NJ: Transaction Publishers, 1994.

Lyotard, Jean-François. *The Postmodern Condition: A Report on Knowledge*. Minneapolis: University of Minnesota Press, 1988.

————. *The Postmodern Explained: Correspondence 1982–1985.* Minneapolis: University of Minnesota Press, 1992.

MacIntyre, Alasdair. *After Virtue: A Study in Moral Theory.* South Bend: University of Notre Dame Press, 1981.

————. *Three Rival Versions of Moral Inquiry.* South Bend: University of Notre Dame Press, 1990.

————. *Whose Justice? Whose Rationality?* South Bend: University of Notre Dame Press, 1988.

Mannheim, Karl. *From Karl Mannheim.* Oxford: Oxford University Press, 1971.

McAllister, Ted V. *Revolt against Modernity: Leo Strauss, Eric Voegelin, and the Search for a Postliberal Order.* Lawrence: University Press of Kansas, 1995.

McDonald, W. Wesley. *Russell Kirk and the Age of Ideology.* Columbia: University of Missouri Press, 2004.

Mehta, Uday Singh. *Liberalism and Empire: A Study in Nineteenth-Century British Liberal Thought.* Chicago: University of Chicago Press, 1999.

Meyer, Frank S. *In Defense of Freedom and Related Essays.* Indianapolis: Liberty Fund, 1996.

Muller, Jerry Z., ed. *Conservatism: An Anthology of Social and Political Thought from David Hume to the Present.* Princeton: Princeton University Press, 1997.

Muncy, Mitchell S., ed. *The End of Democracy? The Judicial Usurpation of Politics.* Dallas: Spence Publishing Company, 1997.

————. *The End of Democracy II: A Crisis of Legitimacy.* Dallas: Spence Publishing Company, 1999.

Nash, George H. *The Conservative Intellectual Movement in America since 1945.* Wilmington: ISI Books, 1996.

Natoli, Joseph, and Linda Hutcheon, eds. *A Postmodern Reader.* New York: State University of New York Press, 1993.

Nisbet, Robert. *Conservatism: Dream and Reality.* New Brunswick, NJ: Transaction Publishers, 2002.

Nock, Albert Jay. *State of the Union: Essays in Social Criticism.* Edited by Charles H. Hamilton. Indianapolis: Liberty Press, 1991.

Oakeshott, Michael. *Rationalism in Politics.* Indianapolis: Liberty Fund, 1991.

Ortega y Gasset, José. *Historical Reason.* New York: Norton, 1984.

————. *History as a System.* New York: Norton, 1961.

————. *The Modern Theme.* New York: Harper Torchbook, 1961.

Pangle, Thomas. *Ennobling of Democracy: The Challenge of the Post-modern Era*. Baltimore: Johns Hopkins University Press 1992.

Panichas, George A., ed. *Modern Age: The First Twenty-Five Years*. Indianapolis: Liberty Fund, 1988.

Panichas, George A., and Claes Ryn, eds. *Irving Babbitt in Our Time*. Washington, DC: Catholic University of America Press, 1986.

Patterson, Dennis. *Law and Truth*. Oxford: Oxford University Press, 1996.

Pelikan, Jaroslav. *The Vindication of Tradition*. New Haven: Yale University Press, 1984.

Person, James E., Jr. *Russell Kirk: A Critical Biography of a Conservative Mind*. Lanham, MD: Madison Books, 1999.

———, ed. *The Unbought Grace of Life: Essays in Honor of Russell Kirk*. Peru, IL: Sherwood Sugden, 1994.

Pieper, Josef. *Hope and History*. San Francisco: Ignatius Press, 1994.

———. *Leisure: The Basis of Culture*. New York: Mentor, 1963.

Pilbeam, Bruce. *Conservatism in Crisis? Anglo-American Conservative Ideology after the Cold War*. New York: Palgrave, 2003.

Pocock, J. G. A. *The Machiavellian Moment: Florentine Political Thought and the Atlantic Republican Tradition*. Princeton: Princeton University Press, 1975.

———. *Politics, Language, and Time: Essays on Political Thought and History*. New York: Atheneum, 1971.

Podhoretz, Norman. *Ex-Friends*. New York: Norton, 1999.

Posner, Richard. *The Problems of Jurisprudence*. Cambridge: Harvard University Press, 1990.

Postrel, Virginia. *The Future and Its Enemies*. New York: Free Press, 1998.

Raimondo, Justin. *Reclaiming the American Right: The Lost Legacy of the Conservative Movement*. Burlingame, CA: Center for Libertarian Studies, 1993.

Reid, John P. *Constitutional History of the American Revolution*. Abridged ed. Madison: University of Wisconsin Press, 1995.

Rossiter, Clinton. *Conservatism in America*. New York: Vintage, 1962.

Rothenberg, Winifred Barr. *From Market-Places to a Market Economy*. Chicago: University of Chicago Press, 1992.

Ryn, Claes. *Will, Imagination, and Reason: Babbitt and Croce and the Problem of Reality*. Washington, DC: Catholic University of America Press, 1986.

Schall, James V., S.J., and John J. Schrems, eds. *On the Intelligibility of Political Philosophy: Essays of Charles N. R. McCoy, S.J.* Washington, DC: Catholic University Press, 1989.

Scotchie, Joseph, ed. *The Paleoconservatives.* New Brunswick, NJ: Transaction Publishers, 1999.

Scruton, Roger. *The Meaning of Conservatism.* Rev. ed. London: Macmillan, 1984.

———. *The West and the Rest: Globalization and the Terrorist Threat.* Wilmington: ISI Books, 2002.

Shain, Barry Alan. *The Myth of American Individualism: The Protestant Origin of American Political Thought.* Princeton: Princeton University Press, 1996.

Sheldrake, Philip. *Spaces for the Sacred: Place, Memory, and Identity.* Baltimore: Johns Hopkins University Press, 2001.

Shils, Edward. *Tradition.* Chicago: University of Chicago Press, 1981.

Simon, Yves. *The Tradition of Natural Law.* New York: Fordham University Press, 1992.

Smant, Kevin J. *Principles and Heresies: Frank S. Meyer and the Shaping of the American Conservative Movement.* Wilmington: ISI Books, 2002.

Spender, Stephen. *The Struggle of the Modern.* Berkeley: University of California Press, 1963.

Stanlis, Peter J. *Edmund Burke and the Natural Law.* Lafayette, LA: Huntington House, 1986.

Stone, Brad Lowell. *Robert Nisbet.* Wilmington: ISI Books, 2001.

Stoner, James R., Jr. *Common Law and Liberal Theory: Coke, Hobbes and the Origins of American Constitutionalism.* Lawrence: University Press of Kansas, 1992.

Tate, Allen. *Essays of Four Decades.* Wilmington: ISI Books, 1999.

Tonsor, Stephen, ed. *Reflections on the French Revolution: A Hillsdale Symposium.* Washington, DC: Regnery, 1990.

Trilling, Lionel. *The Liberal Imagination: Essays on Literature and Politics.* New York: Doubleday, 1953.

Tuan, Yi-Fu. *Space and Place: The Perspective of Experience.* Minneapolis: University of Minnesota Press, 1977.

Tushnet, Mark. *Taking the Constitution Away from the Courts.* Princeton: Princeton University Press, 1999.

Veldman, Meredith. *Fantasy, the Bomb, and the Greening of Britain: Romantic Protest, 1945–1980.* Cambridge: Cambridge University Press, 1994.

Walsh, David. *Guarded by Mystery: Meaning in a Postmodern Age.* Washington, DC: Catholic University of America Press, 1999.

Weaver, Richard M. *Ideas Have Consequences.* Chicago: University of Chicago Press, 1984.

Wedgwood, C. V. *Truth and Opinion: Historical Essays.* New York: Macmillan, 1960.

White, James Boyd. *Heracles' Bow: Essays on the Rhetoric and Poetics of the Law.* Madison: University of Wisconsin Press, 1985.

Will, George. *Men at Work: The Craft of Baseball.* New York: Harper Perennial, 1991.

Yack, Bernard. *The Fetishism of Modernities.* South Bend: University of Notre Dame Press, 1997.

Articles and Essays

Ackerman, Bruce. "The Common Law Constitution of John Marshall Harlan." *New York Law School Law Review* 36 (1992): 23.

Ashford, Nigel. "Russell Kirk as Conservative Thinker." *The Salisbury Review* 2, no. 4 (July 1984): 37–39.

Attarian, John. "Russell Kirk's Political Economy." *Modern Age* 40, no. 1 (Winter 1998): 87–97.

Bainbridge, Stephen M. "Community and Statism: A Conservative Contractarian Critique of Progressive Corporate Law Scholarship." *Cornell Law Review* 82 (1997): 856–904.

Balkin, J. M. "What is a Postmodern Constitutionalism?" *Michigan Law Review* 90 (1992): 1966–90.

Beer, Jeremy M. "Science Genuine and Corrupt: Russell Kirk's Christian Humanism." *Intercollegiate Review* 35, no. 1 (Fall 1999): 28–33.

Berger, Peter. "Our Conservatism and Theirs." *Commentary* (October 1986): 65–66.

Berman, Harold J. "The Origins of Historical Jurisprudence: Coke, Selden, Hale." *Yale Law Review* 103 (1994): 1651–1738.

Berns, Walter. Review of *A Program for Conservatives,* by Russell Kirk. *Review of Politics* 17 (1955): 683–86.

Biddle, Francis. "The Blur of Mediocrity." *New Republic* 129, no. 4 (August 24, 1953): 17–19.

Bix, Brian. "Positively Positivism." *Virginia Law Review* 85 (August 1999): 889–923.

Bliese, John R. E. "Conservatism and the Ideology of 'Growth.'" *Modern Age* 41, no. 2 (Spring 1999): 117–25.

Boarman, Patrick M. "Apostle of a Humane Economy: Remembering Wilhelm Roepke." *Humanitas* 13, no. 1 (2000): 31–67.

Bottum, Joseph. "Christians and Postmoderns." *First Things* 40 (February 1994): 28–32.

Boyle, James. "Anachronism of the Moral Sentiments? Integrity, Postmodernism, and Justice." *Stanford Law Review* 51 (1999): 493–527.

———. "A Process of Denial: Bork and Post-Modern Conservatism." *Yale Journal of Law and the Humanities* 3 (1991): 263–310.

Campbell, William F. "An Economist's Tribute to Russell Kirk." *Intercollegiate Review* 30, no. 1 (Fall 1994): 68–71.

Canavan, Francis, S.J. Review of *The Irony of Liberal Reason*, by Thomas A. Spragens Jr. *Review of Politics* 44, no. 4 (October 1982): 615–16.

———. "Knowledge and Politics." *Thought* 50 (December 1975): 432–37.

Carey, George. "Traditions at War." *Modern Age* 36, no. 3 (Spring 1994): 237–43.

Carr, David. "Modernity, Post-Modernity, and the Philosophy of History." *American Catholic Philosophical Quarterly* 68 (1994): 45.

Chalmers, Gordon Keith. "Goodwill Is Not Enough." *New York Times Book Review* (May 17, 1953): 7, 28.

Champ, Robert. "Russell Kirk's Fiction of Enchantment." *Intercollegiate Review* 30, no. 1 (Fall 1994): 39–42.

Chapman, Gerald W. "The Organic Premise." In *Edmund Burke: Appraisals and Applications*, edited by Daniel E. Ritchie. New Brunswick, NJ: Transaction Books, 1990.

Coombs, Mary. "Outsider Scholarship: The Law Review Stories." *University of Colorado Law Review* 63 (1992).

Cover, Robert M. "Nomos and Narrative." *Harvard Law Review* 97 (1983): 4–68.

Crick, Bernard. "The Strange Quest for an American Conservatism." *Review of Politics* (1953): 359–76.

Delgado, Richard. "Rodrigo's Chronicle." *Yale Law Journal* 101 (1992): 1357–80.

———. "Storytelling for Oppositionists and Others: A Plea for Narrative." *Michigan Law Review* 87 (1988): 2411–41.

Dreher, Rod. "Crunchy Cons." *National Review* 54 (September 30, 2002).

Easterbrook, Gregg. "The New Convergence." *Wired* 10, no. 12 (December 2002).

Farber, Daniel A., and Suzanne Sherry. "Telling Stories Out of School: An Essay on Legal Narratives." *Stanford Law Review* 45 (1993): 807–54.

Fish, Stanley. "Don't Blame Relativism." *The Responsive Community* 12, no. 3 (Summer 2002): 27–31.

Fleming, Thomas. "Selling the Golden Cord." *Chronicles* 22, no. 7 (July 1997): 10.

———. "Thunder on the Right." *Chronicles of Culture* 9, no. 6 (June 1985): 43.

Fortin, Ernest L. "Natural Law and Social Justice." *American Journal of Jurisprudence* (1982): 17.

Francis, Samuel. "Holding the Pass." *Chronicles* 29, no. 9 (September 2004): 34–35.

———. "The Price of Empire." *Chronicles* 22, no. 6 (June 1997): 14–17.

French, Rebecca R. "Lamas, Oracles, Channels, and the Law: Reconsidering Religion and Social Theory." *Yale Journal of Law and the Humanities* 10 (1998): 505–35.

Frohnen, Bruce. "Has Conservatism Lost Its Mind? The Half-Remembered Legacy of Russell Kirk." *Policy Review* (Winter 1994): 62–66.

Frum, David. "The Legacy of Russell Kirk." *New Criterion* 13 (December 1994): 10–16.

———. "Unpatriotic Conservatives." *National Review* (April 7, 2003): 32–40.

Genovese, Eugene. "Captain Kirk." *New Republic* (December 11, 1995): 35–38.

George, Robert. "Natural Law, the Constitution, and the Theory and Practice of Judicial Review." In *Vital Remnants: America's Founding and the Western Tradition,* edited by Gary L. Gregg II. Wilmington: ISI Books, 1999.

Gross, David. "Rethinking Traditions." *Telos* 94 (Winter 1992–1993): 6.

Guroian, Vigen. "*The Conservative Mind* Forty Years Later." *Intercollegiate Review* 30, no. 1 (Fall 1994): 23–26.

———. "Moral Imagination, Humane Letters, and the Renewal of Society." Heritage Lecture No. 636, Heritage Foundation, Washington, DC, May 12, 1999.

Harris, Lee. "The Future of Tradition." *Policy Review*, no. 131 (June–July 2005).

Heilbrunn, Jacob. "The Great Conservative Crackup." *Washington Monthly* (May 2006).

Heineman, Robert. "Conservatism in the U.S.: 1976 to the Present." *Choice* (May 1997): 1451–58.

Henrie, Mark C. "Opposing Strains." *Modern Age* 44, no. 1 (Winter 2002): 24–29.

———. "The Road to the Future." *Intercollegiate Review* 27, no. 1 (Fall 1991): 15–19.

———. "Russell Kirk and the Conservative Heart." *Intercollegiate Review* 38, no. 2 (Spring/Summer 2003): 14–23.

———. "Russell Kirk's Unfounded America." *Intercollegiate Review* 30, no. 1 (Fall 1994): 51–57.

Herberg, Will. "Natural Law and History in Burke's Thought." *Modern Age* 3, no. 3 (Summer 1959): 325–28.

Hittinger, Russell. "Government by Dissent: A Note on Our Judicial Sovereigns." *The World and I* (March 1994): 376–81.

Huntington, Samuel P. "Conservatism as an Ideology." *American Political Science Review* 51 (1957): 454–73.

Hyman, David A. "Lies, Damned Lies, and Narrative." *Indiana Law Journal* 73 (1998): 797–861.

Jamieson, Dale. "The Poverty of Postmodernist Theory." *University of Colorado Law Review* 62 (1991): 577–95.

Jones, Edith. "The Nature of Man According to the Supreme Court." *Texas Review of Law and Politics* 4, no. 1 (Fall 1999): 237–60.

Jordan, Michael. "Me and Mecosta: Studying with Russell Kirk." *Chronicles* 24, no. 4 (April 1999): 35–38.

Judis, John. "The Conservative Crackup." *The American Prospect* 3 (Fall 1990): 30–42.

———. "Three Wise Men." *New Republic* (May 30, 1994): 20–21, 24.

Kalb, James. "The Tyranny of Liberalism." *Modern Age* 42, no. 3 (Summer 2000): 241–52.

Kesler, Charles R. "Natural Law and the Constitution." *Southern California Interdisciplinary Law Journal* 4 (1995): 558.

———. "What's Wrong with Conservatism." Bradley Lecture, American Enterprise Institute, Washington, DC, June 8, 1998.

Kramer, Hilton. "Modernism and Its Enemies." *New Criterion* 4, no. 3 (March 1988): 3.

Kraynak, Robert P. "Toward a Conservative Postmodernism." *Modern Age* 42, no. 3 (Summer 2000): 304–9.

Kronman, Anthony. "Precedent and Tradition." *Yale Law Journal* 99 (1990): 1029–69.

Lawler, Peter A. "Conservative Postmodernism, Postmodern Conservatism." *Intercollegiate Review* 39, no. 1 (Fall 2002): 16–25.

Lawson, Alan. "Is There a Usable Conservatism?" *Intellectual History Newsletter* 11 (June 1989): 16–25.

Lewis, Gordon K. "The Metaphysics of Conservatism." *Western Political Quarterly* (1953): 728–41.

Lilla, Mark. "A Tale of Two Reactions." *New York Review of Books* (May 14, 1998).

Livingston, Michael A. "Postmodernism Meets Practical Reason." *Yale Law Journal* 107 (1998): 1125–49.

Luban, David. "Legal Traditionalism." *Stanford Law Review* 43 (1991): 1035–60.

Lutz, Donald S. "Religious Dimensions in the Development of American Constitutionalism." *Emory Law Journal* 39 (1990): 21–40.

Malvasi, Mark C. "Kirk among the Historians." *Political Science Reviewer* 35 (2006): 132–58.

McClay, Wilfred M. "History and Memory." *University Bookman* 35, no. 4 (Winter 1995): 19.

———. "Is Conservatism Finished?" *Commentary* (January 2007): 13–19.

———. "The Mystic Chords of Memory: Reclaiming American History." Heritage Lecture No. 550, Heritage Foundation, Washington, DC, December 13, 1995.

McDonald, W. Wesley. "The Conservative Mind of Russell Kirk: 'The Permanent Things' in an Age of Ideology." Ph.D. diss., Catholic University, 1982.

———. "Reason, Natural Law, and Moral Imagination in the Thought of Russell Kirk." *Modern Age* 27, no. 1 (Winter 1983): 15–24.

———. "Russell Kirk and the Prospects for Conservatism." *Humanitas* 12, no. 1 (Winter 1999): 56–76.

———. "The Sacred Garden." *Chronicles* 25, no. 4 (April 2000): 29–30.

McPherson, James M. "History: It's Still about Stories." *New York Times Book Review* (September 19, 1999): 35.

Meyer, Frank S. "In Defense of John Stuart Mill." *National Review* 1 (March 28, 1956): 24.

Murphy, Dwight D. Review of *The Roots of American Order* and *Beyond the Dreams of Avarice*, by Russell Kirk. *Journal of Social, Political, and Economic Studies* 17, nos. 3 and 4 (Fall / Winter 1992): 458, 462.

Neuchterlein, James. "The Paleo's Paleo." *First Things* (August / September 1991): 46.

Niemeyer, Gerhard. "Russell Kirk and Ideology." *Intercollegiate Review* 30, no. 1 (Fall 1994): 35–38.

O'Brien, Christopher. "Liberal Studies through International College." *Journal of General Education* 32 (Summer 1980): 159–66.

"On the Future of Conservatism." *Commentary* (February 19, 1997).

Palmer, Tom G. "Myths of Individualism." *Cato Policy Report* 18, no. 5 (September / October 1996): 1–5.

Pieper, Josef. "Tradition: The Concept and Its Claim upon Us." *Modern Age* 36, no. 3 (Spring 1994): 217–28.

Presser, Stephen B. "What Would Burke Think of Law and Economics?" *Harvard Journal of Law and Public Policy* 21 (1997): 147–53.

Quinn, Dermot. "Religion and The Conservative Mind." *Political Science Reviewer* 35 (2006): 200–229.

Ransom, John Crowe. "Empirics in Politics." *Kenyon Review* 15 (1953): 648–54.

Richert, Scott P. "Russell Kirk and the Negation of Ideology." *Chronicles* 29, no. 7 (July 2004): 28–30.

Rieff, David. "Multiculturalism's Silent Partner." *Harper's* (August 1993): 62–72.

Ritchie, Daniel E. "Remembrance of Things Past: Edmund Burke, the Enlightenment, and Postmodernity." *Books and Culture* (March / April 2004): 24–25, 41–42.

Rossiter, Clinton. Review of *The Conservative Mind: From Burke to Santayana*, by Russell Kirk. *American Political Science Review* 47, no. 3 (September 1953): 868–70.

Russello, Gerald J. "Liberal Ends and Republican Means." *Seton Hall Law Review* 28 (1997): 740–60.

Ryn, Claes. "Defining Historicism." *Humanitas* 11, no. 2 (1998): 80–101.

Sabetti, Filippo. "Local Roots of Constitutionalism." *Perspectives on Political Science* 33 (Spring 2004): 70–78.

Schall, James V., S.J. "A Natural Law Bibliography." *American Journal of Jurisprudence* (1995): 1.

Schlag, Pierre J. "The Problem of the Subject." *Texas Law Review* 69 (1991): 1627–1743.

Schmitz, Kenneth L. "What Happens to Tradition When History Overtakes It." *Proceedings of the American Catholic Philosophical Association* 68 (1994): 59.

Scruton, Roger. "Godless Conservatism." *Wall Street Journal* (April 5, 1996): 8.

Sewall, Elizabeth. "The Death of the Imagination." *Logos* 1, no. 1 (Spring 1997): 153.

Shiflett, Dave. "The Yappy Warrior." *National Review Online* (November 19, 2001). http://www.nationalreview.com/shiflett/shiflett111901.shtml.

Shils, Edward. "Tradition and Liberty." In *The Virtue of Civility: Selected Essays on Liberalism, Tradition, and Civil Society by Edward Shils,* edited by Steven Gresby. Indianapolis: Liberty Fund, 1997.

Smith, Rogers M. "Beyond Tocqueville, Myrdal, and Hartz: The Multiple Traditions in America." *American Political Science Review* 87, no. 3 (September 1993): 549–68.

Stanlis, Peter J. "Russell Kirk and the Roots of American Order." (unpublished manuscript).

Stoner, James R., Jr. "Is Tradition Activist? The Common Law of the Family in the Liberal Constitutional World." *University of Colorado Law Review* 73 (Fall 2002): 1291–1306.

Sullivan, Andrew. "The Scolds." *New York Times Magazine* (March 11, 1998): 46–51, 88–91.

———. "Right Turn: What Conservatives Should Learn from 9/11." *New Republic* (December 17, 2001).

Tanner, Stephen L. "Paul Elmer More and the Critical Temper." *Modern Age* 40, no. 2 (Spring 1998): 186–94.

Tate, John W. "The Hermeneutic Circle vs. the Enlightenment." *Telos* 110 (Winter 1998): 9–38.

Theroux, Paul. "The Way to East Coker." *Book World* (March 12, 1972): 4–5.

Topolski, Jerzy. "The Role of Logic and Aesthetics in Constructing Narrative Wholes in Historiography." *History and Theory* 38 (May 1999).

Tushnet, Mark. "Conservative Constitutional Theory." *Tulane Law Review* 59 (March 1985): 910–27.

Watson, George. "Conservatives and the Free Market." *Chronicles* 22, no. 4 (April 1997): 23.

Ways, Max. "Generation to Generation." *Time* 62, no. 1 (July 6, 1953): 88, 90–92.

Weinstein, Michael A. "Irving Babbitt and Postmodernity: Amplitude and Intensity." *Humanitas* 6, no. 1 (1992/1993): 42–48.

Wheeler, Harvey. "Russell Kirk and the New Conservatism." *Shenandoah* (1953): 20–34.

Whitney, Gleaves. "The Swords of Imagination: Russell Kirk's Battle with Modernity" (unpublished manuscript).

Wilhelmsen, Frederick D. "The Wandering Seer of Mecosta." *Intercollegiate Review* 30, no. 1 (Fall 1994): 81–84.

Wills, Garry. "The Day the Enlightenment Went Out." *New York Times* (November 4, 2004): A25.

Wilson, James G. "Justice Diffused: A Comparison of Edmund Burke's Conservatism with the Views of Five Conservative Academic Judges." *Miami University Law Review* 40 (1986): 913–75.

Windschuttle, Keith. "The Real Stuff of History." *New Criterion* 15, no. 7 (March 1997): 4.

Wolfe, Gregory. "Beauty Will Save the World." *Intercollegiate Review* 27, no. 1 (Fall 1991): 27–31.

———. "I Was a Teenage Conservative." *Commonweal* (March 9, 2001): 12–14.

———. "Russell Kirk—The Catholic as Conservative." *Crisis* 11, no. 9 (October 1993): 31–32.

Wolfson, Adam. "Apocalypse Now?" *Weekly Standard* (July 26, 1999): 31–35.

———. "Conservatives and Neoconservatives." *Public Interest* 154 (Winter 2004): 32–49.

Wood, Gordon. "Was America Born Capitalist?" *Wilson Quarterly* (Spring 1999).

Wood, Ralph C. "Russell Kirk, Knight of Cheerful Countenance." *Christian Century* (October 23, 1996): 1015–21.

Wooster, Martin Morse. "Captain Kirk." *American Enterprise* (January/February 1996): 74.

Zoll, Donald Atwell. "The Social Thought of Russell Kirk." *Political Science Reviewer* 2 (Fall 1972): 112–36.

Index

chitecture, 49–50; conservative critiques of, 182, 187, 211; conservative defense of, 202–3; denigration of mystery, 65; dissolving of, 10, 11, 178; failure of, 9; and history, 71, 86, 87, 102; ideology as product of, 60, 62; and imagination, 53–54, 57, 59, 62, 194, 213; Kirk's critique of, 12, 13, 25, 26–27, 32, 38, 52, 65, 178, 197, 203, 207–8; meanings of, 14; and past, 97; and place, 48, 49, 51; political and economic upheavals of, 119; and postmodernism, 177, 211; and progress, 70, 84, 102, 141, 188, 191; and scientism, 46, 191; universalist notions of, 39

Montesquieu, Charles-Louis de, 152, 178

Moral imagination: action tempered by, 65; and Age of Sentiments, 200; Babbitt on, 54, 56, 59, 60; Burke on, 54–55, 118; and experience as means to deeper understanding, 57; and ideology, 108; and intuitive grasp of the good, 152; Kirk's rousing of, 105; in literature, 58; and natural law, 8, 152; and redeemed imagination, 60, 64; regenerating tools of, 66; and service of eternal values, 54; as society's bulwark, 145; and truths, 206

More, Paul Elmer, 29, 198
Morgenthau, Hans, 122
Morley, Felix, 131
Morley, John, 106
Mosca, Gaetano, 5
Muggeridge, Malcolm, 21, 95
Muller, Jerry, 68, 91, 208
Multiculturalism, 81, 102
Mysteries: appreciation of, 186; of historical past, 71, 72; images conveying, 5; of permanent things, 65; place of, 37; respect for, 65; and science, 47
"Myth of Objectivity, The" (Kirk), 85

Narrative: addressing of mysteries, 65; and association of facts, 88; Burke's crafting of, 119–20; communication of, 101; and conservative voice, 11; and construction of legal environment, 156–57, 157n46, 162; and facts, 99; and historical

imagination, 68, 69, 70, 71; history as, 87–88, 90, 103, 184; and Kirk's historical writing, 75, 102; Kirk's use of, 210–11; multiplicity of, 120; necessity of, 43, 206, 208; and postmodernism, 100, 144, 183–84; and tradition, 95, 120

Nash, George, 28, 72
National Review, Kirk's column for, 39
Natural law: and abuse of legal and political system, 149; and Burke, 106, 107, 116, 147; and common law system, 146–47, 151; and constitutional law, 148, 149, 151; and historical imagination, 69; and ideology, 148–49; indirect application of, 154; and individual, 147, 148–49, 151, 163, 170; intuitive understanding of, 151–54; Kirk's definition of, 150, 176; and moral imagination, 8, 152; and reason, 152–53, 154; relationship to positive human law, 147–48, 149, 150

Natural rights, 23, 24, 116, 117
Neoconservatives: and American founding, 22; and democratic capitalism, 112; and economics, 143; liberal globalizers compared to, 113; on Lincoln, 22; and meaning of conservatism, 15; and modernity, 14, 202; and terrorist attacks, 18
Neuhaus, John, 187–88
New Age spiritualism, 45, 93
New Deal, 125, 126
Newman, John Henry, 94
Niebuhr, Reinhold, 83
Niemeyer, Gerhart, 62
Ninth Amendment, 166
Nisbet, Robert, 12n20, 29, 67
Nixon, Richard, 31, 122, 199
Nock, Albert Jay, 29, 36, 44, 124, 156, 181
Nominalists, 152
Novak, Michael, 16, 112
Nozick, Robert, 172

Oakeshott, Michael, 87, 145
O'Brien, Conor Cruise, 107, 118
Occult, 34–35, 36, 37
Old House of Fear, The (Kirk), 34
Order: and conflicting possibilities, 74; as first need of society, 19–20; and history, 79, 83; individual or-